AF413237

Songs of Lost Things

Sonata for the Sun

Monica McCollough

The Writing Tree LLC

For my mother and father

Chapter 1

Twelve

"Inner City Blues" - Marvin Gaye

IT WAS EARLY IN THE MORNING WHEN THE DISSONANCE AND loud screeches of her home, sounding as though falling to destruction, rang Lavender's ears. Her eyes jolted open, and she sat straight up on her mattress. The stern, discontent tone of her father Joshua's voice burst from the kitchen down the hallway. He was angry—yelling and cursing, but she couldn't tell what the cause was just yet. Fury dripped from every syllable, punctuated with the noise of drawers slamming shut and chairs dragging across the linoleum that echoed through the residence. Her mind was still foggy from slumber at first and conjured thoughts of a break-in in progress or of their upstairs neighbors' twins fighting again. Then as the mental clouds cleared and she heard her mother's groans, the reality became lucid and burning.

Oh... Ok, Lavender thought.

She left her bed, slipped through the partially closed door of her bedroom, and walked towards the kitchen. Before completely entering, she could see her mother, Katherine, slumped over in a chair. Her thin twisted mahogany frame folded and shuddered in place. Katherine rubbed her back repeatedly... then her legs...then her arms,

1

never finding comfort in any position, though she tried. Fidgeting, Katherine resolved to rock back and forth as Joshua paced around her in a circle as though performing a strange seance. His eyes were red, his jaws clenched, and he seethed anger. He walked from the refrigerator carrying a can of cold ginger ale and placed it on the table before her.

"Here. Hurry and drink this before you puke all over the damn floor again," he said.

Lavender stood frozen. She had an idea of what had provoked all of this and didn't want to be any closer than necessary. Instead, she continued to watch from just beyond the doorway. To fully know how bad it would be this time, she needed to play voyeur a bit longer. Hear her mother's tone. Lavender wanted to know which *performance* Katherine would give this time. Would it be the theatrics where she spoke of her firmness in haughty defiance of the withdrawal—proclaiming strength and determination to leave it alone? Or maybe, Lavender thought, it would be the "pity act"; distraught, helpless, ashamed, begging even. The "I can't do it without you" lines delivered to her father with raw, shallow emotion? She had seen all these performances before and knew that the ending had consistently been the same.

"I don't want it," Katherine responded.

Joshua ignored the declaration. He grabbed her face with a firm hand, squeezed hard so her lips pierced open, then lifted her head and poured small amounts of the beverage into her barely open mouth. She coughed as if she were near choking to death, and the liquid spilled from around the sides of her lips.

"How the fuck is that helping me?" She asked in a raspy voice, coughing and wiping her mouth.

He scoffed and slung the can back onto the table, splattering more of its contents out, before exiting the kitchen in frustration. Lavender tiptoed back to her room before either could hear or see her and got back into bed. She stared at the ceiling fan as it rattled loudly, adding to the already rhythmic raindrops outside and accompanying snores from her brother's *nasal show* in his adjacent bed. She couldn't fathom how Čhetáŋ (Chay-ton) managed to sleep through so much commotion. Or, how he managed to do so on those other mornings when near identical moments occurred in the kitchen between their parents.

Summer break is already off to a shitty start, she thought.

The rain started early and heavy that morning, and it appeared as though the children would not venture outside at all on this first official day of summer break. However, the clouds broke, and later Lavender and Čhetáŋ excitedly departed the cramped walls of their fourth-floor apartment for their Newark concrete courtyard below.

It had been a long school year, full of the typical grade school activities and pre-pubescent wonder for Lavender and her girlfriends. They were in that awkward phase of budding adolescence. Most of them were between eleven and thirteen years old. Lavender was twelve. They sat on the stoop and squealed at the gossip of who "went with" who, who had or hadn't "done it," who would or wouldn't, and why. It was all glib chatter from those at the crossroads of carrying baby dolls or having their own authentic version to nuzzle and feed.

Lavender couldn't wait to huddle within her circle of peers and contribute to their aimless chitchat. She descended downstairs, her long legs quickly paced one after the other until the midday sun that pierced through the clouds warmed her face. The rays illuminated her honey skin, unveiling the soft tones of sienna beneath the surface in a way only natural radiance could reveal. It was already the afternoon, and she was late to the gathering spot. She'd spent a couple of hours pretending to be asleep and another few procrastinating around her room, waiting for the kitchen hostilities from earlier to damper down.

"Well, I heard Lisa let him tongue kiss her," one proclaimed.

"Uh uh, you lying! I know she didn't," the doubters screeched.

"Yes, she did! I saw it," shouted another.

"When!?" A chorus of five or six gum-popping, lip-smacking, chatty girls voiced in an inquisitive carol at once.

Nadia approached the group and beckoned for Lavender, who brushed her off initially. The conversation of sex and neighborhood squabbles had been much too alluring at that moment.

"Lavender!" Nadia called more forcefully, then pressed her index finger and thumb together and gestured toward her lips. This motion got Lavender to her feet, and she left the cackling crowd to follow Nadia toward the implied retreat for intoxication.

Nadia was her closest friend in the poor and mostly Black neighborhood of Cypress Grove. She was a dark, slender girl with striking Haitian features who often spoke in thick, indiscernible Haitian Creole that Lavender grew to somewhat understand. Nadia's unique traits often left her on the outskirts of the girl cliques. Lavender, whose paternal grandmother Ellen was an Indigenous American of the Oglala Lakota, often resided on the exterior of those circles as well.

Besides her mystifying name, Lavender was also the tallest of all her acquaintances. Her long black curls, which descended to the middle of her back, would fall even lower when she crouched beside her friends — attempting to diminish how much taller she stood. Her distinctness was even more pronounced when she would speak of "cooking frybread" or occasionally respond with "tó" (*you are welcome*) whenever anyone expressed gratitude. The term of politeness was one of only a handful of expressions Joshua managed to pass down to his children that Indian Boarding Schools, distance, and deaths hadn't washed away from his familial memory over the decades. Lavender also spoke with a nearly unplaceable cadence of midwestern, New Jersey, and southern drawl that nobody outside of the four walls of her apartment could truly relate to.

She and Nadia bonded immediately.

The two walked the sidewalk towards Nadia's apartment. The heels of their jelly shoes clicked and clacked against the concrete beneath their feet. Young boys from their school called to Lavender as they passed, remarking on her already blossoming, curvaceous shape.

"Hey, Lavender! Hey girl..." they hollered while making suggestive gestures with their hands, fingers, and groins.

Lavender, as usual, responded with a finger gesture of her own.

Inside Nadia's apartment, there was a trail of disorder in every room. Layers of clothes, toys, and unfinished meals carpeted the entire area. Seven people lived in the tiny three-bedroom apartment, all ranging from five months to forty-five years old, most working various shifts to cover the rent and help the family. It was Nadia's twenty-two-year-old brother, William, who had haphazardly, in a rush for work, left his unfinished blunt accessible to anyone who knew where to look.

Nadia successfully secured the prize from the back of his underwear drawer. Then they made their way to the roof of the building. There, they smoked and hacked through the rolled hashish like the infrequent partakers they tried pretending they were not. They leaned over the edge and blew into the wind as they stared down onto the busy sidewalk below. The isolation and freeing effects of the refreshment allowed Lavender to ease into discussing all that she witnessed that morning, the type of confessions that were not uncommon between them.

"Well, there's nothing you can do about it," Nadia said as she inhaled and twirled one of her long braids between her fingers.

"Does she seem messed up to you? Like, does she seem like she's on something? When you see her?" Lavender asked. It felt more detrimental to Lavender for her friends to notice an issue than the matter of her mother's addiction itself.

"No," Nadia said flatly. "Everyone around here knows someone on something. Who cares. Fuck them," she continued with conviction as they exchanged the blunt again. "I have never seen your mama look crazy. No one says these things because no one sees them. Only you see. If they do, then beat them!"

Nadia then followed that advice with a screeching, "Bann epav!" Lavender laughed hard, always enjoying the inflections of her Haitian insults, but then returned to a contemplative state.

"Why they think I'm stupid though? I can see Čhetáŋ. But I'm no baby. This is like the third time I seen them like that. With daddy fussing, and her looking all...." She shrugged and slapped her hand against the side of her thigh. "They look dumb lying to me about it every time." She was confident that her father could handle everything but was dismayed at her parent's perception of her inability to comprehend. "If they tell me she got the flu or a stomach virus one more time... Nobody gets the flu in June." They both giggled at the foolishness of adults, particularly of parents, but only for a moment.

Lavender grew quiet, walked to the edge of the rooftop, and looked down. She picked up a plastic bottle top she found, flicked it over, and watched to see if she hit anyone below.

Nadia walked nearby, laughing. "You need to stop doing that." Then she twisted her face into a devious and knowing smile. "So... What's happening with Justin? This weekend, no?"

"No, not this weekend. Next Friday. And quit looking at me like that," Lavender replied as Nadia burst into even deeper laughing, which blended with coughing to nearly choke her.

"Li gen yon gwo zozo."

Lavender didn't know all those terms, but she'd heard Nadia refer to penises enough to understand zozo.

"Shut up! I didn't say I was!" She responded.

"It is easy. My sister have sex all the time in the bed next to ours."

"Yah, she do. It's a million of you ashy negroes in there," Lavender snorted.

"Yes, it is easy," Nadia proceeded, ignoring Lavender's gibe. "You have to become a woman someday."

"Yeah, well. It might be next week. It might not. You're no woman yet."

"Oh, but I've seen and touched."

"Your baby brothers don't count," Lavender said.

"You'll have to do something," Nadia suggested while taking a long pull of the marijuana. "He will think that's why you're there."

Lavender took a protracted pause and thought about that last statement and the planned rendezvous she had with Justin Brown, her habitual crush for the past three years. He was a classmate, and unlike herself, he had just started noticing her. They'd begun exchanging flirtatious notes and looks with each other ever since the weather turned warm and had even had a session of heavy petting and kissing.

Next Friday was the day they had tentatively planned to sneak around while his family was out of town. Sex was not explicitly discussed, but the philosophy of their environment and peers usually steered in that direction. She had only just pushed it to the back of her mind behind thoughts of her mother and the haze of weed. But leave it to Nadia to lead her back to more imminent concerns. They remained on the roof a while longer, losing track of time, chatting like two old, experienced women. Before long, evening approached, the cigar shrank and disappeared, their high subsided, and they parted ways.

Chapter 2

The Antihero

"Summertime" - Ella Fitzgerald

As was typical on most nights, once nine P.M. struck, Joshua was setting up on stage at Sapphire Lounge. He was a jazz guitarist there with his band Rhapsody, which had been the main entertainment for the lounge for the greater part of fifteen years. As Joshua pulled cases of instruments and sound equipment onto the stage, his modeled biceps tightened and extended in a repetitive motion. The nightly ritual of lifting musical apparatuses assisted in maintaining his fitness despite his forty-three years. Sweat began to bead on his warm, tan brow and glistened through the edges of his curly hair that he now wore short. Years of Katherine's southern cooking had added a couple of layers around his midsection, and a few worry lines began to show. But otherwise, Joshua looked nearly the same man as he did years prior, wrangling with sound equipment and fidgeting with guitar strings on the platform.

He fell in love with the guitar after his father, Samuel, a carpenter, gifted him an acoustic as a birthday present many years before. The story had been that Samuel left Arkansas during the Great Migration bound for either Seattle or San Francisco when he made a detour to pick up quick labor near Ellsworth Air Force Base in South

Dakota. There, he met and fell in love with a beguiling and somewhat adrift young Lakota girl, and they had a son. Samuel never made it to the west coast. Instead, he remained near Rapid City until Ellen passed away. Eventually, he and Joshua moved together to the northeast. They weren't there long before Samuel, too, would join Ellen in the afterlife, leaving Joshua, still a young man himself, alone to make his own way. The guitar became an integral component in that quest, and Joshua immersed himself in music, which became his primary occupation.

"Hey man," Maurice said. "How you doing? You looking good up there."

"I'm good. You?" Joshua asked although anyone who saw Maurice's state would know the real answer.

"I'm good, I'm good," he said hurriedly.

Joshua attempted to rush the conversation along. "Hey, we're in the middle of getting ready for another set. I'm gonna have to holla at you later, ok?"

"Oh, yeah, that's cool, that's cool." Maurice then tried to give him a handful of crumpled-up dollar bills. Joshua, already understanding what the gesture meant, ignored him and walked past Maurice in haste, nearly knocking him down as he and the band went back on stage to continue their show.

Maurice disappeared, reemerged, then disappeared again and repeated this dance—in and out of the shadows of the nightclub for the remainder of the evening.

In the wee hours of the morning, after Rhapsody's final set was complete and the club was almost empty, he approached Joshua again.

"Hey, hey, y'all was good tonight," Maurice said, walking up seconds after the band had wrapped. Joshua hadn't managed to unplug his guitar from the amplifier before he was pounced upon. Several of his bandmates observing the scene walked away, shaking their heads and grimacing at what Maurice had become. Once a talented drummer in his own right, he'd strayed far from that identity.

Alcohol and drugs were frequent indulgences of Joshua's musical peers, especially those in the late-night circuit he lived in. But the reality of that dynamic rearing its ugly face first by Katherine earlier and now by a former bandmate within mere days of each other had frustrated him.

"I don't have it for you," Joshua said before the question was asked. "It" being any amount of opioid Maurice may have believed his friend had on him to sell or barter. If Maurice had shown up and lingered around the club for as long as he did in search of it, Joshua thought, he must be desperate.

Joshua despised the narcotic. "Tar is the nastiest shit you can fuck with. I would never touch it," he frequently said when he was younger as the drug floated around his scene. It was indicative of Joshua's stratified view of the various substances that drifted about his world. It was truly something he believed and had lived by; until Katherine had shown up strung out on it.

"I know I told you I was gonna get straight, and I have," Maurice said. "It's just been a bad time right now."

The excuses and broken promises delivered by the addicts in Joshua's life were accumulating and rotting with the weight and stench of a landfill.

"It's hard out here. I can't find work," Maurice continued. "You know this recession. Just gotta ease my mind right now 'cause I got a job interview in a couple days, and I can't be like this." The withdrawal symptoms were observable. Joshua disregarded every word of his friend.

Maurice pulled the same crumpled bills from his pocket and tried to hand them off again, and Joshua slapped them away.

"What did I just tell you?" Joshua's expression was rigid, and his brown eyes were piercing when he asked. The commotion drew the attention of a few stragglers left inside the lounge.

"Little Jo'... I... I seen Kathy the other day and...."

The entire time Maurice struggled through his plea for a score, he was being swiftly escorted behind the stage by Joshua's firm grip on the back of his neck and arm. Once a light reddish tan, Joshua's face was now nearly that of a smoldering ember.

Behind the stage, Joshua pressed his hands into Maurice's chest and looked at him with a penetrating gaze. "If you don't leave right now, I promise you, I'm going to beat the shit out of you in here," he said in a hard, low voice. "You hear me?"

The harshness and vitriolic nature of the threat surprised his former friend. Maurice looked wide-eyed, then lowered his head and slid away from Joshua's grasp before he crept out of the rear entrance.

Joshua was left in an enraged and guilt-stricken state. Maurice dragging his desperate body to him, searching for relief, wasn't so outlandish. He'd lugged his rickety shell to him before and had been able to find the relief he sought. What infuriated Joshua the most was that the sight of Maurice was always a reminder of the walking contradiction he'd become in the last several years. Joshua was filling Katherine's syringe, tying her off. Her habit turned him into the begrudged administer of the very thing he had once adamantly railed against and still detested. He was trying to wean her off it himself. He tried to control the situation after cold turkey attempts, and a rehab stint had all failed. He had subsequently become her supplier. Maurice as a hanger-on to this, was the mere consequence of Joshua "helping out a friend" with what remained of what he hadn't administered to her.

Katherine was still naive in navigating the dark corners of the city's addicts and shady dealers. She, after all, was still in a million different ways that same unsuspecting Alabama girl he'd met fourteen years ago who spoke with a southern twang and smiled at strangers passing on the street. It had been one of her more endearing traits to him, but it was also the thing that would leave her susceptible to predators. The real dark creatures whom Joshua knew would use her pretty and tender form in unimaginable ways if she became one of the frequent fiends attempting to tame that beast.

Joshua procured the heroine himself. Making sure of its quality, that it wasn't mixed with anything. He'd lived in those streets for almost three decades and knew whom to trust. He made sure he gave her less and less with each injection. Making her promise that "if it came to it," she'd only come to him. He didn't want to hear about her in any alley like a "junkie."

None of those promises worked. He would discover her in some stage of relapse on multiple occasions. Katherine had either been too ashamed to ask him outright in her quests or she'd fallen back into old scenes and old friends and couldn't resist it in her presence. It had always been after she'd already relapsed from her own sources or was noticeably strung out that he tried his methods. Three times in the last six years, he had to do this. He would slowly bring her back around every time, nursing her through the muscle cramps, diarrhea, and sweats. Trying to reduce the dependency and the effects. He called it "a soft landing." Yesterday morning in the kitchen was the fourth time, and he was beginning to understand it as an untenable cycle he couldn't fix alone.

When Joshua returned home that evening, things were relatively back to normal. Lavender remained home to watch Katherine and help her with her "flu" as usual and as Joshua instructed. Lavender had cleaned up, cooked, and brought dinner to her mother's bedroom before she turned in for the night. Čhetáŋ, who was only seven, was oblivious to most of the underlying subtext of what was happening. He was always too wrapped up in video games and his friends. He spent most of that day playing stickball in the street and that evening watching Angus MacGyver escape death and entrapment with nothing more than a Swiss Army knife, his intellect, and luck.

It was about two A.M. As soon as Joshua entered, he found his way to his wife in their bedroom. The anger and disappointment from the previous morning had evaporated, and the scene with Maurice had only filled him with bitter regret and more resolve to find a way to make things right again. All he wanted was a quiet moment with her. He could be grating in his insults when Katherine would relapse, but just as quickly, back to the tender temperament she'd fallen in love with.

She was still up, as she often was, even now as her body ached and revolted, waiting on him. He laid down beside her for a moment and kissed her gently. She smiled.

"You taste Lavender's frybread she cooked me? It's in the fridge. She's getting good," Katherine said.

He turned over and faced her. "Nah, I didn't. I'll have to get some."

A curl of her hair fell against her shoulder, reflecting the dim light of the lamp on the nightstand. Joshua took in a long drink of her form, lying there in that light. She had a slender but soft and delicate face, naturally long lashes, mahogany skin, and dark hair that curled against her elegant neck. The features all worked together to make her the prototypical, classic black doll or the model she had once aspired to be. Her peeling lips, with freshly applied balm, curved to the perfect shape—a shape he enjoyed kissing.

"You remember when I used to roll up to the diner on 'Sophisticated Saturdays' at the club every Saturday night when I got off," he asked.

"Every Saturday night? You mean every Sunday morning."

"True. I had your nose wide open and real quick too. You were fast!" He laughed.

"Oh no... There ain't nothing that sent my nose wide open. You in there, ordering the same shit over and over every night," Katherine whispered. Her voice was still strained and hoarse from retching.

"What? That was brilliant. What other nigga you know ordering sweet potatoes and chamomile tea at three in the morning?" Joshua grinned. "Them jokers were all bacon, eggs, and patty melts. But not me. I was chamomile. That was different. You liked it."

"I liked your curly hair, your lips, and your eyes. I ain't never seen nobody Black look like you where I was from. You was fine! Fuck some goddamn tea!"

They both laughed. How absurd chance encounters like those

could ignite what would end in nuptials and new lives entering the world. As trying and frustrating as her addiction was, it always dissolved into moments like these. Too often, their days and exchanges were full of suspicion and stress about money and the children. Oddly, the relapses would reunite them with the passion that otherwise eroded into the monotony of daily routine.

"I want you to try rehab again. Paid this time. Whatever it costs," Joshua said as he stroked her hair.

"I'm good. I'll be fine."

"You said that before."

"Joshua, come on! I've gone years without touching it, too, and you know that. Sometimes I don't take things too serious. But you know, when I do, I commit. I'm stubborn. I'm taking it serious." She turned and looked towards the ceiling and then down at her hands, which she was now inexplicably examining. "I'm realizing that I can't be around it at all. I can't even be with the same people. It's too easy to fall back in that way. You know, I was thinking I could just hang here and there. But I can't. Can't trust everybody you with to be about your best interest." She exhaled a long breath.

"I hear you. And you are stubborn, Lord knows I know," he smiled. "But..."

"I know," she interrupted. "I'll do what you need me to."

He listened to her words and hoped that they proved true. She buried her face into his chest and breathed him in. He held her, and they quickly changed topics towards the children.

Chapter 3

The Prodigy

"To Be Young, Gifted and Black" - Donny Hathaway

Lavender didn't sleep much that night. She knew that in a day, she'd be sitting on Justin's bed alone with only him and all that implied. It didn't help ease her nerves either when Joshua woke her early, hours later, at only nine A.M. for a guitar lesson. She could never understand how someone who played at night clubs until near dawn could be up and bright-eyed only a few hours later.

"Amášte Adair!" Joshua called to her.

Amášte (A-mah-shday) was her middle name. The name Joshua chose to be her first. It was a term from the world he felt was stolen from him by the "education" his mother received at the Indian boarding school. A world further torn away when she succumbed to the lasting damage from her younger battle with tuberculosis. It had robbed him of that heritage outside of knowing a few Oglala words and stories Ellen managed to retain, and he attempted to pass down. He remembered his mother saying Amášte meant something akin to "the sun shining on." He always thought it would be a lovely name for a daughter, even with knowing the naming tradition in his culture didn't always work that way.

Lavender, on the other hand, was something Katherine had

chosen instead that had to grow on him. It was apparently her favorite color, the color of her Amethyst birthstone and one of the flowers her mother always grew in their garden in Alabama. It was the ties to the flower and Earth that eventually won him over to Katherine's desire for the name. And how that name also still fit with Amášte and the narrative his fat infant daughter told of herself when he bounced her on his knee.

When the second "Amášte!" hit Lavender's ears and shook her brain from slumber, she looked at her old Michael Jackson alarm clock and knew then that whatever plans she thought she had for another lazy day of summer break were now changed. Before she could fully rise, Joshua stood a few feet from her in her room, hovering with his guitar in hand.

"Come on. Up on the roof," he said.

There was no time to search for an excuse. She was ambushed by his command and her own inability to shake out the haze of sleep enough to garner a reason for why it was too early and taxing for such an excursion. Čhetáŋ was still asleep in the bed beside hers, yet Joshua never bothered him for such lessons. He had been a lost cause musically. He was more eager to run aimlessly around the street, hitting at the old, filthy tennis balls that had been used by the neighborhood boys for eternity in games of stickball. Or, pretending as if he were some action hero, leaping from their furniture and landing in karate poses.

Joshua and Katherine had compromised with Čhetáŋ's naming in the same way they'd approached Lavender's. Joshua knew Čhetáŋ meant hawk. He had also learned of several Oglala heroes who'd carried it as part of their name during his attempt at reconnecting.

When the boy was first born, he was perceptive and active. He almost sailed from Katherine's arms at the sound of his father's voice and big sister's touch. Katherine gave him the middle name Chase, and Joshua proudly called his first son "Čhetáŋ." Honoring his past. Fitting, Joshua believed for the already watchful and energetic infant. Joshua had placed all of that intention behind his first son's name, only later to have Čhetáŋ declare by six years old that he'd rather go by "Chase" because it was "easier" for his friends to say. Also, Čhetáŋ said, it made him "sound fast" like he knew he was.

When it came to the music tutelage, Katherine was content to let her baby boy run free and guarded him against the early practices Joshua pushed on his true musical progeny. Čhetáŋ would kick and scream in protest of the sessions that, while Lavender despised the ungodly hours in which she was roused for practice, didn't object to them as vehemently. She already had Joshua's musical ear, even "more so," as he would often tell her. Therefore, she was the one who suffered the brunt of the early morning lessons on weekends, school breaks, and any downtime Joshua had in between pauses of work and chores.

The rooftop was their space of reprieve as it had been for her and Nadia. It offered peace and a literal ability to float above the busy denizens below. Up there, Joshua and Lavender carried their guitars and sat on the roof's flat surface on blankets to escape all the chaos that dwelled beneath their feet.

"You been practicing?" He asked.

"Yeah."

"You lie. I saw the dust on it." He pointed downwards towards her guitar case and swiped it with his finger, removing the tiniest film of grit. He shook his head. "What you wanna play?"

"Um... I don't really know. I don't care. You got me up. You come up with something."

Joshua thought for a second, then broke into something that felt befitting of the setting; Gershwin's "Summertime." He sped up its arrangement a bit, making it more playful and less melancholy.

"I don't like it like that," Lavender said.

"You don't even really know what this is."

"Yes, I do." She then took her guitar and began to play it slower, in D-minor and how she saw it to be. Hers was looser, less polished, and had a sadder feel. She had only ever heard Joshua play it once. But, she had it just that quickly, as if she had spent months practicing and interpreted it in her own way. This was why she, not Čhetáŋ, was up on the hot rooftop at nine in the morning.

"Aw... that's good. I guess you have been listening and practicing," he said, happy with his daughter but also used to her rapid absorption of music, so keeping his praise a bit restrained. "I really want you to take this seriously. I want you to get into that Arts High School in a couple of years."

Lavender wasn't entirely sure about that. It seemed so far off. The school was full of music and ballet nerds in her eyes and would also take her away from her current group of friends.

"I don't know, Daddy. That's a long time from now."

"It's not that long. A couple of years, and you gotta audition and apply a year out. It's a good opportunity."

She shrugged, not wanting to think about some distant high school in her first week of summer break. They played there for several more minutes. It was the proverbial icebreaker. Their rooftop music lessons always parlayed themselves into deeper conversations beyond keys and chords.

"So, how was your momma yesterday?"

"Oh... she was ok. She didn't throw up."

He looked at her. "So, do you know why she was sick?"

"No... why? You said she had the flu, right?"

"Yeah....." Joshua paused after his response and stared down at the ground. He didn't know how to proceed, but Lavender felt he was teetering on whether to reveal more. So, she helped him along.

"Well... I know it's not the flu. I've known that a while," she said, and a look of surprise and slight relief spread across his brow.

"And?" Joshua wondered what more she might also understand.

"She's... she's on drugs, ain't she? A junkie?" Lavender said with a dullness.

He paused, deciding how best to approach the topic and this new understanding between them.

"Yes, she is, but... don't call her that. She's not that."

"But that's what she is," Lavender insisted.

"It ain't that simple. Nobody comes up sayin' 'Hey, I wanna be hooked on drugs'."

"That still don't change what she is."

"Well, you just don't call her that. She's addicted. She's sick. But she's still your mother," Joshua said.

Lavender allowed his words to settle in her mind for what they were worth.

"How did you know?" He asked.

"I ain't dumb. I heard y'all yesterday morning and a couple times before that. When she's sick, it's not normal sick, and she'll be weird. I seen her ankle one morning up close too. Like... bruised and red?"

His face went pale. He was astounded at how matter-of-fact she was. How much she'd observed.

"When... when did it all start?" Lavender asked. "Was she always, and I was too young to know?"

When did it all start was a question he'd asked himself a million times. In his ventures, they'd done their fair amount of partying together when they were younger, especially before Čhetáŋ was born. He'd introduced her to some crowds that he later came to regret. There was no telling what truly initiated it when she hung with that cast of characters, and he wasn't around. When he'd inquired before, Katherine could only vaguely recall drinking, entertaining, and trusting the wrong people. She said she would have a cloudy mind and didn't particularly pay attention to what she was being handed to smoke or snort in that fog. He blamed himself. She was still so green then. She still was.

"I don't really know, baby," was all he could manage.

"So. Whatcha gonna do?" Lavender asked.

"I've been doing everything I know to. I might try a real rehab place, an expensive one. You'll have to look after Čhetáŋ then. Does he know anything?"

"Čhetáŋ? Čhetáŋ be in his own world. I wasn't gonna say nothing if he didn't."

"That's good, and don't," Joshua said. He searched for the right words, words of optimism for the young yet reasonable mind before him. "It'll get better. She'll get it together. I'ma take care of it and take care of all of us, like always."

She smiled, wanting to believe in his words but unsure how it would all work out. They continued with their music for a while longer. As the sun gradually lifted towards noon and the coolish morning air was overtaken by heat and humidity, their lesson drew to a close. Lavender was relieved they had the discussion but grew nervous, knowing what the next day was supposed to bring.

Chapter 4

Wingtips

"Maggot Brain" - Funkadelic

THINGS WERE QUIET AT HOME, AND KATHERINE WAS RETURNING to her old self. She wasn't as sick, and much of her energy was restored. She resumed some of her domestic affairs, crafting succulent cuisine or mending garments and sewing new ones. She also returned to barking commands to the children about what daily chores needed to be completed. When she wasn't doing that, Katherine bounced between sleeping long hours or working on some new "project."

Katherine always had new plans in hopes of being released from her job at the diner. She wanted to do something creative. It was what she had hoped for when she moved north so many years ago. If she couldn't have that, she at least wanted something different than the 14 years she'd spent flipping burgers and pouring coffee at the 24-hour diner on Ferguson St.

Lavender remembered many of her mother's large business ideas and creative impulses. She could faintly recall when Katherine operated a catering business out of their kitchen right before Čhetáŋ was born. Lavender was only four then but could remember empty carry-out plates and how the kitchen always smelled of fried foods, coconut, and pineapple for cake fillings. That didn't last long. There was always more money going out than coming in, and trying to conceal the business operations, as it was a lease violation, was a hassle. It ended up more trouble than it was worth, and Katherine was often exhausted, still working diner shifts and attempting to make her own kitchen business profitable.

There was the time she took acting classes, trying to pick back up and make connections from when she'd had a modicum of experience and achievement on the stage in her younger years and at a conservatory. But that also proved too difficult. It was expensive, and unlike when she had graced stages previously, she now had two children — one of whom was a crying toddler at the time. Before her recent relapse, her new enterprise was going on local casting calls. She wanted to "get her face back out there," as she'd tried many years before marriage, children, and bad habits.

"Lavender," Katherine said through clenched teeth as she wiped lipstick from them, giving herself a last look over in the bathroom mirror. It was the brunch hour. She had just finished her makeup, and Lavender had only now emerged from her bedroom and crept down the hall, appearing half-sedated from drowsiness. "I cooked some bacon and biscuits. Your brother almost ate it all up from you. But you tell him I said to get his ass from in front of them cartoons and help you clean the house today while I'm gone."

Katherine had already charged her to take care of things during the day so that she and Joshua could run their errands or take odd jobs when possible. She was old enough to manage herself and babysit during daylight hours. Now that summer break was upon them and Lavender was a burgeoning mature teenager who could take on more responsibility, Katherine wanted to seize the opportunity. She wanted to start going to New York for small auditions and reconnect with some old acting acquaintances from her past. "Hopefully," Katherine told her daughter, "I'll get some commercials, nothing major."

A dry, skeptical, "Yeah, Momma," was Lavender's only response at the time to that bit of information.

Lavender was dubious but not totally dismissive. She knew that what she saw as her mother's "whimsical" pursuits was what led to her conception in the first place. One would have to be a bit daring to leave their small world in a humble Alabama town to travel thousands of miles on a hope and prayer of a modeling and acting career. All simply because she had the height, "the face," and a modest amount of success in her southern hamlet.

Katherine was 19, thin, and five-foot-nine of legs when she left Montgomery. She ended up in Newark after a stint at a conservatory. She met Joshua on the late shift of her restaurant job after the few modeling opportunities she did have, dried up. Two years later, she had Lavender. A courthouse wedding followed, five years ensued, and Čhetáŋ came. The next seven years were a series of overdue bills, daycare centers, job rejections, backaches, failed businesses, added pounds, and creases to the once youthful and elegant face she thought would be in magazines and on billboards. When Katherine glared into a mirror, it was only a painful reflection of the dreams and sacrifices her father had poured into her withering away.

Katherine grabbed her purse and unfolded the piece of paper in her hand with two addresses and descriptions, both casting calls. One was for a non-speaking role: "Female/ Black or Hispanic/ 30-40 years old/ Attractive/ To play bartender at dance club." She wasn't excited about that one, but the second casting description: "Female/ Black / 25 - 30 / Southern/ To play a school teacher to urban youth" made her hopeful. She would be thrilled to get either.

"Listen to this y'all." She read the second description aloud to Lavender and Čhetáŋ before she got ready to leave. "What y'all think?"

"I think you ain't 25 or 30," Lavender said bluntly.

"Ooh, that's you, Momma!" Čhetáŋ replied.

"Thank you, my sweet boy." Katherine leaned down and kissed his face.

Lavender rolled her eyes at the *momma's boy* and sucked her teeth at how the "twins" doted on each other. How unfair it was to her that Čhetáŋ, a boy, had been more the spitting image of her model-like mother than she was. He had been bestowed with long lashes, deep brown eyes, and perfect rows of teeth. She had more of her mother's complexion, being darker than her brother, but felt cursed that the only other trait of Katherine's she inherited was that annoying tendency to be nearly half a foot taller than everyone else.

"I'm telling you the truth," Lavender fired back. "He just trying to get something."

"Nuh, uh! You a lie!" Čhetáŋ elbowed her, and she pushed him back.

"Uh huh. I heard my *real* child," Katherine teased, then folded the paper back into her hand and headed out of the door.

A few hours later, Joshua came home with bags of groceries that he dumped on the kitchen counter, then quickly headed to his bedroom. He lit a cigar and reclined back into his favorite chair in the corner with his feet on the mattress. Lavender didn't disturb him on evenings before a gig at the club. He'd often try to relax, knowing he'd be pulling an all-nighter, particularly on a Thursday, one of their busier times. It wasn't until a few hours later, when she heard him picking at some notes on the guitar, that she ventured into the room. It was a sad song he played, one she was unfamiliar with, but it piqued her interest as all the somber-sounding minor chord arrangements usually did.

Upon entering, she noticed the sneakers, socks, belt, and t-shirt he'd worn lying across the floor. While his pristine new wingtips, gray slacks, and white button-down shirt, which Katherine had ironed, rested neatly on a half-made bed. Joshua was usually a stickler for order and tidiness. The room being messy demonstrated just how tired he was.

"Somebody got some new shoes!" Lavender noted as Joshua paused his playing and smiled. "That what y'all playing tonight?"

"This? No way," he laughed.

"Why you laugh? It doesn't sound like y'all stuff but...."

He stopped for a moment and put out his cigar. "You know what this song is called," he asked. "Maggot Brain."

"What the...? Maggot Brain?" Lavender twisted her face. "I don't even know what that means, but it sounds gross. Sound like some white folk shi... I mean mess."

He laughed. "It ain't no white folk's mess. It's Black folks' psychedelic funk and rock. I ain't doing it no justice on this acoustic. You need to hear it amped." He formed an O with his mouth. "Ooh, it's sweet."

When he mentioned *amped*, Lavender headed towards his other guitar case lying against the back wall and pulled out the electric Gibson Les Paul.

He gave her a warning glance. "Girl."

"I ain't gonna scratch it. When you gonna teach me how to play it with the amp and everything?"

He sucked his teeth, walked over, and retrieved his precious instrument—one of the most expensive things he owned. "You think you ready?"

"Yeah," Lavender replied.

"I don't know, you act like you tired of the lessons we have now."

"Daddy, they're getting kinda lame. I can play anything on the acoustic. If you gon' drag me up at the crack of dawn, at least let it be something new."

He snickered a bit at the hubris of her words. "You're good, but you don't know everything. I'll show you something next week. I'll see when's a day I can get in the club early. Can't be amping up in the house. You gon' get us evicted. I damn sure ain't bringing all that on the roof."

She smiled, nodding her head affirmatively.

"I think you'll like it. It's easier in a lot of ways than acoustic," Joshua continued.

"That's cool but still don't make practice early in the morning," she said and pressed her hands together as though begging.

He shook his head and rose to his feet. "If you wanna do well at something, you gotta get up early, child. Otherwise, you get beat by the folks half as good, but who got their ass outta bed."

"Is this like the early bird, worm stuff old folks say?"

He playfully tapped her on her head. "Exactly. Now, I gotta get ready to go. Don't you and Čhetáŋ be fighting tonight either."

"Can't make promises like that, Daddy. Let me beat him, just a little."

Joshua shook his head. "No ma'am. That boy gon' be bigger than you one day, and he's gonna remember."

Chapter 5

Prelude to Sunday
"For All We Know" - Roberta Flack, Donny Hathaway

Thursday nights at Sapphire were bustling. It was easily its busiest night of the week. People preferred spending their Friday and Saturday evenings in the sweat and funk of dance clubs and psychedelic lights. However, Thursdays were well suited as opening acts to the ruckus of the weekend, and Joshua's band had become that prelude. It was a full house and so gorged with energy that Rhapsody went through two straight sets without stopping. It was nearly eleven-thirty before Joshua sat his pick on the stool and announced over the microphone that they would "take ten." Sweat poured from all the musicians, not only because they were playing so vigorously but because the club was warm and at capacity.

"Hey man, let's go out back and get away from all these negros for a minute," Gerald said to Joshua as they began their intermission. He was the bass guitarist—a tall, round man in his forties with a head and beard peppered with gray. Joshua agreed, and they took hurried steps to the rear of the club, dabbing sweat from their necks with handkerchiefs as they moved along.

"You got a light?" Joshua asked as he stuck a cigarette between his lips. He grabbed a cold soda from the refrigerator in the back before exiting and reminded Gerald not to let the tricky door shut, or they'd have to walk all the way back to the front to re-enter.

"Yes. I know," Gerald replied in a mocking tone.

Outside, the June temperature was only tepidly better, but at least it was open and not the stale air their lungs had been recycling for three hours.

"Man, these longer sets better be worth me sweating through this new shirt," Gerald complained as he popped the collar on his eggplant-colored top with large sweat stains under each armpit and down the back. "Nate really need to add some more AC units up in there or something. Niggas gon' quit comin'!"

"Ain't nobody tell you to wear that hot ass long sleeve shirt tonight," Joshua laughed.

"It ain't the sleeves, man."

"The lighter," Joshua demanded. "And what we playing next?"

"Nigga, you're the one made the set list."

Joshua snickered. "Hell, I got kids. I forgot. Is it the Ornette Coleman or...."

Before Joshua could finish, a figure emerged from the alley beside the building next to them. Joshua squinted his eyes for better recognition, then sighed and dropped his head after realizing who it was. Maurice. Again.

"Hey! Hey Jo!?"

"Shit," he said to Gerald. "Help me get rid of this dude."

Gerald shook his head and blew a large cloud of smoke into the sky. "I ain't in all that," he sneered. "That's your man."

"Used to be."

"Good luck with that." Gerald gave him a sympathetic nudge on his shoulder. "I'll see you in a few."

Joshua's companion went back inside as Maurice moved closer, looking as disheveled as he did the last time Joshua saw him, perhaps worse. His eyes were wild, and all the withdrawal symptoms showed in his every movement.

"Shit, man," Joshua started. "Why you coming out of the dark looking crazy, scaring me?"

"I'm hurtin.'" His sorrowful eyes reflected regret and desperation.

"Yeah?" Joshua continued to smoke. "I'm sorry. I can't help you. I told you before I ain't got nothin', and you gotta quit coming up here like this too."

"Jo, man, please. I know you and Kathy still...."

"Don't speak my wife's name. And don't worry about what we doin'. Ain't got shit to do with you!" Joshua's face grew red, and his jaws tightened with every word.

"Nah, man, ain't like that. If you can just... like a cap. One cap. I just need a little. You have a little, I know."

"What the fuck you ain't understanding?" Joshua snapped back, then turned to re-enter the club. He soon realized that Gerald had indeed allowed the door to shut, locking him out.

"Dammit!" Joshua exclaimed, and he banged on the door, hoping Gerald was still close enough to hear him on the other side.

"Jo!" Maurice screamed. His voice filled with the angst of some wounded animal caught in a snare. "Well... give me some money then."

Joshua jerked his face around in aggravation. "Nigga, I know you crazy now. I know you stupid. I ain't giving you shit." He threw his cigarette to the ground and started banging on the door even harder. After a few more minutes of no response, he began to walk towards the entrance. *I'm whipping Gerald & Maurice's ass for making me take this walk*, he thought. His new Wingtip Oxford hard-bottom shoes were beginning to ache his feet.

Maurice rushed to step in front of his path. "Jo, if you ain't got it, I know you can let me borrow a few dollars. I'll pay you back tomorrow!"

"Are you deaf? You're really asking for a beating if you don't get from in front of me. I will beat your ass. I ain't playing."

Maurice took one step to the side, scratching his face wildly. "I ain't asking you," Maurice said. Then he brandished a .45 Smith & Wesson pistol.

Joshua frowned, and his mouth went agape. "Are you fucking kidding me?"

"I know you got money on you. You just being difficult," Maurice continued. Joshua couldn't believe his ears.

"I know you not...." Joshua muttered, still stunned. "This how you doing me?"

"Look I'm sorry. But you just don't know, Jo."

"The hell I don't."

They locked eyes in a silence that felt like a never-ending plunge.

"I'm not giving you another damn thing. Now, what?" Joshua said with defiance. His heart raced. Every muscle in his body had contracted at once, ready to recoil from the adrenaline. He knew Maurice to be many things, but violent wasn't one of them. Joshua could see Maurice's hands were unsteady; his face dripped with sweat, and his trembles extended from his hand through the rest of his diminished body. He looked afraid, Joshua realized. *The moment this fool flinches, it's gon' take the hands of God to keep me from killing him.*

The two stared at each other for one more eternal second before Maurice moved to steady the bottom of the gun with his other hand. Joshua took a small, slow step towards him and calmly lifted both his hands as though in surrender.

"Maurice..."

The shot was loud, and despite Maurice's limp and unfocused posture, he managed to hit him anyway. Joshua grabbed the side of his neck where the blood began to pour, and fell to his knees.

"You shot me? The fuck?"

"Why you come at me? I wasn't gon' shoot! I swear! It's just a graze. I wasn't trying to shoot!"

Though Maurice insisted he barely hit his friend, Joshua's collapse toward the ground was definitive.

"You gon' be alright. I'ma, I'ma call an ambulance right now. This an accident. I'm going right now!" Maurice said as he pulled Joshua's wallet from his back pocket. He stuffed the pistol and the wallet into his pants and ran back into the dark alley. Joshua laid still, looking up at his former friend and bandmate, clutching his neck until his grasp became so weak it relaxed completely.

Chapter 6

Query to Stars

"Round Midnight" - Ella Fitzgerald

It was two A.M. when the loud banging at the door of the Adair apartment roused Lavender from sleep. She was so confused that it seemed part of the dream her mind was crafting. It wasn't until the persistent racket and her mother's loud wails that she left her bewildered state to realize what she had heard existed in the real world. She leaped forward and sprinted towards the sound of unbearable sobbing. Lavender entered the living room to see Katherine hunched over on the floor like grotesque origami. She resembled the folded figure from the scene in the kitchen that first summer morning, yet far more foreboding this time. An older black man held her, Lavender could see, but his face was hidden in the shadows. She did recognize Gerald, who stood with a police officer near the front door. He looked like he'd seen an apparition. All the color was gone from his face. His shirt was messy, and an eerie peculiar shade stained a large swathe of it. Dull sienna browns had overlain the deep violets his shirt cast, resulting in a heavy obsidian hue. It looked like a hole, like an abyss. Lavender had known him nearly half of her life as a longtime friend and bandmate to her father. He deemed himself their uncle of sorts, wholly jovial and cheerful—a jokester. She could not understand the face of this man before her now. He was a frightening dichotomy of familiar and stranger. She trembled and folded her arms tightly against her chest as the goose-bumps rose.

Gerald saw her standing in the doorway, and before he could speak, Čhetáŋ came to stand beside her, wiping the sleep from his eyelids.

"Nate..." Gerald nodded toward the children.

Nate looked up and over his shoulder, while continuing to bear Katherine's weight with his other arm. Lavender finally recognized him as Sapphire's manager. He left Katherine's side as Gerald stepped in to relieve him and came to Lavender. Her heart sank lower and lower as she kept her eyes moving back and forth between all the adults in the room.

What is it? What is this?

When the low, almost whisper "Somebody shot your daddy... He, he passed on," came to her ears, everything stopped. "He passed on, baby."

Even after Nate said it again, she remained paralyzed. Her feet grew heavy like they were submerged in congealing cement. The heaviness crept up her legs until it brought her down and down and seemingly pulled her through the floor and away to some other adjacent world. It felt like another plane. One, where she could clearly see her mother's body on the floor, see her brother's opened mouth and tearful eyes, but she couldn't hear them. She couldn't hear her own screams nor grasp the air her lungs needed for breaths.

"No. No! No, Gerald!" Katherine shouted. It was that anguish that brought Lavender back into the moment despite her mind railing against the return.

"What you mean?" Lavender asked Nate. Yet, it was a question for everyone there and no one in particular—a query for the stars.

He looked into her weeping, red eyes with no words to offer.

She wrapped her arms around her brother as he sobbed into her nightgown and screamed his wretched pleas.

"Why did this happen? What happened?" Lavender begged.

No one had the words to express to the child how her father had warm flesh, vigor, and shared purpose at an evening's discourse and a few hours later be the end note of a song ringing to silence, dissipating in every direction. There was no sufficient language for that.

She and Čhetáŋ crumpled to the floor as Gerald's low discussions with the police officers became static in the distance, and Nate continued to try to console them all.

Eventually, Ms. Jolene, a neighbor, and frequent babysitter, appeared in the doorway with her white hair in rollers, peeking from underneath her scarf. She was still in a housecoat and slippers. Katherine managed to communicate well enough that Ms. Jolene was the best fit to come and help with the children while she composed herself and went with the others to see about the morbid business of his remains.

Lavender and Čhetáŋ sat in the middle of the floor for hours, sobbing on and off again as waves against a riverbank. Ms. Jolene allowed them to be after she tried to pray for them upon first entering.

"Dear God, only you know. Grant these children peace. Give their momma the strength she needs to handle this trial, oh Lord. We know all things have a purpose, and we know even this work for the good, and ..." She stopped. Her voice cracked, "...Amen."

She closed her eyes and allowed their grief to flood unabridged from her spiritual invocations and fruitless attempts of consolation. That open valve of emotion was the only thing to stop the pressure from splitting their hearts. The relative quietness was only interrupted by the shrieking of emergency service sirens on the street below or the intermittent wailing from one of the children. Lavender cloaked her brother as she used to when he was a baby.

"Family has to protect each other and stay together," Joshua would say as she caressed baby Čhetáŋ's head with her small hands at five. It was those words that she heard again now while she rocked him, and they both drifted on surfs of pain, sometimes buoyantly, while at other times swept under.

Chapter 7

A Sweet Coating

"They Reminisce Over You (T.R.O.Y.)" -
Pete Rock & CL Smooth

The service was a well-attended event. Bethel Baptist Church burst at the seams with friends, fans, musicians, and people from the neighborhood. So many had known Joshua personally or knew of him through his long time at Sapphire. There was such a crowd that Lavender wondered if many of them were present just to "be nosy." Hearing how that "Indian guitar man" had gotten shot and desired to be among the masses.

Through tears, she still recognized several "stoop" girls—Lisa, Claudette, and Stacey. She didn't completely fracture in her emotions until she saw Nadia crying as she entered with her entire family. Even Justin, who gave her a slight embrace and whispered condolences at the graveside, came with his father and brother. It wasn't until then, seeing him, that she even recalled the date they'd planned. It had been for that previous Friday night—the same day she'd learned hours before that she'd lost him. Joshua was gone.

The eulogy, instrumental and vocal solos exalted the sanctuary in the name of a quiet man who didn't practice organized religion and had only visited the church twice. Gerald had insisted on using the chapel he belonged to, making all the arrangements, and having a homegoing befitting his friend. It was a foreign and audacious spectacle for Lavender and Čhetáŋ, who viewed it all with curiosity. So much so that there were moments their minds drifted, and they weren't acutely focused on the casket before them but wondered about various performers and speakers.

"This man... he saved my life!" One older gentleman professed. "I was homeless for a while, and I know folks at the club don't know, but Josh would let me sneak in, stay the night. Even leave me a plate when he could. Give you the shirt off his back."

Another boy spoke about how Joshua had stepped in and rescued him from a group trying to rob him once. "He ain't have no fear, just saw somebody who needed help."

Lavender pondered all these stories she'd never heard before, from people she'd never seen before, orating on this heroic being. She couldn't help but wonder where the savior was for him that night. Who would be that for them all now?

The funeral director did an artful job of concealing the hole in his lower neck, further camouflaged by the top collar of the light gray shirt that went with the charcoal suit and black tie Lavender chose. She also added his capo, guitar strap, one of his picks, and a long thick braid of her hair inside the casket.

The morning after the shooting, she went to her bathroom with scissors and rage and performed the Lakota custom of mourning as best as she understood it. She was unsure if she honored the tradition of the shedding correctly. However, she recalled the one picture she knew of Joshua as a teenager with an untamed mane and how he told her he cut it all off after his mother died and never grew it that long again. Lavender regretted not paying closer attention to the bits of Oglala culture Joshua knew and tried to impart. Now she understood what he meant by "lost" or "stolen things" as it pertained to his past. Her connection to that knowledge and inheritance was gone now, and even if she'd butchered her crown, she didn't care how ragged or unappealing her disheveled ends looked—they looked how she felt.

After she did it, Čhetáŋ gasped at the sight. "What you do?"

Katherine just stared with a blank look at Lavender's head, barely acknowledging her daughter's tattered and shoulder-length hair, never offering assistance to manicure it. Her haircut was at least in a better, more polished condition now after her grandmother gave it a loving trim.

When Katherine's mother, Mary, came from Alabama to offer support, the first thing she did was shape Lavender's cut into something presentable enough to carry for the funeral.

"I'm ready for the shit to be over," an exhausted Lavender whispered in a low voice so only Čhetáŋ could hear. They sat on the sofa of their living room as some of the last of the visitors came by, dropping off food and giving their final condolences in the funeral's aftermath.

"When will it?" Čhetáŋ asked.

She shrugged her shoulders and ran her fingers through her hair, still getting accustomed to its lightness—or rather its absence, from her neck.

"I heard Grandma was staying a while," Čhetáŋ continued. "I heard her on the phone with Aunt Liz." He laid his head on her lap, and she began stroking his soft curls, straightening his tie, and removing lint from the shirt collar she'd ironed for him that morning.

Mary and Gerald received most of the guests as Katherine hid in her bedroom the way she'd done most of the week.

After the bedlam of the funeral, the graveside service, the fresh raw emotional flare-ups, and the flood of visitors, only Mary and occasionally Gerald were left to help with rebuilding what the new reality would be.

Mary was a petite and slender woman with a voice like the Alaga syrup she used to carry with her on trips to Newark—sweet but heavy and thick, a betrayal of what was expected from the frame that carried it. She hadn't seen her grandchildren in almost seven years but wasted no time entering in, trying to glean as much information as possible about their lives and who they were now.

"What you need Grandma to do? Cook? Go to the store? Clean?"

She asked them. Lavender found herself having to help the "helper" navigate her new environment as she assisted around the apartment. "Where's this go?" "How I get to the washateria 'round here?" "What station the stories be on?" Mary would ask. "Don't y'all got a corner store? Walk with me to it."

It was a barrage. It was mildly worrisome and feigned helplessness that even Lavender recognized as a willful distraction but still acquiesced to.

~

It was several days after Joshua's burial, and they all sat at the kitchen table over the breakfast Mary had prepared. "You know when you going back to work," she asked Katherine. "I ain't meaning no pressure, but I'm trying to plan, give Lizzy an idea. You talk to her?"

"Briefly," Katherine said before narrowing her lips and folding her arms into a tight knot. "Once. It was about a day after you got here. Lizzy said, 'Sorry 'bout your husband,' then said, 'We gon' be good,' and finally wanted to know how long you would be here. I ain't talked to her no more after that."

"Oh," Mary sort of half groaned. "Do you know 'bout work and whatnot yet? Askin' cause Lizzy..."

"I don't know momma. Lizzy a grown woman who can be without you for a little while."

"I was jus' askin' baby," Mary sighed. Any discussions about Elizabeth usually drew the ire of Katherine. "Well... we'll work it out."

"I still gotta deal with these police," Katherine continued.

Mary looked at the children. Čhetáŋ slowly consumed his bacon and eggs, while Lavender only drank her juice. "Why don't y'all finish all that up in the other room? Watch some TV," Mary suggested.

They obeyed, but it made no difference to Lavender. She knew she'd not miss the conversation and took her seat in the living room, making sure she plopped down in the chair closest to the words being spoken.

"What the police saying," Mary asked now that the kitchen was free of minors.

"They looking for a man who was a friend of ours. Used to play with Joshua. Gerald said he left him with Maurice, and that's the last time he saw him alive." Her voice cracked a bit. She pulled a cigarette from her purse and lit it, taking a deep pull before exhaling through her nose. She walked to the pantry, pulled a bottle of vodka out, and filled her glass of juice nearly halfway with the liquid. Mary opened her mouth to say something but relented.

"I do gotta get back to work. I'm all out of sick and bereavement time, and them people ain't gonna hold that job for me. Gerald helped, but I spent a lot of savings on the burial."

Katherine took large sips of the beverage with one hand and alternated with pulls from her Kool cigarette with the other in a crude juggling performance of self-medication.

Lavender could smell the smoke from the other room and hear the stress of the conversation in Katherine's voice despite Čhetáŋ's loud flipping of television channels.

"I probably need to work as much overtime as possible. But I still gotta straighten out all Joshua's stuff. Meet with the bank, insurance, and creditors. I guess it's good the kids out of school, but at least if they was, I know they could go there most of the day, I wouldn't have to worry 'bout what they doing. I gotta think about that too now."

"Well, about that," Mary interrupted. "I was thinkin' 'bout all you had to do. I can't help you with that too much, but I can take the kids with me. They can stay with us a couple weeks 'til you can sort through all the business up here. It can be just like it was when y'all used to visit in the summer."

Lavender could only decipher every few words over the television and through their soft tones, but she picked up the essence of Mary's suggestion. She remembered their trips to Alabama every other summer before Čhetáŋ was born. She recalled Mary's "blackberry slang cobbler," attending church services in a small, sweaty sanctuary and playing in the dirt in her grandmother's garden. But what stood out most was the near atmospheric shift surrounding her thoughts on her Aunt Elizabeth. Even in her current recollection, those memories were consumed with shadowy, indiscernible murkiness.

"Or," Mary proceeded, "You can move back home after. You alone here. At least for a little...."

"I ain't going back there," Katherine cut in. "And I ain't alone. I got friends. I got family here. I made a life. You see how full that church was the other day? We have people here. You think I wanna come back there with nothing and hear Lizzy's mouth?"

"I'm not saying that, I...."

"Yes, you are," Katherine interrupted Mary again, "It took so much to get me here already. You know that."

Mary sipped her coffee and allowed the temperature to cool on the conversation. "Well, let me take the chil'ren for a while like I said."

Katherine sat still for a moment, continuing her juggler's act—left hand, drink, right hand, smoke.

"And 'fore you say it, it ain't outta my way. I ain't spent much time with them, none at all really. I wanna do it," Mary pleaded once more.

"They can be a handful, is all," Katherine said. "Lavender think she grown, got a smart mouth, and Čhetáŋ," a grin flashed across Katherine's face, "Well Chase, cause that's what he'll want you calling him, he just runs wild playin'."

"You forget I raised two myself already?" Mary said and smiled.

Lavender relaxed back in her chair. "We going to Alabama now," she said, just over a whisper to Čhetáŋ.

"Huh?" He lazily responded without turning from the television.

She didn't waste another word of explanation. She readied her thoughts for yet another transition in what had already been a devastating past few weeks.

They agreed on the children's trip to Alabama, and the subsequent days were filled with a tug-of-war between Lavender wanting to remain and the adults insisting and then demanding her acceptance of the inevitable.

"You can take Čhetáŋ. Momma needs me. I can help. I'm not a baby!" Lavender declared repeatedly. She even expanded the amount and intensity of her house chores, hoping that the extra sweeping and mopping would prove her usefulness there at home. It was futile.

Five days after they buried Joshua, Lavender and Čhetáŋ were packing two weeks' worth of belongings to head down to Montgomery, Alabama.

Čhetáŋ was excited by the venture. He had dozens of questions for his grandmother, as he had never been outside the tri-state area in his entire life. He only knew what he'd seen in books or heard Katherine recount.

"Is there like those little buildings to go to the bathroom? And water wells and stuff?"

"Little buildings? Where the hell you think I'm from?" Katherine replied to some of his more fantastical assumptions.

On and on he went, all the way up to the day they were boarding the bus.

"Will there be cows and stuff? Horses? Cotton?" Čhetáŋ continued his interrogation.

"This ain't slavery, fool." Lavender snapped back as they walked through the bus terminal. She'd finally tired of his *silly* questions.

Katherine solemnly laughed at them as she helped roll Mary's suitcase.

"You might see some of those things on the way, but not where I live at, baby. You'll see."

Mary stood to the side while the children said their goodbyes. Lavender's eyes were spigots, and Čhetáŋ, who'd been too curious over his destination to notice her anguish before, finally recognized her grief.

"It won't be but for a little while," he said, attempting to comfort her. "I miss Daddy too." He quieted into his own melancholy and held his sister's hand.

Katherine pulled them both in close to her. "Babies, I love you," she said through tears. "Y'all gon' have a good time there. Be good for me and your daddy, ok?" She took Lavender's face between her fingers. "Look after your brother. Be strong. You're a smart girl."

She wiped Lavender's cheeks and kissed her, stepping back to observe her fully as though it was her first time seeing her daughter. "You look just like him," she said. "Strong and beautiful." Then she backed away to hug Mary. "I'll be checking in. I'll let you know the status on everything. Don't know how long this kind of stuff takes."

Mary nodded, and the three boarded the bus.

Lavender took a seat across the aisle from her grandmother and Čhetáŋ by the window where she could still see her mother looking on. Katherine found her face in the pane, smiled, and waved. But the only response she received was Lavender's skeptical, somber eyes gazing back.

Chapter 8

Honeysuckle Offenses

"Here I Am (Come And Take Me)" - Al Green

It was almost a day's drive between Newark and Montgomery. Not an easy journey for an older woman, an unwilling preteen, and a seven-year-old who was antsy over being cooped up longer than thirty minutes at a time. Nevertheless, they managed the trip without losing their wits or enraging the other passengers.

Their Greyhound bus pulled into the station in Montgomery around midnight. To Čhetáŋ's disappointment, it was dark when they passed the few cotton fields that existed along the interstate, and he missed them.

"You'll catch them when you go back," Mary assured him.

The brief walk from the bus before they reached the cool air-conditioned climate of the depot was thick, *soupy* déjà vu to Lavender. She recalled how when she was younger, she would pretend that marching through Montgomery's "gooey" air was like crossing the swamp in her "Liza Lou and the Yeller Belly Swamp" book. *I remember this now,* she thought, even as she struggled to make sense of much else.

They weren't at the station long before a full-figured, deep-brown woman with two children in tow, commanded the attention of everyone there as she approached. Her hair was tied up in a head-scarf. She wore a faded Disney World t-shirt and blue jean shorts a size smaller than was needed. The woman loudly criticized the small boy walking with her for not keeping pace as she sashayed forward. She then chastised the older girl for not making him keep up.

"Oh, there go Lizzy," Mary said, nodding toward the vexed woman moving through the room.

There was no warm greeting when she reached them—just a mild "Hey," as she stopped near Mary.

"This your Aunt Elizabeth, Čhetáŋ," Mary said, "and your cousins Jason and Keshia. Lavender, I know you remember everybody, 'cept Jason."

Jason hadn't been born yet the last time Lavender was in Montgomery. He was a plump boy with sandy hair, clinging to his sister before eventually running to Mary. They all looked at each other in silence, paralyzed by awkwardness.

"Aww boy!" Elizabeth exclaimed as Jason latched on to her mother. She then began to tug and pull on Mary's luggage and bark commands to her children as they trailed out of the station.

"Y'all mama sent y'all down here like you was fixin' to live," Elizabeth muttered, complaining about all their bags as they made their way towards an old Cadillac Fleetwood illegally parked on the curb just outside the doors.

When they exited the station, the heat and humidity enveloped Lavender once more, and by the time they were at the car, she wore a sheet of perspiration.

It was dark and too late for them to observe the neighborhood or explore Mary's home. Elizabeth helped them in, uttered what few words she had to say to Mary only, then left. They called Katherine, who sounded half asleep, to let her know they'd made it, then proceeded to bed.

The following morning Lavender slept until almost noon. The smell of Conecuh sausages, eggs, and biscuits filled her nostrils and titillated her to consciousness. When she got up, she immediately went to find Čhetáŋ, who'd slept in Elizabeth's old room while she'd rested in Katherine's adjacent chambers. Having a room to herself for the first time since he'd been born, even if only for a couple of weeks, was perhaps the one thing she believed to be positive out of the entire visit. However, she found that she lacked sound rest without his presence that night. When she finally left her room, she could already hear him excited over some topic in the kitchen.

"Grandma, any kids live around here?"

"Yeah, there's plenty. I can take you by a couple nice neighbors I know later." Mary glanced up to see Lavender creeping into the room. "Good morning, sleepy head."

"Hey," she responded in a groggy voice.

"Go on 'head and feed your face."

Lavender fixed her plate and devoured large portions of everything, including the plum preserves she hadn't had for years but still remembered—her eyes growing large when she saw the jar. She paused as the sweetness melted on her tongue, and the aroma lingered on her fingers from where the jelly had merged with her bread.

"I see somebody finally got they appetite back," Mary noticed. "Y'all can hang 'round here for a little while but come by the store this afternoon. I'ma need help, and it'll give y'all something to do."

"Store?" Čhetáŋ asked.

"Yeah. Lavender, you remember it? Two blocks down on the right. You need me to walk with you?"

"No ma'am, I got it," Lavender said between bites.

The store, Freeman's Grocery, was a small mom-and-pop which Mary and her late husband, Ernest, owned. Lavender remembered how as a child, she thought they were rich because they had their own bodega like those back home. Whenever she was there, she was implored to help tidy things up, which granted her access to all the sweets from the shelves she wanted. Being closer to Čhetáŋ's age then, she recalled the excitement she had about doing "adult labor." That was then.

I ain't come down here to work, she thought.

"Cool!" Čhetáŋ exclaimed in contrast.

Just then, a loud bang of the screen door slamming shut interrupted them as Kenneth walked in, sweaty after cutting Mary's grass.

"Ma," he announced, wiping his brow with a towel. Mary winced at the entry and salutation. "I'm finished. Oh..." He spotted the two youths at the table. "Good morning, Cha-tin and Lavender? I say that right?"

"Not really," Čhetáŋ responded. "Most people don't say it right. I like to be called Chase anyway. That's my middle name."

"Ok. Yes sir. Chase, it is. I know I won't forget those names." He joined them and grabbed a biscuit as he sat.

"Hey y'all, this Kenny, Jason's daddy," Mary announced before darting out of the room.

He was *different,* Lavender intuited. He lacked the southern drawl she'd heard from everyone since they arrived. He sat across from her with a friendly smile that she forced her mouth to repay and turned up the corners of her lips. He had a chestnut complexion and a low haircut with waves brushed into submission. Lavender thought he had a handsome face and couldn't help but wonder how someone like her aunt had managed to get him. He was also friendly, and Elizabeth had been anything but that so far.

"Where you from?" Lavender asked before she could catch herself.

"Massachusetts."

Her expression was curious, and he noticed.

"Military. I got stationed at Foshee." He glanced over Čhetáŋ, "How old are you, little man? I got somebody bigger than Jason I can play ball with now. For a little while at least."

The mention of "ball" made Čhetáŋ instantly enthralled and ready to morph into a chatterbox.

"You in the army?" Čhetáŋ asked. "My granddaddy was in the army too."

"No, he wasn't. He worked for an Air Force base," Lavender chimed in. Neither of them correctly conveyed the nature of Samuel's work at the commissary in a civilian role back in Rapid City.

"Same thing," Čhetáŋ said.

"How is it the same thing, fool?"

The infighting between the two tickled Kenny. "No, I'm not in the Army," he continued. "Foshee is Air Force. I guess like your grandfather worked. But I'm not even in it anymore. I do construction."

"Here you go," Mary said, reentering the kitchen. She handed Kenneth some cash as he gathered himself to leave. Before he did, he invited everyone to a cookout he and Elizabeth were putting together later in the day.

"I want you all to come, ok?"

"Ok," Čhetáŋ ensured as if he had the authority to promise anything.

When they finished their breakfast and spent some time at the store, Mary found the energy to honor Kenneth's request. Sheridan Heights was only a fifteen-minute drive from Ridgecrest, but it felt like an eternity to Lavender as she and Čhetáŋ both took in the terrain of the unfamiliar city.

Elizabeth and Kenneth's home was a modest ranch style with a spacious backyard. When they arrived, a few cars were parked on the street, and Lisa Lisa's "I Wonder If I Take You Home" blasted from beyond the fence. Once inside, the fragrance of cigarettes, barbecue, and beer welcomed them before anyone else officially could. Several rowdy games of Spades and Dominoes were all happening at once. Elizabeth, finally noticing her newest guests, approached with a drink and cigarette in one hand as Jason walked close to her hip, holding the other.

"Y'all, come get you a plate," she said.

There was barbecue chicken, steak, burgers, and franks. There were sides of corn on the cob, potato salad, baked beans, a four-layer chocolate cake, and a platter of cookies. Čhetáŋ's eyes grew large, and despite the snacks he'd just filled up on from the store, he loaded his plate with a bit of everything.

Lavender, however, considered her memories of friends who'd returned fattened from their visits "down south" and opted for only the chicken and corn.

Elizabeth noticed. "What's the matter? You don't like this food?"

"Oh, it's good. I'm just not hungry."

Elizabeth sucked her teeth, then turned up her cup and took a big gulp. "Kathy ain't cook for y'all up there or something? Y'all eat fancy city stuff or Navajo food?"

Lavender was confused. She didn't know her aunt well enough to gauge if she was drunk, ignorant, or intentionally rude. "No... I mean, yes, she cooked. And we ain't Navajo, but that's not why...."

"Lizzy, leave these chil'ren alone in peace," Mary interrupted.

Elizabeth lazily walked away, and Mary pointed out a place they could eat in an unoccupied corner.

"You don't worry about Lizzy. She always talkin' and lettin' a little of nothin' bother her."

Lavender nodded, sat with Čhetáŋ and Mary, and picked at her plate. Čhetáŋ soon got up and ventured off to play with his cousins in their rooms. At ages five and nine, Jason and Keisha were equidistant apart in years from him, and he quickly sought camaraderie from both.

Later, after feeling abandoned by her brother, Lavender announced to Mary that she would find him. It was also her opportunity to snoop around Elizabeth's place on her own.

She walked through the four-bedroom, two-and-a-half-bath house and thought of how tiny their New Jersey apartment was in comparison. She and Nadia would've loved to live somewhere this spacious, not crowded by the presence of stacked bodies and the loudness of the street outside their windows. But there was also a sort of boredom that abounded without those urban cues, and she'd miss that, she thought.

Lavender passed by a door that led to another exterior corridor where she first smelled it, then noticed Kenneth sitting alone outside smoking. He observed her creeping, unattended, appearing lost.

"Hey," he called out and opened the door for her. "You alright? You lost?"

"No, I'm good." She smiled, and her eyes landed on his hand of interest as the fumes of what was indeed marijuana lingered underneath the canopy.

"Aww, I know that look. I know where you're from." He laughed hardily. "No ma'am. You're not getting me in trouble."

"What?"

"I know you're a 'Brick City' girl. I was a city kid way back when too. Smokin', drinking, thinking I was grown. And no ma'am. Your grandmother would kill me on this day."

"I ain't even say anything."

He smiled a doubtful grin.

"You been to Newark?" She asked.

"Oh yeah. We used to go down to New York all the time to hang out. I had a couple of partners that lived across the river."

She gave Kenneth another look over. He wore a pair of white and black Jordan 9s with long denim shorts, an oversized black Polo shirt, and a gold chain "Jesus piece." He looked like any of the guys she was used to seeing on her corner back home.

"How you liking it down here so far in 'The Gump?'"

"The Gump?" She asked.

"Yeah, that's what they call it, 'The Gump.'"

"Eww, that's even countrier than I already thought."

Kenneth laughed.

"How do you think I'm liking it?" Lavender continued.

"It's an adjustment. But it's good you have family. I didn't have anything when I got stationed here."

"I guess," she paused, considering her next words. "Your girlfriend or your wife or whatever she is..." She stopped before saying too much.

He smiled. "Elizabeth? She has her ways. You just have to know how to maneuver around them." He swayed his hands in a swerving motion, like a vehicle dodging some unintentional object in the road. Lavender envisioned something more akin to a willful oncoming tractor-trailer. "And she's sweet too. When she wants to be, there's that."

"Well, she's weird. I'm staying out of her way while we're here." He grinned at that. "You seem cool. Like y'all don't go together," Lavender said, and he looked surprised. "Sorry."

He pulled a tallboy can of Colt 45 from where it was huddled beside him and cracked it open. It was sweating with condensation and almost slipped from his fingers before he took a drink.

"You get older, you'll understand. Sometimes you don't have control over who you like. Your aunt is real pretty, like all you Freeman women. I've seen your momma's pictures. And Lizzy, she definitely got another side to her." He smiled to himself.

Lavender shrugged her shoulders, thinking about how she never considered herself as having the "Freeman look." She peered out past the fence as the music changed to a blues song. "You need to go put on something better than this," she said.

He laughed. "You're alright, Lavender," then he passed his beer to her. "You can have the rest of this."

She looked at his offer with suspicion but realized it was genuine as nearly half of the can was still full.

"Thank you!"

"Just don't get me in trouble. Hold your liquor," Kenneth instructed.

"Of course, this is nothing." She gulped the remaining liquid down as quickly as possible.

"Now, go get you some food or gum or something to hide that, and go inside now before you smell like me and I still get in trouble." He gave her a serious look with the directive.

She nodded, already feeling the effects of the malt, trying to appear the mature, experienced drinker she'd portrayed herself as before heading indoors. Effects of the alcohol aside, she felt relief from the exchange. It was one of the few interactions she'd had with anyone here where she didn't feel her guard needed to be up as it was with her aunt. Or be on her most proper behavior as with Mary.

~

Their visit moved at a snail's pace for Lavender. As much as she had balked at assisting Mary at the store, she had to admit that it helped break up the hours of monotony and keep her mind from wallowing in sadness. She'd cried herself to sleep her first three nights there, away from home, the wound of Joshua being gone still fresh and the loneliness of being away from her friends was palpable. Čhetáŋ's experience had been the opposite. He mourned his father, but also happily rose every morning alongside Mary and the glorious smells of her cooking. He ate his weight in jelly, bread, and sausage. Then went out into the neighborhood, playing with the kids Mary had introduced him to—already gaining a reputation as a formidable base-ball player. It was as if he'd transformed Mary's street into his Cypress Grove block, reshaping his new terrain into a province that gave him most of his wishes. Sometimes the kids played kickball in one of the open fields near Mary's house. There, he'd run barefoot in the dirt, wrestle in the grass, and try to catch cicadas. He learned that the odd smell that permeated the air derived from a peculiar white, yellowish flower that grew along every fence. With enough precision, its bottom could be plucked and relieved of a long "string" that released a minute drop of nectar.

When he approached Lavender in excitement one afternoon with the honeysuckle and the new skill he learned of how to free it of its ambrosia, her response to him was a disappointing, "Who the fuck is doing all of that for that one little drop?"

Čhetáŋ took to the south, like a flock of birds to the air. Lavender took to it like a fish on land.

Every time Katherine called to check on them, the very first question from Lavender was when they could return home. The answer was never simple. It always "depended" on something, or some new, unexpected issue would arise, according to Katherine. The two weeks paraded on.

"It's not all about you," Katherine insisted over the phone one evening to Lavender. "Momma says Čhetáŋ is having a good time. You just makin' yourself miserable. Y'all staying a little longer would be good and help me out."

"No!" Lavender shouted.

Katherine revealed that Maurice had been arrested and the process would be lingering.

"I wanna be there momma. I wanna see that asshole."

"Why? What good would it do? I don't want y'all here for that. You already worked up," Katherine said. "I don't want y'all 'round this. Y'all need to have a summer—a decent one with whatever's left of it. Away from the bullshit. Away from these reminders, I gotta see every day."

This was the way of their next several conversations. Into week three. Then, into week four. It was a battle of wills until finally, on a late-June Sunday afternoon, Mary announced between the second helping of lima beans and smothered pork chops, "I'm keepin' y'all the rest of the summer! Ain't that good!"

Čhetáŋ yelped with glee while Lavender almost choked. Lavender remained quiet while Čhetáŋ expounded verbosely about the things he'd now get to do with Kenneth and Jason. There was fishing, baseball, basketball, and boxing even. Things Kenneth—who'd taken him under his wing—had told him about from his military days. It was a list of things Čhetáŋ apparently never realized he was missing. He spent all his life without brothers and with a father whose only use for a nylon string was for his classical guitar rather than entrapping bass along riverbanks with them.

Later in the quiet of the evening, after all the Sunday prayers, feasting, and planning for their remaining days there, Lavender crept into Mary's bedroom, where she lay partially under the covers. Only the reflection of the flickering lights from the small television illuminated her face.

"Baby? What is it?" Mary asked.

Even in the twilight, Lavender's expression wore her unease like an emblazoned sign that screamed caution, and Mary noticed.

"You should take us back," Lavender said. "You should take us back, and you stay with us. Up there. Stay with us in Newark."

Mary sighed, exhausted by this merry-go-round. "Lavender, we don' went through this. You know I can't stay. I got too much business here. I got the store. I have to help Lizzy with the grandbabies. This easiest for everybody now. You big enough to see that. Be a good girl."

"You don't know. You don't get it," Lavender said.

"What you talkin' 'bout child? What you mean?"

Lavender exhaled with worry, "Nothing." Then she stuffed her hands into her pants pockets and left her grandmother, never truly able to articulate her concerns.

"You don't sound good, baby," Mary said only a couple of minutes into the call. Katherine had few words, and those she expressed were pained and near whispers.

"How the hell I'm supposed to sound, momma?"

Mary was unaccustomed to that edge in her daughter's voice and nervously spouted, "Just the chil'ren... they worried. Wanna know what's going on. About the case and...."

"They ain't gotta worry. Tell 'em they don't. Why are you talkin' to them about it anyway?" Katherine paused for a moment. "The nigga took the plea deal. That's the case. I'm working two, sometimes three shifts at work and still barely making a dent. That's what's going on. Anything else?"

"Kathy..." Mary sensed the stress but still tried to extract as much information as possible and proceeded delicately. "Well, baby... Why didn't you call and let us know? At least baby girl. She's old enough, and I ain't have no answers when she asks. Just, we been waiting to hear is all."

"Cause what's to tell momma? That white folks don't give a shit when a Black man get killed? Charging Maurice with manslaughter? How the fuck robbery, manslaughter? Just cause he called them after he did the shit? They was trying to close this case so fast. Be done with it. Cause they don't care. They can't even..." Katherine's voice went hoarse. "They can't even find his wallet! He killed him to take his shit! I know it because I know how these people are, and he gon' get away with it too. Nobody cares about what's right."

Mary was quiet, searching for words of encouragement and could offer few.

"Well baby, I'm just gon' continue to pray and ...."

"What has God done in this?" Katherine said.

They ended the call shortly after.

~

It was July. Mary's phone had once rung in an almost rhythmic consistent pattern with calls from Katherine. However, as the family became more settled into the new routine, those calls came less and less.

"No messages either?" Lavender asked periodically whenever she hadn't heard from her mother.

"No news is good news. She ain't worried 'bout y'all. She knows Grandma got you." Mary spoke with confidence even after feeling concerned following the last conversations she had with her daughter.

As they neared the end of summer and the week they'd tentatively planned for their return, Katherine's communication remained unsteady. Mary had at one time made it clear to the children regarding her phone bill—"I ain't paying for y'all to run ya mouths to your little friends back home"—long-distance calls were strictly reserved for conversing with Katherine. But by August, Mary relented on that edict to try to connect with her daughter however possible.

Lavender reached out to Nadia as soon as she got that permission.

"Hey Lavender! I miss you! You on your way back?" Nadia blurted out with excitement when she heard her friend's voice on the line. Lavender hadn't spoken to her since they left and now sought any insight she could provide on Katherine from her vantage point in Cyprus Grove.

"I miss you too."

It took all Lavender had to bury the embarrassment and concern in her tone that she was certain would rise to the surface. The sadness grew upon hearing Nadia's voice, and she considered how unsure she was of when she'd see her again. But Lavender remained composed.

"You seen my momma around any?"

"Um... now that you say... no. Not in weeks."

Lavender received a similar response when she spoke to Ms. Jolene, who also asked to chat with Mary for a bit. Mary never revealed the details of what was said between them, but Lavender was perceptive enough to notice her grandmother's altered mood after the call ended with her former babysitter.

Still, Mary gingerly nudged the children towards preparing for their return. She reminded them about gathering their things and any novelties or trinkets they wanted to take back. "We gon' hear something soon. The moment we hear 'bout the when's and where's of what she needs us to do, just a matter of gettin' back up there then."

While her words still carried the same spirit of reassurance regarding their return, they lacked the previous tenacity. As if words that had to trudge through mucky apprehension to even make their way into the world. Lavender had barely unpacked her bags to begin with, remaining ready the leave at any moment.

Chapter 9

Going Home

"No Love Dying Here" - Gregory Porter

"The answering machine doesn't pick up no more, Grandma. We had one. It just rings now. She get rid of it?" Lavender asked Mary. It was the closing days of what should've been the finishing preparations for their exodus from Montgomery. Instead, the endeavor lacked direction or specifics because Katherine had become a mystery and remained elusive in those final weeks.

"I don't know. Why? What reason would she do that for?" Mary asked.

Lavender shrugged, "You never know." She had asked it rhetorically anyway. She understood Mary would not know the answer but wanted her grandmother to feel the apprehension that had been growing in her since their arrival.

Within a few days, Mary announced she was traveling to Newark and a show of relief, and a smile grew on Lavender's face after receiving the news. But then her grandmother announced, "Alone. I'm going to Newark alone," and Lavender's expression turned sour.

"Alone? Why!? Why can't we come? Why can't I? How are you gonna go back and not bring us?"

It was almost mid-August, and the void of information surrounding Katherine had reached its pinnacle.

"Cause I need to see what's going on 'fore I send or haul y'all up there."

"That don't make no sense!" Lavender said in an elevated tone, and Mary bristled.

"Ain't gotta make sense to you gal! It's what's gon' happen!"

Lavender burst into tears. The outpouring almost felt like recompense for the months of stoicism she had otherwise shown. She cried out, her pulse raced, and her breathing was rapid, bordering on hyperventilation.

"Baby, breathe! Calm yourself!" Mary insisted, wiping and fanning Lavender's face with her hand. Once that initial wave subsided, Mary continued. "You and your brother stayin' with Lizzy for a couple days. Only a couple. Then I'll be back."

"No, Grandma, please." Lavender's breaths were easier now, but her eyes still flashed anguish.

"Ain't no ways around it. Ain't no changing it now child. We gotta do it like this, now. It's gon' all be fine. You'll see."

Within a day, Mary boarded a plane to Newark. She'd managed to track Gerald's number down with assistance from Lavender, the operator, and some sleuthing of her own. He had been such a help in those days after Joshua's funeral that Mary figured he'd be a great companion and aide again. He was her escort once she landed at Newark Liberty International, and after brief pleasantries, they immediately went about the business at hand.

When they approached the door to Katherine's apartment, it had an eviction notice taped to it—issued in the past two days. The key still worked, and they entered, announcing themselves to echoes and hollowness as no soul abounded inside. A mass of clutter and chaos filled the apartment. The refrigerator was empty, and the pantry was depleted of all content. Every corner seemed to have trash or mail—envelopes with "Past Due" written on the front. They waited hours for Katherine to show, with nothing but small talk and the occasional scavenges through loose items to break the silence.

"I think we should get you to your hotel Mrs. Freeman. We can leave her a note if she comes back," Gerald eventually said.

She agreed with a disappointed nod and then exited while he locked up behind them. Out of the corner of her eye, Mary sensed the slightest movement from the direction of the stairwell and elevator corridor. It was Katherine emerging from the darkness at a slow, lumbering pace. She carried a quart of milk and one carton of eggs. Her hair was up in a messy bun, and the clothes she wore fell loose as tapestry.

Mary gasped. Gerald squinted as though trying to discover the identity of the doppelgänger before him.

"Kathy... " Mary muttered.

Katherine looked up at the two of them and then coiled her head against her clavicle like a tortoise seeking the safety of its shell.

"What y'all doin' here?" She mumbled.

"Came lookin' for you," Gerald said.

They all reentered the apartment, where Gerald left them alone. Other than their rustling feet through the debris on the floor as they walked, it was quiet between the two women for what felt like an eternity.

"Kathy, what you doin'? What's happening with you?" Mary asked.

Katherine ran her fingers up the sides of her bun and sat at the kitchen table.

"I'm dog-tired. Is what's happening," she finally said.

Mary pulled out the chair across from her and plopped down.

"Where all ya stuff? The children's? Why it's like this here? Why you ain't say you were getting put out?"

"I couldn't work anything out with the landlord, so I'm moving us to a smaller place and got things in storage in the meantime. It's just like this cause I ain't get a chance to straighten up. And if he gon' evict me, I ain't cleaning. They can have most of this shit anyway. I ain't gon' make it easy," Katherine said with contempt.

"I could've helped ya with money for a while at least. Why you ain't..."

"What money momma?" Katherine scoffed. "From the store and your Social Security check? I already got a new place anyway, like I said."

"Kathy, come home," Mary insisted.

"No. I'm making a way," Katherine said as she removed herself from the table and placed her meager groceries in the refrigerator. "Children just gon' be a little behind schedule at school, that's all. Their daddy died. The school knows this."

"Kathy, what you into up here? What you not tellin' me?" Mary asked.

"Huh?"

"I said, what are you into? Liquor? Pills? Something else?"

"I don't know what you trying to say. I do drink some. And? What of it? I can. That ain't got nothin' to do with nothin'."

"The hell it don't when ya got kids. How I'm s'posed to send my grands up here? To how you are?" Mary sucked her teeth.

"Then what then? You gon' take them or somethin'?"

"Oh girl," Mary hissed.

"Momma?"

They stared at each other in silence.

"Prove to me you doin' right by 'em, and I'll see," Mary responded.

"Prove? I could come and get them whenever I want. They mine!" Katherine slapped her hand against her chest as she said it.

"If that's what you wanted you would'a been don' that. You would've called, and I wouldn't be here."

They returned to their staring postures. Katherine broke from the gaze and looked past Mary towards one of their wallet-sized family photos still taped to the refrigerator door. She closed her eyes, opening them only when Mary approached and cupped her daughter's hands inside her own.

"Look, momma..." Katherine exhaled. "I just still need a little more time. Just a little more, that's all. I'm working hard and already got a place like I said. You see what I'm trying to deal with, with the money and stuff, is all."

"You choosing that, Kathy. You always been stubborn, and that's been for good and bad, but bullheaded, nonetheless. If ya need more time, that's fine. But better be worth it. Ain't no use tryin' to get blood from a stone here."

Chapter 10

Reluctant Sleuth

"Grandma's Hands" - Bill Withers

"That's how you sweep at your house?" Elizabeth asked as Lavender made a sluggish march through her chores at the store. It had been less than a day since Lavender had to digest the news that she and Čhetáŋ would be residents of their southern dwelling a bit longer. All Mary would say over the phone when she called from Newark was that they'd "talk about it when she got back." Lavender worked through her errands with more disdain than usual after that, and it was apparent to anyone watching. Elizabeth was always watching. In their brief stay with their aunt, Lavender felt like Elizabeth examined and critiqued their every action—especially hers.

When Mary returned—two days later than planned—Lavender noticed her grandmother's mood was somber and a bit distant. Even her smile and natural congenial manner did little to disguise it. The only answers Mary gave when questioned about what happened in Newark when she rested for a short time at Elizabeth's, were "fine" and "We've worked something out." The answers were insufficient for Lavender but not scant enough that she desired to remain under her aunt's roof one moment longer than necessary for clarity.

"Let's get us home, Kenny. I'm tired," Mary said less than five minutes after entering through Elizabeth's front doors.

When they arrived at Mary's house, she quickly sent Čhetáŋ to bed, granting him an assortment of allowances she hadn't all summer. She let him watch his television after hours and sent him in with his favorite sweets—apparently unconcerned with the ants and roaches she'd once said they'd draw.

Lavender was close to bursting, waiting for a moment when she and Mary could be alone. Her grandmother's return flight, car ride from the airport, and their trip back to Ridgecrest transpired in measures of days, not hours, in Lavender's mind.

Once the door to Čhetáŋ's room shut and he was content in a cocoon of oblivion for the night, Lavender started with the questions without pause. "It's bad? What happened? What momma say? When is she bringing us back?" She asked.

Mary looked at her, not speaking, just moving toward her bedroom in a slow glide. She beckoned for Lavender to follow her in. Mary closed the door behind them and turned her television on to nothing in particular—only for background noise loud enough to insulate their discussion.

She sat on the bed and exhaled. "Lavender, I got there... I got there and..." She sighed. "Well, that ain't y'all home no more, first off."

Lavender frowned, unable to comprehend. Mary explained it in plain terms. She told her about the eviction notice, the mess the place was in, and how all their things were missing. "In storage, as Kathy put it," Mary said. She also told Lavender how her mother secured another apartment on Warren Avenue.

"Warren Avenue?" Lavender's voice turned into a nervous reverberation.

"Don't you worry none. I went over there," Mary continued. "I told her I ain't havin' y'all livin' there."

Mary never slowed her dissemination of information. Her words weren't explosive revelations, needing time to be processed. She spoke them like they were matter-of-fact, inconsequential drivel that she needed to purge herself of.

"I told her that neighborhood ain't fit for an ol' stray cat, but she say that's all she can afford," she continued. "I told her to come home. She keeps sayin' no and that she already signed a lease. That y'all can make it fine there." Mary clasped her hands together. "That's when we get to arguin'. Right in Gerald's car. And I tell her I ain't bringin' y'all back like that."

Lavender's body was still and fixed to her place on the bed. Each of Mary's words had been a shot of venom to her ears, paralyzing her.

"She ain't right. But she won't tell me nothing goin' on," said Mary. "Gerald say he don't know nothing, and your daddy didn't tell him anything personal like that, but... he can see she ain't right either."

Lavender read between the words of what it felt Mary was implying.

Like she's on something? The same thing she'd asked Nadia if she had noticed about her mother.

Mary began sobbing, "Jesus, why all this?"

Lavender slid next to her on the bed and reached to hold her hands. She noticed they were warm and clammy as she had been clenching them tightly as she retold the story.

"It's alright Grandma," Lavender assured her. "She... she's been like this before, off and on. Just for a little while though. But then, she's back, and everything is good again. Daddy..." She stopped. She was about to say how Katherine's rebound was only a matter of time, as it always had been. Then it dawned on her that the person who usually set Katherine's course back right was no longer here.

Mary noticed Lavender's hesitation and how the girl's expression shifted. They both seemed to reach the same understanding in that moment. "I asked Gerald to keep an eye out and let me know if anything happens 'til I can get back again," Mary said.

"You going back?"

"She says she comin' to get y'all, but the lease is for six months.

She can't do nothin' about that. It's signed and since it is, she sound determined to make that work. I don't know what I'm gon' do," Mary wiped her face. "I ain't lettin' y'all stay there that's for sure. I ain't lettin' y'all go nowhere 'til I know what's goin' on and feel right about it."

Chapter 11

Certified Mail

"Back in the Day" - Ahmad Lewis

THE HEAT OF SEPTEMBER BEGAN TO SUBSIDE. IT WAS NO LONGER suffocating and oppressive but gave way to infrequent fluxes of cool breaths that announced Autumn's certainty. Lavender had detested the season's punishing warmth, yet the noticeable change served as no relief either. It tormented her in other ways—a reminder of what was lost and that there were things still left unanchored.

When she thought about it, it wasn't the day Mary first mentioned lawyers. Or the times she overheard her arguing with Katherine, using words like "temporary guardianship" and "probate court." It wasn't even when her grandmother made a last-minute trip to the airport and returned later that night to tell them she had "rights" now. It was the day they drove past their respective new schools—Fitzgerald Junior High and Floyd Elementary—that reality set in for Lavender.

Čhetáŋ was inconsolable when he learned *home* would have to wait, while Lavender was resolute to not shed any more tears over what she couldn't change. Instead, she'd taken to chastising her brother about what she saw as his excessive outbursts of emotion over something *any idiot could've seen coming*. It was her way of playing

66

the antagonist after he'd spent the entire summer absorbed in play, enamored by excursions with "the fellas," as he called Kenneth and Jason, and ignoring every concern she would mention.

"I wanna go home! Y'all can just take us back!" Čhetáŋ hollered the morning before they were to shop for school clothes at a local consignment store.

"Take us where, stupid? I told you momma got rid of our place."

"You're lying!"

"Why would I lie? Go on, call her! You heard from her since we're supposed to be back? No! Stop crying, damn fool!"

Mary's hand was quick to Lavender's backside. It surprised her but delighted Čhetáŋ.

"Don't talk to him like that! Just cause you hurtin' don't mean you get to hurt him."

Similar scenes of arguments, weeping, and remorse would play out for weeks before they started school and as they acclimated into the academic year. Nothing served to boost their morale, not even the calls from Katherine when she had updates and hopeful promises about the coming months.

Lavender tried viewing their circumstance as just a bizarre detour with the end destination of "home," still in full view. After all, temporary guardianship was called temporary for a reason, and six months wasn't "too long." Lavender would turn these thoughts over often in her mind. *Returning in time to start the new semester wouldn't be so bad*, Lavender considered. However, Mary was adamant about them not living in what she viewed as the squalor of the new apartment and neighborhood Katherine had relocated to.

"We can do 'til January, Čhetáŋ," Lavender would say to him occasionally. "You ain't gonna wanna live on 'Killer Warren Ave' anyway. Be glad Grandma stopped that. She, Gerald, and momma can find something way better, and we'll be back."

The intermittent soothing of his emotions had served well enough to get them through the early autumn months, months peppered with bad report cards, school altercations, and uncomfortable run-ins with Elizabeth.

Occasionally, Mary had the entire family over for a Sunday dinner, where those kinds of bitter exchanges with Elizabeth would often occur.

"You know why I give y'all a hard time?" Elizabeth directed the random question at her niece during one of these meals. Jason, Keshia, and Čhetáŋ were busy playing in the living room, and Lavender sat at the dining room table across from Kenneth when Elizabeth came in with trays of food and in one of her moods. "It's cause how else y'all gon' learn responsibility? Your momma don't know nothin' about that, and my momma ain't gon' do shit but baby y'all. See, right now, why your little ass ain't in the kitchen helping?"

Lavender slid the chair from underneath her and began to stand, only to have Elizabeth suck her teeth at the motion.

"It's too late now." Then Elizabeth placed the food on the table with a thud.

Lavender sat in silence. She rolled her eyes once her aunt exited, then glanced at the man across from her.

"It's not you, baby girl. It's shit from way back, with your momma," he said, never looking up from the vibrating pager in his hands.

"You know what it is?" Lavender asked in a low voice.

He quit tinkering with the device. "Something about how she left when they were young and when you guys' granddad was sick. I don't know, something like that."

She peered with a pensive look before Kenneth gently touched her hand. "If you ask me, though, I just think she was jealous," he said, smiling. "Apparently, your momma was a big deal, at least around here back in the day. You probably remind her of that."

She gave a bashful grin, still wondering about the depths of their dispute while feeling fortunate she only had to deal with Elizabeth on occasion. She never bothered with further investigation into their past disputes whenever Katherine called home—calls that had now dwindled to about twice a week. Those conversations were brief and infrequent enough as they were. Lavender reasoned that the ancient feud between those two *old ladies* wouldn't matter after she was back in Newark anyway. She was more concerned with her mother's inconsistency.

She tried to heed Katherine's pleas for patience when she expressed frustration with her sparse communication and what felt like disarray.

"I'm off at three, sometimes four in the morning. When I'm up, y'all at school. When I'm sleeping, y'all up. I'm trying."

I'm trying. Lavender replayed Katherine's explanations of what she was enduring without Joshua, all alone for the first time in almost fifteen years. She tried to understand.

Halloween came and passed. Then Thanksgiving. Their feast was large and absent Katherine, who couldn't spare the expense to travel. She called that afternoon before work, not having the holiday off, allegedly.

"Happy Thanksgiving y'all. Love you," rang from the speaker-phone. She coughed excessively but otherwise sounded content. The family gorged and didn't think much of the unassuming call.

Two weeks later, Mary heard from Gerald.

"Mrs. Freeman, sorry it's late."

"Ain't never late for you, Gerald. What's going on?" Mary regarded him as *her eyes* in Newark and never tired of his calls, no matter the hour.

He hesitated a second. "Well... it might be nothing, but...Kathy asked me to do something that didn't seem quite right."

Mary braced for what it might be.

"She had me go over to storage and get some things out. But, well, one was Joshua's, Les Paul. Said she was gonna ship it down for Lavender."

Mary breathed a nervous sigh of relief. "Oh. That's ok ain't it? Well, I don't really know what a Les Paul is, you say."

"It's an electric guitar. It was Joshua's baby."

Mary, still confused, "I don't know nothing 'bout all that. Alright for her to have, but I ain't about a lotta racket either."

He chuckled for a second. "Not exactly how it works, Mrs. Freeman. She won't make much sound at all without an amp."

"Oh? Well, what's wrong then?"

He exhaled, "It's just that, that's a real nice instrument, and with the case and all, it'll take almost seventy dollars alone to ship and... well... maybe Kathy wants her to have it for Christmas or something, but...."

"But what?" Mary was ready for him to come out with it.

"Well, Mrs. Mary, why would you spend all that when you're trying to save money and when the person it's for is supposed to be here in two months anyway?"

Chapter 12

Calluses

"Here We Go Again!" - Portrait

TABS: E3, A0-A2... DOWN, UP, DOWN... G, EM, C...

"Redemption Song," by Bob Marley, timidly flowed from Lavender's fingertips through the guitar as if the instrument feared its own voice. Chords that when wielded with boldness, could both incite rebellion or croon in a calming nature to quiet the manic. However, Gerald was correct. Without the amplifier, Joshua's mighty Les Paul was less than a soft purr. Still, Lavender appreciated the tranquility. It allowed her to practice without disturbing the house while also concealing the flaws that months without playing had almost calcified.

She believed it was impossible to forget the first song Joshua taught her. When she plucked the first few strings, she knew she had some brushing up to do. It came back to memory fast enough, but her fingers had softened. Even by nylon string standards, they were pulp. This was nickel-plated steel, and her fingers ached from pressing them against the fretboard. She'd have to re-fortify her fingertips again, a frustrating endeavor to regain her playing levels and gain calluses.

The way she got her hands on Joshua's Les Paul—the one he chastised her about touching—wasn't unrecognized by her. It was that cruel irony that kept her away from playing it weeks after it arrived. The massive box landed just days before Christmas and required the formal signature of one, *Lavender Amášte Adair*.

She didn't know what to make of it, never receiving certified mail or much mail at all before. It was from Katherine, and Lavender's first instinct was that it must be good news. Mary was somber in its reception, however. She already had a notion of what the package could mean.

"Wonder what it is?" Lavender questioned aloud.

"Why only you get something?" Čhetáŋ wondered with a perplexed look.

When she opened it, Lavender squealed with joy initially. That feeling then gave way to a forlorn mood that she remained in for days. Mary joined her in sullenness. The parcel was just more confirmation of looming trouble.

A few weeks later, another sizable package arrived of several large crate-size boxes, this time addressed to both Čhetáŋ and Lavender from Gerald. Čhetáŋ was excited at the haul until they opened each crate and discovered they all contained the same sort of item—cassettes. There were tens of hundreds of standard cassettes and older 8-track cartridges.

"What in the world!?" Mary exclaimed upon receiving the shipments at her home. She made an urgent phone call to "her eyes" in New Jersey.

"Mr. Gerald, I know you said you was sending the children they daddy music, but I ain't know you meant all this! What we supposed to do with it? Altogether, these things can fill a closet, flo' to ceiling'!"

Gerald explained that in those crates were nearly two decades of Joshua's shows. Some were from his days with Rhapsody, but much was from times before, including solo gigs. "I had to decide what to take in the quick time they gave me before they seized everything. I figured these were the most valuable, sentimentally at least."

As with their Cypress Grove apartment, the self-storage unit Katherine had leased also went into default. Mary would've argued against spending all the money it took to mail those cassettes—cash Gerald collected from the rest of the band. She would've preferred the children's winter clothes and shoes for the coming months be sent or the money itself instead of boxes of music she had nowhere to store.

Lavender asked her grandmother where she could put them.

"I don't know. Put 'em outside under the carport." Mary instructed.

"The carport that leaks when it rains hard? The carport that somebody stole your wheelbarrow from?" Lavender asked. "No, I'm not putting them there."

"Well, where you think they goin'? Ain't no room at the store either," Mary explained.

Lavender happily stacked them two bins across and three high at the foot and the side of her bed. It made navigating the room awkward but gave her easy access as she played a different tape every night. It also provided a barrier of semi-privacy. Mary, with few exceptions, didn't allow them to close the doors to their rooms, and Lavender's bed faced the hallway. She could now lie near the foot, almost completely hidden behind them. The new layout—being unfriendly to older knees—also kept her grandmother from entering as freely as before. Lavender stretched across the bed, wearing headphones, listening to one tape at a time, surrounded by the others. Without thinking about it, she created a cavern that swaddled her in Joshua's essence.

The guitar and the cassette shipments were the only significant developments in the continued Katherine and Newark saga over the holiday season. Lavender and Čhetáŋ received clothes from Mary and Elizabeth and a refurbished Sega game console that Mary claimed came from Katherine for Christmas. Kenneth bought Čhetáŋ a football and slipped Lavender the 2Pac CD she wasn't supposed to have. Kenneth promised to get her a CD player when she mentioned the only one she had was attached to her stereo in Newark. That stereo was also now in limbo alongside their other belongings due to Katherine's delinquency on her self-storage unit.

Katherine had an answer for that—as she did regarding all uncomfortable discussions during their family calls. "I ain't feel like it made sense to keep paying that storage, so I just... I sold off some of me and Joshua's things and I'm keeping the rest in the children's rooms. They're not here with me. Remember?" Katherine never missed an opportunity to make a dig at the temporary guardianship Mary had gained, even though Katherine had reluctantly agreed to it.

She had answers and affirmative explanations for almost every aspect of her wandering and fickleness.

"I got a job interview coming up. It's gon' pay better, be better hours, and then, I can really make it happen. Don't make sense to try for the same ol' thing that will get me to the same spot I'm in now," Katherine said while discussing a new opportunity. She then explained the role was as an assistant for an entertainment lawyer,

Čhetáŋ yelled, "Good luck!"

Mary went on about how it sounded interesting.

Lavender frowned, recalling the other forays into the entertainment sector Katherine had tried before.

"And what of the apartment?" Mary asked. "'Bout getting a better one?"

"I can't do nothing there until after I hear about the jobs." Words Lavender had heard so often now, it was just a discorded refrain of a song—a rhythmic chant and predictable cadence.

"So, guess you talkin' even later now? Gettin' them back," Mary asked. Her voice was slight, but the question drilled to the core issue.

"Momma, what you want? I can't see into the future. I'm trying.

You told me what I had wasn't good enough, so I'm trying for better. Now you sayin' that ain't good enough either?"

Every phone call followed this path, going from initial pleasantness to frustrating debates over plans and the feasibility thereof.

Mary planned to revisit Katherine to see the conditions for herself. "Ain't no meat on them bones, 'til I can see," she told Lavender, who'd grown into her main confidant in matters. But before she could schedule her return, Gerald called with a word of warning.

"I ain't saying you'd be wasting your money and time, Mrs. Freeman. Can't tell you how to feel, but you may come all the way here and never lay eyes on her. Y'all don't get steady word from her there, and I can barely track her down here with my schedule and not knowing hers. And..." He hesitated. "I know you had thoughts about her being on something... I guess, well, I've seen it enough to know what that looks like. When I did see her last, weeks ago, she had that look, desperate like." He cleared his throat. "You work these clubs long enough, and you hear things. People I'm hearing her name brought up with ain't good. Don't mean it's certain, but...."

Mary felt like he was too ashamed to speak in explicit terms. His mumbling on and on about how things "seemed" and "looked" only made her desire to return to Newark feel more urgent. She booked her flight and hotel anyway. When she finally did get in touch with Katherine on the phone, she made her intentions plain. "Ain't no wait and see when I come this time, Kathy. I'm old and can't keep all this up. I need to see you livin' decent and workin'. I need to see who you 'sociating with, or I need you to have your tail on the plane back with me!"

Katherine quietly agreed to all her terms and a tenuous calm followed.

The week of Mary's scheduled visit, Katherine's communication faded to total silence once more. Gerald didn't fare any better, and Mary seesawed between fury and fear of the worst.

"I'm done with it this time!" Mary would rage one instance in front of the children or to Elizabeth. Then burst into spontaneous tears the next, "Jesus, please, put yo' protective hedges 'round my child. Let her be safe, Father." She contacted authorities but had to wait the allotted time for "missing" individuals before anything could be done.

∼

This is a pre-paid call from [pauses and phone clicks] 'Katherine,' an inmate at Essex County Correctional Facility... Do you accept? The automated voice rang out when Lavender answered the phone the evening after they sought police help, wondering about her whereabouts.

"Momma?"

"Lavender, what you... Where momma at?"

"She's grocery shopping." A long pause ensued. "Hello?" Lavender could hear what sounded like sniffling. "Momma?"

"I'm sorry... Baby, I'm sorry."

"You in damn jail!?" Lavender asked.

More silence.

"I'm sorry."

"Sorry for what?"

"I can't do better by y'all right now," Katherine said, weeping.

"So, what you saying?" Lavender's face was fire. She could feel the burning and tightening around her throat, making it hard to even express that rage. Through clenched teeth, the words eventually flowed unbound. "Say it," Lavender demanded. "Say what you sorry for. You ain't got no way for us to get back, do you? We ain't got nothing to come back to? That why you fuckin' up? It's because you don't want us back. Ain't that right?"

Katherine sobbed, struggling to answer. Lavender didn't relent. She wanted her to say what was now the irrefutable conclusion in her mind. That, that entire summer away had only been a test, a test for the kind of reprieve her mother had wanted.

"Ok, you ain't gotta say it," Lavender continued. "I knew that when you put us on the bus. You looked like somebody who just got set free."

"That ain't true! It ain't!"

"It is!" Lavender screamed back.

The automated voice announced the time was down to a minute, but it didn't dull Lavender's onslaught. "I don't believe you! You weren't ever doing nothing to get us back there!"

"Don't talk to me like that. Lavender. I, I just needed a little break. Joshua held a lot of stuff together. Things ain't work out in the end. One day you'll see how stuff don't always fall in place and..."

"Bullshit. Mothers don't get breaks from their kids. I'll never see that!" Lavender's emotions came flooding out. She was angry at Katherine and at herself for allowing the tears she'd mostly warded off for months to pour when her only desire was to prove her indifference to *that woman.*

Čhetáŋ entered the room, confused by all the tension in his sister's voice.

"What's wrong?" He asked.

"Put Chase on the phone," Katherine asked, needing a break from Lavender's sharp attacks.

"No!"

"Lavender!" Katherine demanded.

"For what? So, you can lie to him too?"

"Is that momma," Čhetáŋ asked, looking on in bewilderment.

A lifetime transpired in the sixty seconds of what was left of the collect call.

"Lavender? Lavender?" Katherine exhaled a deep, weighty breath. "Just, please tell momma where I'm at, and I'll call her when..."

The cold, automated voice interrupted again to declare their time had expired. Lavender slung the phone to the floor and stormed past Čhetáŋ, who stood frozen with his mouth agape. He finally mumbled something to her, but she couldn't hear him. Pounding rage filled her ears. It was distorted chords thundering from chamber to chamber in her head—loud, off-key notes of friction, sending currents of heat over her. She slammed and locked the door to her room and paced the floor, ignoring Čhetáŋ's pleas and his banging until he went away. Nothing soothed her.

She eventually collapsed into her cradle at the foot of the bed behind all of Joshua's music and extracted the first cassette her fingertips found as she reached into one of the bins. She opened the case, placed it into the Walkman, and hit play. A sad tune opened, slow, and tampered down. Some man's voice boomed through, surprising her. Joshua's bands were usually instrumental quartets, rarely utilizing vocalists at all. She almost fast-forwarded past the first number, wanting to hear something spotlighting only her father. Yet even that simple operation required a level of focus and energy she couldn't find.

The voice kept singing, "What kind of fool am I." It was a song by Sammy Davis Jr. about being empty and never knowing love. A melancholy jazz number of a man reflecting on the self-sabotage he imposed in relationships, leaving him alone. The song's topic, perspective, and downtrodden nature would seem too paradoxical to grip an adolescent girl's attention. Yet somehow, she couldn't move past it, playing it over and over again.

Chapter 13

Distractions

"Keep Ya Head Up" - 2Pac

Lavender gripped the girl's hair between her fingers with a tight pull so that escape was a hopeless cause. She slammed her fist into the side of the girl's temple as hard as she could.

Crack!

The circling crowd in the hallway shouted as if the school's walls were the interior of a Roman coliseum. They erupted even louder when Lavender pinned her to the floor and pummeled her from above— head, face, body, face, face, face, on and on. Lavender dealt blow after blow to any exposed area she could find.

Eventually, a resource officer grabbed her, freeing the defenseless, bloodied soul whose only miscalculation that day was making a show of pointing out Lavender's "repeat jeans" that she'd worn for the third time that week. She and Čhetáŋ were still without large options in their wardrobes after theirs never made it down from Newark, and Mary was doing her best to replace them one piece at a time. Repetition in their attire was not uncommon.

"Lavender, you got them same ugly gray jeans on from Monday and Wednesday!"

It was the last sentence the girl uttered before receiving the

79

lumps that swelled on the side of her face and head. The girl clawed and cursed as security restrained her.

"Let me go!" She screamed.

"Yeah, let her go!" Lavender said from within the enveloped arms of the other massive guard. She was unscathed, laughing and largely pleased with herself.

It was the second fight of her eighth-grade school year, and there were still four months to go. Lavender sometimes felt disoriented as to how she made it to her second year of junior high anyway, her first being such a blur. She recalled doing just enough to pass classes and a couple of instances where Mary sobbed in parent-teacher conferences, accruing enough sympathy and perhaps guilt that the few points Lavender was short of matriculating "appeared" by the time final grades were entered.

"We doin' the best we can... This my first year havin' 'em down here on my own. Sometimes they go weeks without hearing from their momma. She's been struggling, and I'm workin' and trying to help them keep up. It's too much at times..." Mary's words to instructors were all true, but sometimes Lavender cringed hearing them out loud, as though they were scripted in a film about someone else.

Čhetáŋ had adjusted much better than she had. But he wasn't dealing with *wild hormones* yet, nor what that meant alongside *gossipy girls* like she was, Lavender concluded. Whenever report cards came, and hers resembled sketches of tiny protruding half-moons next to each course down the page, she reminded Mary of that fact.

Lavender missed her own chatty cliques of girls from Cyprus Grove. She missed Nadia. The smell of the stairwell near the girl's bathroom would sometimes dredge up memories of her old building —aged, soured linoleum flooring, a tinge of mildew in the air. Lavender had stopped calling her old cohorts now. She used to call Nadia whenever Mary allowed, but that grew too painful. Cypress Grove was now a world she was far removed from, full of strange news and unfamiliar names of people she had no context for. It was also embarrassing.

Everyone knew why she wasn't there among them as she should've been, engaging in neighborhood talk on their stoop or pursuing matters of the heart like her affair with Justin Brown. Her father was murdered. Her mother was lost. And those were things Lavender would rather not be constantly reminded of in discussions about *The Grove.*

Čhetáŋ's slow detachment from Newark was similar, except he at least managed new acquaintances. Lavender remained peculiar and awkward but absent her Haitian companion of a similar distinction to ease that loneliness.

When she received a classical guitar as a gift, it was at least a reunion of sorts with a familiar friend and another diversion from reality. Kenneth purchased a new one for her after overhearing her repeatedly strumming those faint sounds on the Les Paul as he performed errands around Mary's house.

"Can't nobody hear that, you know," he mentioned in passing.

She had her bedroom window open on a mild January day, and he hovered just outside, clearing gutters. "No shit, Sherlock," she said through the screen. "Grandma won't buy me the amplifier."

He laughed.

The following afternoon Mary presented her with the new instrument, telling her she'd saved enough to buy a used one. Kenneth hadn't wanted any acknowledgment lest he have to deal with Elizabeth's questions about it.

"Don't keep up a whole lot of racket, now," Mary advised before releasing it to her.

Lavender gleamed even brighter than when she'd received the Les Paul. She knew this machine intimately, and this instrument didn't come with the same sad memories.

"You just sit down," Lavender instructed Mary.

She gave it a quick tune, then dazzled with a series of complicated finger-picking songs. Mary transformed into a giddy seal, clapping, squealing, and flailing in admiration.

"Oooh baby, good job! Good job! Well done!"

"What did you think? That they were ly— I mean, tellin' stories when Momma and Čhetáŋ said I was good?"

"Guess I just had to hear for myself."

"I played the other guitar," Lavender said.

"Nah, you tried to hide in your room," Mary pointed out, then immediately began requests. "You know some gospel songs you can play on this acoustic?"

"It's a classical guitar, Grandma."

"Oh, whatever it is. Can you?" Mary asked.

Lavender played the few she knew, then worked her way through more with her grandmother's assistance. They went on in this manner for over an hour that evening. Mary called out titles, and Lavender picked through them with ease. If she was unfamiliar with a song, Mary hummed it, and without her being pitch-perfect, Lavender could translate Mary's voice into the correct notes. Then, parrot it back with the proper tabs and chords as though it were only a faded memory that needed the right prompt for recollection. The impromptu "musical doubles" became weekly affairs, sometimes extending well into the night, providing each with appreciated distraction.

The rain droplets landed on Čhetáŋ's hand as he held onto the bullpen railing at the local ball field. The thunder from the fleeting storm had been loud enough to run every other living creature into hiding. Yet that didn't deter him from running out and sliding into the grass with Jason, making complete muddy spectacles of themselves.

"Y'all quit that foolishness," Kenneth yelled from home plate. "I don't wanna be out in this weather if y'all ain't gonna be serious."

Čhetáŋ straightened up, put his glove on, and yelled, "Ok, I'm ready!"

Kenneth leaned back, tossed the ball into the air, and swung his bat, hitting a near line-drive toward Čhetáŋ. The boy raised his glove in a smooth, quick reflex and deflected the ball away from causing him any injury. His reaction was so swift that he nearly caught the incoming projectile.

"Oh, I'm so sorry Chase! You good? That was my fault. I didn't...." Kenneth began, panting and jogging towards him.

"Dammit! I almost had it too! You see that?" Čhetáŋ said with glee. "Do it again!"

"Chase you're crazy. I ain't doing that again." Kenneth said, looking concerned and giving Čhetáŋ a look over before exhaling. "I didn't mean to hit it at you like that the first time. That came off the bat all wrong. But shit. You're quick!"

"I know. But I didn't catch it. I could have. I wanna try again."

"I couldn't do that again even if I tried. And I'm not trying again," Kenneth grunted. "You may have something there. I'm not gonna lie. You got some reflexes. Quick as a cat, as they say."

They'd been at the field for nearly two hours. The grass was in rough shape, but it was the closest field for miles. It was the most accessible one Čhetáŋ had ever been free to play on. It made his stickball days in front of their old apartment feel small to him.

"Did your daddy hit to you like this? Cause you're good, especially for your age."

"Nah." A slight southern drawl was beginning to form in Čhetáŋ's tone. "He didn't really have time with his music jobs." A hint of regret flashed over his face. "Daddy used to take me to see the Yankees, though. Plus, we ain't have no fields like this up there by me, so this is cool. Best I had!"

"I think I'll get you in Little League or something at the youth center this coming season if your grandma alright with it. You like that?"

"Hell yes!" Čhetáŋ exclaimed, with a smile that spanned his face. Then he tossed Jason the ball to have his time at bat.

"Daddy me too?" Jason asked.

"We'll see. You only ever talk about ball when I bring you out here with your cousin."

They played until sunset, and again every free sunny afternoon Kenneth was available. It became their routine. The promise of joining an actual team gave Čhetáŋ purpose and even more preoccupation with the sport. He threw tennis balls against the side of the house to practice pitches and increase his reaction time when it ricocheted back. He traded cards at school, networking and making deals like a street hustler. It expanded his world and gave him social opportunities. It became his distraction.

When spring approached, Kenneth fulfilled his promise. Early one Saturday morning, he picked Čhetáŋ up and helped him begin his new endeavor as a youth ballplayer. He stood with him in the long line for sign-up, spoke with the coach, gathered the additional paperwork for Mary to sign off on, then brought Čhetáŋ back home. After that, Kenneth disappeared without explanation for weeks. He had been somber during the entire process, and Čhetáŋ noticed. However, after being chastised for asking questions about his Aunt Elizabeth and Kenneth barging into the store and screaming at each other just a few days before, Čhetáŋ took the advice of "staying out of grown folks' business" to heart.

Elizabeth and Kenneth stormed into Freeman's Grocery, cursing and running off the few customers inside. Lavender and Čhetáŋ were in the middle of chores, and Mary was attending the register when they burst in, one behind the other like vehicles in a wild car chase.

"I don't give a shit about you coming up here! How long you been talkin' to this nigga!?" Kenneth demanded while trying to grab her wrist. Elizabeth did a wave of her arm and escaped his grip.

"The fuck you talkin' 'bout? We just friends. We only been friends this whole time."

"Don't no nigga fly from California for no fucking 'friend,' and you looking like this," Kenneth said, mere inches away from her face.

Elizabeth flinched. "You crazy? That man ain't come from California for me. He's working." She looked at him with lips that bordered on laughing, which only infuriated him more. Lavender thought that risky and bold of her to do a breath away from this sizable, fit, and boiling man.

Her aunt donned mascara, rouge, and dramatic lip gloss. Her hair wrapped, framing her face and directing one's eyes to the accentuated cleavage in her form-fitting dress. She was made up and looked like one of the girls from The Notorious B.I.G.'s "One More Chance" video Lavender decided, and *too old for all that*.

"What is goin' on?" Mary asked, annoyed that they'd do this at the store. "Why y'all bringin' this foolishness here? Y'all don' run what little business we got right on out."

"Ask your daughter. Ask her about Jamal," Kenneth said.

All eight pairs of eyes that remained in the store focused on Elizabeth.

"What the hell y'all lookin' at? This man has lost his mind."

"Who's Jamal?" Čhetáŋ whispered a notch louder than discretion required, and Lavender nudged him hard with her elbow.

Mary stepped from behind the counter to stand between the embattled couple.

"Lavender, watch the register 'til I get back," she instructed. Then she gathered the adults. "Come on here." Mary ushered them towards the employee and storage area in the rear of the store. Kenneth looked at Lavender; his tense, inflamed face softened for a moment before shuffling away.

The shouting and anger could still be heard from behind the closed doors, over the street traffic, and over the radio that played R&B music. Kenneth's voice was the angriest and loudest of the three, yet Lavender nor Čhetáŋ could discern any specifics of what was said, turning to each other and occasionally shrugging their shoulders.

After that evening, Kenneth stayed only long enough to sign Čhetáŋ up for his baseball team, then disappeared for nearly a month.

In Kenneth's absence, the bulk of the store duties were left to Mary and the children. Freeman's Grocery didn't have the foot traffic it once did, but Kenneth filled in between his intermittent construction work and was there most days by closing time. He handled the strenuous inventory labor, did the shelf stocking, broke down shipping boxes, and discarded the trash. Now those tasks needed to be spread between the rest of the family. Elizabeth had her banking job and children to feed before she could journey over, so she, Keshia, and Jason were only available for a couple of hours near closing. This left most of the preliminary labor to Čhetáŋ and Lavender.

Lavender and Elizabeth managed to work well together early on without any quarrels. That was until Čhetáŋ dropped an entire case of bottled tea on the floor right after Elizabeth had just finished cleaning it. It was late one Thursday evening, and everyone was already exhausted from the week and itching for the weekend to relieve them as quickly as possible.

"Goddammit, clumsy ass boy! Pay attention to what you doin'! I just cleaned that, and we was fixin' to go! Now look at all this shit!"

Lavender was just as frustrated with him. School had been tiring that day, she was fatigued, and he'd been careless, skipping about, not being cautious with the store's merchandise. Nevertheless, in Lavender's mind, only three other people besides herself could unleash on him in that manner. One was in the grave, another was out of earshot in the rear of the store, and the last one, Katherine, was as far as they knew, about two weeks away from a sentencing date for yet another shoplifting charge.

"Don't talk to him like that. It doesn't take all that."

Elizabeth's head turned ninety degrees in Lavender's direction, with a face that read as both surprise and fury. Elizabeth's cheeks were varnished with a slight smirk that Lavender could only interpret as psychosis. Elizabeth had been antagonistic enough towards her without provocation. Now that she raised her voice at her aunt, Lavender expected a physical fight.

"Oh girl. I been waitin' for you to say somethin' smart to me."

Waiting? Really? Lavender thought.

"You walk around with your nose turned up. Everybody gotta accommodate your feelings. Now you big enough to try to tell me how I'm gon' talk to somebody? In my own business? What I've been running since before you was thought about?" Elizabeth paused, raising her brow. "Well?"

"Well? Well, what?" *What is this lady talking about?*

Čhetáŋ giggled before quickly composing himself.

"Something funny boy?" Elizabeth snapped.

"No ma'am."

Lavender moved to get paper towels to soak up the liquid and directed Čhetáŋ to bring a broom and dustpan for the glass. But Elizabeth wasn't finished. She muttered under her breath, occasionally inflecting specific words she wanted to resound throughout the room.

Something, blah, blah, something... "Y'all ain't had enough ass whippings"... *blah, blah, something else...*"Got ere'body babying you, walkin' on eggshells. Pretty this, guitar that! Flattery ain't doin' nothin' for you!"

Lavender rolled her eyes and turned away. She was confused, frustrated, and ready to go home. It was all gibberish as far as she was concerned, and she mostly tuned it out. Ramblings from a woman who was *off* that had nothing to do with her and more about a history she didn't understand.

Blah, blah, blah, something else... Elizabeth kept going... "How y'all are cleaning it is wrong and stupid, anyway," she said.

"Well, you come do it then," Lavender insisted, not truly meaning for the words to live outside of her head. Perhaps that's why they were little more than a murmur. But there the words were, out, roaming free and landing on Elizabeth's ears, who'd dropped her cleaning cloth and began stomping forward like a bull. She pointed her finger in Lavender's face, nearly touching her nose.

"What you say!?"

Just then, Mary reentered the room in time to interrupt the impending duel.

"Lizzy what's going on in here.... Lawd! Look at this mess! I ain't cleanin' this!"

"This grandson of yours did it," Elizabeth said before returning to her previous focus and whispering at her niece. "Be glad my momma is out here. Keep talkin' to me like that. She won't always be."

Later that night, when they were finally home, Lavender went to Mary's room to go over music together as had grown customary between the two. Mary gently shook her head, vetoing the notion. "Too tired tonight baby," and sat down on the bed. Lavender nodded in confirmation and turned to leave but paused before she did.

"Grandma, what's wrong with your daughter?"

Mary laughed, "Which one?" Then she kicked off her shoes and rubbed her feet. Lavender picked up her orthopedic sneakers and stuck them in the closet for her. "If you talkin' 'bout Lizzy, she always been high-strung. But that girl ain't gon' do too much of nothin'. Just wear her emotions all out and easy."

"Well, I don't know. If you hadn't come out tonight, we may have been fighting."

"Nah now. Don't do that. Don't disrespect your auntie."

"It's her! It's been her since we got here! She's all cursing at Čhetáŋ and running up in my face."

"I'll talk to her. But she having a hard time. Ain't easy when your man just leaves like that."

Lavender rolled her eyes but looked away as she did, to not be perceived as disrespecting another elder in the same evening.

"Did you know, she took all the care of your granddaddy 'fore he died? She was at Ernest's side day and night." Mary took an extended breath, as a swimmer would, before submerging into deeper waters. "He had COPD cause he smoked like a train. Lizzy helped him with his oxygen tank, even clearin' that mucus. Then it got real bad after his stroke, and I, I couldn't do nothin' without her. When she commit to somethin', she'll give 'til she 'bout spent sometimes. God's truth."

Lavender thought about how she'd never seen that side of her aunt, which was immediately followed by another pressing thought.

"Where was momma in all this?"

"Oh, child, that's when she was in New York, with her modeling and theater and whatnot. She was doin' pretty good at the time too. Ernest was so proud. I think I might still have a playbill or two from some shows she was in, while in New York that she sent."

Lavender had learned a little about Katherine's theater days when she was younger. However, she didn't know her mother managed to land jobs in New York City. That she'd actually found some measure of success with her creative zeal, and it wasn't all wishful dreaming. She also didn't know about what all her grandparents and aunt dealt with while Katherine was off entertaining.

"What happened then? What happened with all the stuff she was doing in New York? How come I never saw all this or saw her in anything?"

"Sweet girl," Mary kissed her on her forehead and smiled. "Why you think you ain't ever hear nothin', huh?"

Lavender paused in brief contemplation. Oh. *I happened.*

Chapter 14

Just a Hunch

"I Used to Love H.E.R." - Common

AFTER THREE AND A HALF WEEKS AWAY, KENNETH SLOWLY returned to the fold and his routine. Few people were happier over this development than Čhetáŋ, who ran into his arms the first morning he showed up back at Mary's to help with the yard.

"Hey Chase," he said to Čhetáŋ before turning towards Lavender. "Hey, you."

Čhetáŋ squeezed him tightly, then flinched as if having a sudden realization. "You back for good, or you leaving again?"

Everyone shook their heads and laughed, but all were also wondering the same thing.

"We'll see, I guess," Kenneth said.

He and Čhetáŋ bagged the leaves in the yard. Then Kenneth did light weed removal and the mulching Mary had asked about for months. Lavender could see them from the kitchen window as she washed dishes, waiting for any opportunity to get answers she knew she couldn't get elsewhere. Once Čhetáŋ came in to clean up, she threw her sweater on and dashed towards the front yard.

"Hey, Uncle Kenny."

"Hey. You come to help?"

"What do I look like?" She said with a scowl.

He smiled momentarily, but that soon evaporated to a more drab expression.

"I know it's not my business, but... everything alright now? You really back?" Lavender asked.

He was ankle-deep in soil and wood chips and never stopped shoveling. "Didn't folks tell you to stay out of..."

"Grown folks' business? Yes," she returned. "But I turn fourteen in a few months. I'm damn near grown. Besides that, I'm nosy."

"Yeah?" He finally stopped. "Can you hand me my flask right there?" He pointed towards his jacket on the ground. A chrome canteen peeked from the inside pocket. He took a long swig, then gestured if she wanted any. "It's gin. Straight gin."

She twisted her face and stuck out her tongue, expressing her repulsion of the beverage that lacked any chaser.

"I guess I can tell you," he began. "Might be this liquor making me dumb, though. Don't tell your brother Chase none of this. He might slip and say something."

Lavender nodded, then waited with bated breath.

"I found out Jason ain't mine."

She looked surprised. He let the shovel fall to the ground, then plopped down on the patio step, bringing the flask to his lips as he did.

"I should've known. Hell, when I met Liz, I was still marri..." He cut himself short. "I ain't no perfect man. I got kicked out the Air Force over all that. So, if she did dirt, then she just did."

Lavender didn't understand what all of that meant regarding the Air Force, but she didn't interrupt him.

"She still could've told me. If she had doubts, well, she could've said something." He stared towards the street with a dulled gaze. "Last month when we were fighting at the store. That's when the nigga showed up at the house. I remembered his face actually, since before me and Liz was together, together. He lives in California now, though. Traveling nurse, I learned. But Lizzy stayed in contact with him this whole time." Kenneth shook his head and took a moment before continuing.

"He's working in Atlanta for a bit, so drove down to see her... or them, or whatever. My contract job got canceled that day, and I went home early and they were standing in my driveway when I get there, all laughing it up." He turned towards Lavender. "I almost shot this nigga, we got into it that hard."

A shiver ran down her at the word *shot*. "Then what," she asked.

"Nothing. He left and that's when me and your aunt start fighting."

She had never seen *this* Kenneth. Yes, he often had his pistol at his waist when they closed the store at night for security, but he never seemed violent or jealous. Nor had she ever seen him be this defeated, drowning his sorrows in dry gin.

"I don't get it. Where does Jason come in at?" Lavender asked.

"I'm trying to tell you. After I questioned her enough about why this dude from when we first got together was still in the picture, why she'd still be in contact with this man for seven years, I told her I wanted a test done. She cussed me out, even swung on me, but I ain't give a shit. I told her the only way I was staying was if she did get the test. If she wouldn't, then I knew the truth. She finally agreed and..." he waved his hand. "He's not mine. Since he's not, he's Jamal's, the only other one she was messing with at the time. At least that's what she says. Who the hell knows until she runs him down for a test, I guess. I don't care about all of that anyway." He pounded his fist into his leg. "I'm the only daddy he knows. He's my son, you feel me? She swears she hasn't been lying the whole time, and she was only in touch with Jamal, being friendly, but who knows. Maybe she really thought Jason was mine. Doesn't matter now anyway."

Lavender was suspended in place. She couldn't fathom discovering that your only son, wasn't yours at all.

"I'm sorry Uncle Kenny. I'm so sorry." Even calling him *Uncle* now felt awkward to her despite it never being his official designation since he and Elizabeth weren't married. She then dropped her head in embarrassment after having nothing more profound to offer.

"Ain't your fault, baby girl." Sweat beaded on his face and trickled down his neck. "You know, you the only person I've told all that to. You're an old soul. Easy to talk to."

She smiled.

"You got your own shit anyway," Kenneth continued. "What's up with your moms?"

"I don't wanna talk about it. She ain't shit either."

"Goddamn Freeman sisters," Kenneth said, spewing gin as he snorted.

"Goddamn Freeman sisters," she parroted back.

They both erupted into a fit of laughter.

"I'm staying... by the way," he said after composing himself. "Long as I can, at least."

"That's good." She was happy to hear it. He was one of the few who'd been consistently kind to her. He'd looked after Čhetáŋ in ways she would never have been able to. And, if for nothing else, Kenneth had been an appreciated buffer between her and Elizabeth and the hard work of the store.

Chapter 15

Preacher's Boy

"Come and Talk to Me" - Jodeci

Lavender had her eyes on Cedric Harris the entire school year. He was the statuesque, umber-complected, ninth-grade point guard who'd been so good that he'd played for the varsity basketball team since he was twelve. His shy gazes in passing suggested he had noticed her as well.

Lavender had shed several cherubic layers in the two years of being in Alabama in exchange for something more ample and shapely. "Solid" was what Mary called it. Lavender was certain genetics were the culprit, but Čhetáŋ teased her that she was "getting fat from Grandma's cooking."

It was hard not to notice whenever she stepped into her once reliable jeans or how she had grown to a C-cup seemingly overnight. She stared in the mirror, her sienna goldish skin, flat stomach, and curvy hips reflecting back. She thought at times she looked like Katherine at a similar age, yet without that slim contour that had encouraged her mother to pursue opportunities on the runway. The increased male gaze was testimony to Lavender's maturing figure. However, the only attention she longed for was from the long, athletic basketball player with the thick Southern accent.

The mutual feelings expanded when they shared a PE period, only exchanging smiles at first. That progressed to handwritten, intricately folded, juvenile notes discussing each other's preferences over one topic or another:

"You like OutKast?"

"Who?"

"You prolly only listen to New York folks being from up there. I'ma play you my tape. Can I have your number?"

Before long, they were "going together." Finding each other for quick moments to share in the cafeteria, holding hands in the hallways, kissing in the corners of classroom entryways with more heavy petting and caressing hidden behind bleachers. Their romance was much to the chagrin of scores of female schoolmates Lavender already didn't have a rapport with who had pined for him since primary school. There was palpable tension in the hallways from the other girls when they were together. Instead of allowing a few arrant looks and whispers to become irritants, as she would have before, Lavender comported herself with her best behavior. Mary even noted the shift.

"I ain't heard from none of your teachers in a while. I'm proud of ya. You gettin' along, doin' better?"

"Yes ma'am. I'm talking to this boy now, and..."

"No, you not," Mary responded and returned to what she was doing at the moment.

Whenever Lavender tried pressing her further on the topic of "boyfriends" and dating, Mary's response was typically to remind her of how she was "barely passing'" her classes as is. "Last thing you need to be worried 'bout is some nappy-headed boy," she'd say, ending such discussions.

Cedric's ministerial father had a similar viewpoint about him dating, preferring he focus on academics and basketball. Even if openly courting each other was possible, Lavender thought she wasn't the caliber of young lady his conservative parents would approve of anyway. In those moments of reflection, she decided she should attempt toeing the line in case a possibility of genuine courtship emerged.

"I don't wanna fuck things up."

"Like, whatchu mean," Cedric asked once during their evening covert phone calls.

"You know. You're Cedric Harris, number twenty-three, preacher's kid, B honor roll."

"So what? That don't matter. I like you—a lot. You pretty and smart, way smarter than ya let on, and quiet like. But you'll fight, too. Ere'body knows that by now."

They both snickered.

"Yeah, but... your daddy finds out you're messing with a girl, especially one with my grades and all, he'll snatch you out of Fitzgerald so fast."

"Probably," he laughed, "But you worth that."

She blushed.

Cedric wasn't supposed to attend their school. He'd been using a relative's address in the city to enroll there. He and his family lived in a "one-traffic-light town" an entire county away called Fort Deposit. Bizarre as Lavender found it, Montgomery was the "big city" to lots of people from similar places as his. And Fitzgerald, as well as several other urban schools in Montgomery, were reputed as nurseries for young Black athletes. Budding talent in those halls was often heavily recruited and given scholarships to the more affluent private high schools on the city's east side. And that's where the real exposure and offers lined up. It was more opportunity and a bigger stage than his town offered.

"I wanted to test myself against these 'Gump' boys and get seen," he told her when she asked how he ended up at Fitzgerald. "That's what I told my daddy them anyway, so they'd let me come. But really,

I guess I just wanted the hell out of 'Tha Fote,'" he said, putting heavy emphasis on his town's nickname.

Their distance and strict guardians made connecting outside of school almost impossible. So, it came as a pleasant surprise to Lavender when she overheard Čhetáŋ and Kenneth talking about a series of weekend games his youth baseball team had possibly lined up in Lowndes County—Cedric's County.

"What I hear you say about Lowndes County?" She asked them.

"Nothing," Kenneth said. "Just Chase's team is setting up games with a program there. It's a little bit of a drive, so, trying to plan that out. Why?" He lifted his brow, giving her a contemplative glare. He and Čhetáŋ had discussed his baseball team at length since the season approached, and Lavender hadn't once taken an interest.

"Just wondering. I may wanna go," she said as Kenneth and Čhetáŋ looked at each other, then back at her.

It was the first practical opportunity to see Cedric outside Fitzgerald. Even if they couldn't engineer a real date out of it, perhaps they could manage *something else?* Something more involved than what they'd been doing behind bleachers and in dark corners at school. Things that had been on her mind about doing with him.

Her cheeks reddened, remembering Cedric's strained attempts at seduction over the phone. Awkward conversations with her ear pressed to the receiver, simultaneously listening to him stutter; and also for any indications that Mary had picked up the phone in another room.

"I wanna kiss you all over," Cedric would say.

"Yeah? And then what?" Lavender's ears perked up, expecting a sexy response that would tease her increasing urges and send her mind pondering on things she was curious about.

"Um... um, I don't know. Whatever you wanna do," he said.

A smoother Casanova probably would've been embarrassed at the falter. A habitual player, she considered, would've had the words formulated and ready to fire that Cedric simply couldn't bring himself to articulate. That made it *sweeter.*

"Hellooo... Lavender?" Kenneth waved his hands in front of her. She'd been lost in thought over Cedric and hadn't heard his call. "What you thinking about that got you all red in the face?"

"Huh? What? I'm not."

"Yeah right. Your grandmother's been yelling for you to get the phone," Kenneth told her.

She staggered over to where Mary was and grabbed the receiver. "Hello?"

"Hey baby."

"Oh... Hey Momma."

"Whatcha doin'? Whatcha been up to?"

She hadn't spoken to Katherine in nearly three weeks. She'd been up to many things, she wanted to say—*a boy, fights with your sister, moving on without you.* "Nothing," Lavender said instead.

"I hear you did better last report card. I'm glad. And that you're... adjusting maybe?"

"Well, I'm not failing and didn't have all D's last time. So yeah, I guess."

"You happier then?"

Lavender didn't respond. Katherine hesitated before continuing as though just realizing the pitfalls the question posed—a vast expanse of craters with anger and resentment waiting at the bottom of them all. She quickly moved beyond that query.

"I uh, finished my few days in county and I got some community service left. But I wanna try to be down after, for your birthday."

Down? "You mean, come down here?"

"Yes. I should be able to make that happen. You like that?"

Lavender didn't know what to think. April 29th was only a couple of months away, and nothing Katherine communicated in recent conversations with them indicated she could travel to Alabama so soon.

"I mean if you can. Čhetáŋ will be happy. He'll be starting base-ball by then. He'd love it if you could be here for that," Lavender said.

"That's what I'll do then! I'll be there. And after I'm there, we can sit down and talk about what our next moves together gon' be. Don't say nothing to your brother though. I want Chase to be surprised. It'll be a real good reunion."

"Sure," Lavender answered, curt and airy.

"I love you baby girl."

"Love you too." She handed the phone back to her grandmother.

"What she say," Mary asked.

"Nothing, but she's trying to come down in April and wants to surprise Čhetáŋ."

"She sounds good, don't she?" Mary beamed, appearing more optimistic than Lavender had seen in some time.

"Yes ma'am. I guess she does."

"I'm so glad," Mary went on. "Probably won't hear from Gerald too much longer anyway. He told me they movin' back to Chicago to help with his momma who got dementia. Kathy keep sounding this good and doing better, we may soon be able to go up for a visit. Or get her to finally move back. And, well, it's all in God's plans anyway, but He workin' it out." Mary left it there.

Lavender didn't realize Gerald would be leaving the area. It wasn't as though he was Katherine's warden, but he had done his best to keep them informed of things or when situations appeared precari-ous. He'd saved Joshua's music when no one else would've thought to, and she was grateful. For now, *momma sounded like momma*, Lavender reasoned. But she didn't want to jinx anything and shook all positive considerations from her thoughts.

Chapter 16

Weird Science

"Optimistic" - Sounds of Blackness

"Something ain't right." Lavender strummed a couple of chords on the Yamaha, the classical guitar Mary bought her by way of Kenneth. It had buzzed through the last several plays.

"Whatcha mean? Sounds the same to me," Mary said.

"Me too," Čhetáŋ agreed.

"That's cause y'all not musicians like me."

Mary smiled at her granddaughter's self-assessment while Čhetáŋ only snorted.

"Whatcha think it is then?" Mary asked.

Lavender shrugged her shoulders. Joshua taught her a few things about tuning, cleaning, and replacing strings. Beyond that, she was at a virtual loss.

Mary suggested she and Čhetáŋ walk a few streets over to TB's Music Store, which they often passed going to and from home. The two proceeded to the establishment, pacing along the asphalt, maneuvering around vehicles, and returning smiles to waving seniors on their porches. Despite it being a tepid March day, Lavender wore a good layer of sweat by the time they reached the store from hauling the instrument in its case without any assistance.

100

"Nope. You tell me not to touch it. I ain't touching it," Čhetáŋ said, wearing a facetious grin. "I'm just here for moral support."

When they entered, a wrinkled man as dark as indigo under the fluorescent lights and hair as white as lace greeted them.

"Afternoon, young folk. How can I help y'all?" The man was Titus Bynum as it read on the aged paper taped to the wall behind him at the counter.

Lavender explained her trouble, and he took the guitar from its case. She noticed he had a slight tremor in his hands when they rested on the counter, but it was absent when he played a couple of the chords. "Umm hmm..." He tinkered with the tuning machine. "Hmmm..." he played again. "Yeah, that's it." He sounded like a physician examining a patient, Lavender thought.

"What is it?" She asked.

"Your tuners loose."

"Oh. Ok? How much is that to fix?"

He looked at her, then turned to Čhetáŋ. "I ain't never seen y'all before. Who your people's is?"

"Mary Freeman is our grandmother," Lavender said.

"I know Mary. Y'all got a store 'round the corner." They both nodded affirmatively. He delayed his response for several seconds, then said, "Leave it with me a couple days, I'll getcha fixed up."

"That's it?"

"You want mo'?" Titus asked.

"No sir."

"Alright then."

Two days passed, and Lavender returned to the store. Titus handed her the instrument, and she played a couple of chords to test it out. It sounded as good as before—perhaps clearer.

"Ok there! You might know whatcha doin'," Titus said, regarding her plucking through a few notes.

She thanked him, then began to look around the store with curiosity before leaving. She saw a bulletin board with flyers and local announcements tacked to it. One dingy leaflet, hidden beneath several layers of fresher ads, got her attention as a portion read, "Music lessons."

She wrung it free from behind the others and read it: *Evening Music lesson —trumpet, piano, and guitar... $20/hr.*

"These lessons, they include electric guitar?"

Titus looked a bit confused before recognition flooded his face. "Oh, that. Yeah, it did. But that's old. Ain't nobody ask 'bout that in a while now."

"Oh? You know who was teaching?"

"I was," he said in a flat tone.

Lavender took a long look at him and noticed the tremor in his hands again. "You still teach?"

"Maybe." Now it was him taking a thoughtful gaze at the curious pupil.

From there, she suggested some sort of future teacher-student relationship, pending she *sees what he can do*, naturally, and maybe they could *discuss pricing*. Titus smiled at her negotiating tactics. "We'll see," he said.

When Lavender arrived home after, Elizabeth was there, quiet and reserved, staring at the changing scenes of the television.

"All fixed up?" Mary asked.

"Yes."

"Well, how it sound then?"

Lavender pulled the guitar out, sat on the sofa, and played the beginning chords of James Cleveland's "God Is." Mary's favorite song. She was proud of having taught herself the piece, considering she'd only listened to it twice. It was played on piano, but she had figured out the right chords and cadence to apply to her instrument.

Mary relaxed back into her recliner, drinking in the melody as though parched from the absence of song while the guitar was in the shop. Elizabeth sat on the other end of the sofa from Lavender, indulging as well.

Mary smiled, "That sounds good as always baby. Still can't figure out what you thought was wrong. All sound good to me."

Elizabeth whispered, "Yeah... that's good. You can play," then grew quiet again. A speckle of dust landing would've reverberated; it grew so still after the compliment.

Later, Lavender learned from Čhetáŋ that Kenneth and Elizabeth had been "at it" again. That he wasn't always home every night, was drinking a lot, and there'd been some talk about a "lady friend." It was all information Čhetáŋ gleaned from Keshia and from eavesdropping on phone conversations when he pretended to be distracted by the television or video games.

"He can't leave again. Grandma can't take me to practice and my games. Damn sure can't throw and hit with me." Čhetáŋ stated, worried about playing if Kenneth wasn't around. Lavender nodded along. She, too, was concerned. She needed baseball to work for other reasons, at least for the immediate future.

When Elizabeth and their cousins randomly stayed over a couple of nights to "get away," it confirmed things were still on fragile footing at the other Freeman household. During one of these occasions, Lavender and the bulk of the family migrated between the kitchen and the living room, awash in the commotion of various activities. The television blasted a rerun of "The Cosby Show," dishes clattered as the women cleaned, Lavender and Keshia worked on homework, and the boys ran rambunctiously through the hall, throwing a Nerf ball. Then, "*Clack, splat, rattle!*" The racket came from Lavender's room.

She rushed to her doorway to see Jason lying on the floor, buried under mounds of tapes. He had somehow managed to overturn several bins of Joshua's music, cassettes were dislodged from their cases, and some had their "guts"—the magnetic film itself—wrinkled and protruding.

Lavender became a coiled firing pin when she saw the fate of Joshua's tapes. Her eyes were iron sights, homed in on its target, Jason, still stumbling to his feet.

"What the hell you doing in here!? Get out of my shit!" She screamed before pulling Jason by his arm up and away from the mass of wreckage left, some of which had been catapulted across the room.

"I told him not to," a timid Čhetáŋ admitted from just inside the threshold. "The ball rolled by your bed, and…"

She slung Jason halfway across the floor and ran to gather up the recordings that lay as a field of debris. Her cousin landed inches from Elizabeth as she arrived just in time to witness Lavender launching her son across the room.

"The hell you doing? Don't put your hands on my child like that!"

"Keep your child out of my shit then!"

"Who you talkin' to?"

"You… I'm talkin' to all of you," gesturing from Elizabeth to her children to Čhetáŋ.

"I'm fixin' to knock your…"

"Come do it!" Lavender yelled. "Do it!"

Elizabeth was seconds from fulfilling her threat, lunging forward with quick steps and grabbing Lavender by the collar of her t-shirt when Mary walked in.

"Hold on! Stop now! Y'all stop all this!" Mary screamed. The intensity of Mary's pleas for calm was enough to pause the pending violence, and Elizabeth released her grip on Lavender, roughly flinging the fabric away as she did.

Elizabeth turned to catch her mother's eyes. "Who keeps all this shit piled up like a junkyard in their room anyway? Momma, you're wrong for letting her keep all this mess in here. Never woulda been us."

"He shouldn't have been in here!" Lavender insisted. She walked with caution across the floor, slowly picking up tapes as she went about, getting misty-eyed when she came across one here or there that seemed damaged beyond hope. It was a steep fall from the top of the mount where the highest cassettes were. Their outer cases protected most of them, but the height and weight with which a few came under caused them to crack and spew their film.

She crouched on the floor crying when Čhetáŋ and her cousins attempted to assist.

"Don't touch it! Don't touch none of his stuff," she said in response.

Everyone left her in the room except for Mary, who waited a few seconds before kneeling beside her.

"Shh, shh, now," her grandmother whispered, embracing her.

Mary began gathering some of the cassettes into bunches, attempting to arrange them to the best of her ability.

"I'm not ever gonna get all these organized right again like they were. I'm not going to even get to hear some of these ever," Lavender cried.

"You will. I'll help you." Mary looked at the scene and the untenable nature of allowing them to occupy space and sit stagnant for the foreseeable future. "Lizzy right though. We gotta find someplace for all this, not how you been havin' 'em. Really ain't safe, God's truth."

The best Lavender could do that evening was pile all the stray, fallen, and exposed tapes in one of the two now empty crates that hit the floor and spilled its cargo. She needed to assess them meticulously, listen to them, and find the corresponding labels and order. As far as what to do with them all afterward, she hadn't the faintest idea. Every conceivable option she'd thought of didn't work in some way. Their store didn't have any extra space. Their attic had room but not the right climate, which ranged from an ice box in Winter to the Sun's surface in Summer. That would ruin the collection in less than a year. An outdoor storage unit large enough would be expensive and would still run into climate and weather issues. What she needed was a climate-controlled storage space like the one they had been in before Katherine lost that too. But she had no money for it and knew better than to ask Mary, knowing her grandmother was barely getting them by as it was.

When Cedric called later, the sadness in her voice was discernible as she told him what happened.

Then he responded, "Well, we did this thing in my Science class...."

Lavender stood a few feet from Mary's garden holding a shovel and wearing her least favorite clothes, her grandmother's gardening gloves, and an old pair of swimming goggles she found in her mother's room.

"This is stupid," Čhetáŋ said. She had managed to recruit him into the odd endeavor by promising a percentage of whatever birthday money she would receive soon. "Won't it still like flood inside and get little bugs in?"

"You know of something better that can help right now? Ok then. Shut up," Lavender snapped. "Now...," she fidgeted about, looking for her ruler, "it's important that we go below the frost line. Cedric said you gotta get under the frost line cause of condensation and freezing. That's like 6 inches deep, so the whole thing gotta be under that."

"What he know about it?" Čhetáŋ asked.

"He's smart and listens in class, and he told me so."

"Alright! Ok, whatever, as long as I ain't gotta keep hearing about Cedric this and that."

They dug all evening, following Cedric's coaching on best practices for stashing away valuables underground. This included using insulation, burying "uphill," and utilizing steel wool to test for moisture. His Science class had done a time capsule project where they buried an entire fifty-gallon drum full of books and other keepsakes from his class.

"Are you sure this will work?" She asked Cedric when he gave her the instructions and detailed list of what she would need.

"Guess they'll know in thirty years," he laughed.

Lavender wasn't amused but also didn't intend on waiting three decades to check on her "capsules." She would attend to this regularly, she thought. And as soon as she had a better way, she would be done with the primitive method.

Mary watched from the kitchen window and had nothing to offer except demand that they not "mess up her squash" or "smash her elephant ears or lavender," which grew closest to the area. She also kept herself amused, referring to her granddaughter in her garden attire as "the mad scientist."

They buried four large containers that day. What remained were the tapes that had fallen, which she needed to sort, appraise, and access anyway. Mary purchased several shallower bins for those, and Lavender slid them underneath her bed until she could secure them or possibly bury them later.

With the issue of the tapes at bay for a while, she was ready to focus on a celebratory affair—her *big* fourteenth.

Chapter 17

———

Out of the Park

"Feenin'" - Jodeci

Čhetáŋ's weekend games had been going on for over a month. Lavender attended most of them so that it wouldn't look suspicious for her to tag along when the series near Fort Deposit began. However, spending half of her Saturday mornings in the stands watching nine and ten-year-olds struggle to even make contact with slowly pitched balls was the epitome of boredom to her. It was only bearable when Mary didn't attend.

On the weekends without Mary, Kenneth was more relaxed, often drinking beers concealed within his thermos that he was liberal with sharing when it came to her. Lavender wondered how difficult things were with Elizabeth if, even on mornings surrounded by children, he couldn't go without the liquid reprieve.

As mundane as most of the games were, she had to admit that Čhetáŋ was one of the best players on the field. His team was the Cougars, and he was their best hitter, pitcher, catcher, and most fierce competitor. He was also humorous. Čhetáŋ would loudly rant about the lackadaisical play of his teammates and their errors. Then he'd lift wads of Big Chomp bubble gum—the kind that impersonated chewing tobacco—into his mouth and press it towards the bottom

108

corner of his inner lip. The gum was the one thing he had requested for games. He wanted to look like Barry Bonds, chewing, dipping, and spitting.

"Call the job... cause this a strike," Čhetáŋ said from the mound while pitching. It was during one of his baseball games that Mary hadn't attended, and only Kenneth and Lavender were there, supporting him in the stands.

"Chase, hush up and pitch the ball, boy!" His coach yelled back.

Kenneth couldn't control his laughter. "Ooh, that was bad. That was so bad! He'll never write comedy, that's for damn sure," he said, his voice echoing throughout the park. Kenneth almost keeled over from amusement before turning to Lavender, "Chase so crazy, but this might be his thing for real. What you think?"

His observation was keen even with the scent of malt liquor on his breath.

"Whatever keeps him busy and out of my business," Lavender said.

"Oh, you don't care?"

"I'm just... glad to get out of the house."

"Sure." Kenneth's prying eyes looked her over. "You got something else going on. Something else on your mind?"

"Huh?"

"*Huh?*" He teased. "You out here just to get out of the house? Even though you're bored?"

Lavender shrugged, not understanding what he implied.

They returned to their spectator roles only to witness the Cougars lose again.

Čhetáŋ was quiet and brooding, and his sister was slightly intoxicated when Kenneth dropped them off at home. Mary had finished the weekend cleaning and Sunday dinner, and she rested in her favorite living room chair as they walked in. The aromas of bleach, lemon, lavender, and cornbread stung Lavender's nostrils as the combination of fragrances was like smelling salts to rouse her to brief clarity.

"Y'all win?" Mary asked.

A simultaneous "No" followed, and Čhetáŋ stomped towards his room while Lavender did her best to suppress laughter.

Mary shook her head. "Your momma called."

Katherine had done a better job of communicating with the family after her last legal lapse. She had to spend three weeks in on a misdemeanor shoplifting charge. The time had seemed beneficial.

"She say anything about my birthday? And...," Lavender whispered, "...coming?"

"No. Asked how we all was and talked about having to find another job again. But nothing 'bout coming down."

Lavender's brow furrowed, and her lips constricted as she processed the information. She didn't allow the trepidation she felt to dwell long. Katherine still had nearly a month left to make the visit happen. But Lavender would need to know soon to coordinate the meetup details with Cedric, as the games in Fort Deposit were upon them. That did not end up the way she had hoped.

She thought there would be a trip there every Saturday for a month while the series ran—four chances to be with Cedric outside of school. As it turned out, team parents couldn't commit to that rigor. At best, she would have two weekends in Cedric's town with an option for a third, depending on how things worked out around Easter. The most fortuitous thing that had emerged from her scheme was the knowledge that the park they would play in was within walking distance of his house.

"That what you wearing?" Čhetáŋ asked the morning they were to set off for the Lowndes County game. Lavender was in a form-fitting white top tucked inside a pair of short-shorts, an oversized belt, black boots, and a long sleeve plaid shirt as there was still a slight chill in the air. Her legs were exposed to her thigh and sleek from the generous amount of baby oil she had slathered on them. It was nothing that overtly said, "seeing a boy I like today," but it was far more effort than she had put into dressing for any of Čhetáŋ's other previous contests.

She rushed outside to sit on the porch and wait for Kenneth before Mary, who wasn't joining them—another fortuitous occurrence—could see her and object to the outfit.

"You look nice. Where you goin'? With us?" Kenneth joked when he pulled up.

"Hush," she nodded before hopping into the back seat while they waited on Čhetáŋ.

It was a forty-minute ride. Lavender bit her nails the entire way and barely spoke a word.

When they arrived, a few boys were already on the field, and there was a parking lot of parents toting coolers and lawn chairs. She looked around and didn't see Cedric, so she proceeded to find a seat in the limited-capacity bleachers.

The first inning came and went, then the second. There was still no Cedric. She bounced her knees as she sat towards the edge of the aluminum seat, vibrating the entire row, then peering from the field to the road behind them. In a final gaze, Lavender observed two figures approaching from across the barren lot. The longer she squinted at them, the clearer it became that it was Cedric and a girl. As they drew closer, he said something to the girl, pointed, then headed back in the direction they came from.

The girl was tall and dark-skinned with box braids. Lavender had never seen her before, but there was a familiarity about her face. She looked at Lavender and nodded. Lavender returned the gesture, then turned towards Kenneth, who was next to her, to make sure he didn't observe the undercover operation in progress.

The girl stepped forward. "Hey Lavender!"

"Oh hey. What you doing here?"

"Nothing. I was walking by, being nosy."

Lavender winced. *Such a terrible lie.*

"Whatchu doin' way out here?" The girl continued.

"Watching my little brother play."

"Oh. Wanna hang out a little bit?"

Lavender turned to Kenneth with her brows raised.

"Where you all going?" He asked.

"Oh, just walkin', prolly to my auntie hair shop down the road," the girl said. "That's it."

"Lavender, how you know this girl?' He asked.

"Um, she went to Fitzgerald last year."

He rubbed his face, then something in the game caught his attention, and he yelled commands at Čhetáŋ. "Fine, just be back before the game over. I'm not trying to track you down."

Kenneth wore an annoyed expression, but Lavender smiled, thanked him, and ran off.

Once Lavender and the young lady were down the road a bit, Lavender turned to her with gratitude.

"Thanks for doing this," she said.

"Ain't nothing. Lil cousin does stuff like this for me all the time. So, I'm just paying him back. I'm Wendy, by the way."

It was all Wendy had to say for the rest of the ten-minute hike. When they made it in front of a red brick house with yellow trim, she spoke again.

"My aunt and uncle all the way over in Montgomery theyselves. They shouldn't be back 'til late, but I'll be next door anyway. If I hear them back early or something, Cedric know I'll bang on the back door. You can come get me if you need to, to go back." She pointed Lavender towards his door, where he stood just inside, flashing a smile. "Don't y'all get me in no trouble either. If some shit go bad, I wasn't here."

Lavender nodded, went up the walkway, climbed the front steps, and embraced him. She could smell the butterscotch ChapStick that graciously coated his lips, the peppermint he crunched on, and Old Spice which she thought had to be his father's.

"Sorry, I was late. I had to wait on her," Cedric said. "You look real pretty. How was y'all walk? You think yo' uncle saw where you was goin'? What time you think you need to leave? You hot? Need somethin' to drink?" He was a loquacious bundle of nerves and anxious rambling. "Wanna come to my room?"

Lavender, on the other hand, was virtually mute, nodding yes and following him as he pulled her further inside.

Michael Jordan and Dominique Wilkins posters were plastered on every wall. Books and homework covered his desk. In the back corner was an aquarium for Billy, his pet iguana. A miniature basketball goal was mounted on the back of his closet door, with clothes everywhere except on the bed.

"Look at Billy," Lavender giggled, pointing at the tank. Cedric smiled before rattling off everything he needed to do to care for his pet.

Oh my God. A nerd. She thought. *But a cute one.*

"I woulda cleaned up, but if I did, my momma would've known somethin' was up."

An awkward silence filled the room as they settled on the bed. There was an unspoken understanding that they needed to hurry with whatever their intentions were. But rushing such a moment felt strange and clumsy for both. Cedrick hugged her and then held her hand in his lap.

"So... You good?"

"Yeah." Her shivering body saying otherwise.

He put his hand on her leg and kissed her. She kissed back. He moved his fingers up her thigh, and she kissed him harder. They undressed until each was down to just undergarments. Both still too bashful to get fully disrobed in the open and had to get under the covers before being bare. Cedric reached for the condom he had on his nightstand. He told her he was no virgin; however, Lavender thought he seemed nervous.

"Let me know if you want me to stop," he said. Lavender didn't want him to, but then she did.

She kept her mouth closed, though, grimacing from the initial discomfort and whimpered softly with each movement. A small amount of panic began to infiltrate her thoughts—*pregnancy* and *punishment,* flashing like hot neon signs in her head. She considered telling him to slow down or stop altogether. She knew it would hurt, but nothing the girls on the old stoop said had adequately prepared her for it. Then in a slow beat, all the fear and ache were overcome by another sensation. Soon there were no other distant thoughts, and for a few moments right before it was all over—pleasure.

"You ok?" He asked while brushing her curls away from her face.

"Yes," she smiled. *That was something.* Something maybe worth another try soon, she considered.

Lavender returned to the field just in time to watch the players shake each other's hands in the post-game line. Kenneth looked around and noticed her, waving his hand for her to hurry towards them. She saw Čhetáŋ jumping and excited and assumed they'd won.

"Y'all win, huh."

"Yeah! You weren't watching?" Čhetáŋ asked.

"Nope, she was off with *her friend,*" Kenneth said. Lavender was unable to perceive if it was sarcasm or doubt in his inflection of "friend."

"I did good, too! Coach says I'm hitting over 600!"

"That can't be right," Kenneth twisted his face.

"Uh huh, Coach Davis said."

"I mean, I guess. You hit a lot, and little niggas throwing cantaloupes out there," Kenneth grinned.

Lavender didn't understand what any of that meant. Her mind was focused on what had just transpired and how it felt. Her thoughts were brandished all over her face.

"You alright?" Kenneth asked.

"Yeah."

"You sure? Cause you look all, I don't know, goofy or something."

Chapter 18

Yellow Cake & Metal

"You Remind Me" - Mary J. Blige

EXACTLY TWO WEEKS *UNTIL FOURTEEN,* AND WHEN THE PHONE rang late that night, Lavender had a gut feeling of who and what it was about.

"Yeah, I figured. It's fine. You wanna talk to Čhetáŋ?"

"I know it ain't fine," Katherine spoke in an exhausted voice. "I know you mad."

The news of her securing employment after a tumultuous two years was a positive revelation. But it meant getting the time off to come to Alabama as a new hire, with a record no less, was unlikely.

"Then why'd you promise... Promise, again?" Lavender asked. She had fortified her emotions so much during these years to avoid mourning over high hopes. Whenever she did let her guard down and was dealt a blow, Lavender blamed only herself for entertaining dreams.

"Cause I didn't know it would happen this soon. I thought I would have time, I guess," Katherine tried to reemphasize.

"Yes. Understood." It was a curt response. "Chase, get the phone," Lavender called and dropped the receiver.

She was relieved in a sense. Without worrying about Katherine

115

coming and the many ways that could be disruptive, she could get back to her life. Her new life.

On the Cougars' second and final outing to Fort Deposit, Lavender couldn't manage another tryst with Cedric because their "cover," Wendy, was out of town. Mary also decided to ride along, and there was no drinking nor any sneaking off that Saturday. Cedric came by the field, but Lavender was confined to the middle seat of a Kenneth and Mary "sandwich" for the entirety of the game. She could only smile and flirt with him from a distance.

That first Saturday afternoon that ended in Cedric's bed had stirred feelings in her. Lavender's mind would stray to their intertwined limbs at all hours, in improbable moments: English class, Math, cleaning at the store. She couldn't readily subdue these fresh thoughts with her and Cedric's typical rendezvouses in school hallways and quick moments hidden in the gym. She longed for that same intimacy again. It was punishment, Lavender believed, that all of these urges also ended up coinciding with the separation Spring Break forced upon them as well.

"I miss you." She admitted over the phone at the onset of their spring vacation.

"Miss you too." His voice warmed her and made her prickly to the point that she would find her hand in places descending below her navel, like an almost involuntary compulsion.

"I'll really miss you next year," he continued, thinking of the approaching end of the academic calendar year.

Cedric would be leaving for high school and departing Fitzgerald regardless, but his gamble with the Montgomery zip code usage had paid off, and not only would he be moving on to a new school, but one way across town. He averaged twenty-three points and nine rebounds and had his name routinely noted in the *Montgomery Journal* newspaper that season. His parents were sending him to Horizons Catholic Preparatory School after the coach there scouted him and offered tuition assistance while a "sponsor" would cover the difference.

They're not even Catholic, Lavender thought. Most people, quiet as it was kept, also knew Cedric lived nowhere near the westside address he added to forms. She pondered on how doors opened and exceptions unanimously made for Black boys who performed feats of athleticism with their bodies. She thought about Čhetáŋ and if his baseball would be the same.

Horizons Catholic Preparatory was less than ten miles away, but for most of her peers, it may as well have been in another nation, culturally.

"Daddy real happy, bragging and all. Talkin' bout how good a school I'm finna go to and away from this riffraff over here." Cedric laughed, but Lavender knew she likely would've been included in the *riffraff*.

A sudden coldness filled her. The sustainability of this courtship, or whatever it was they had, was always in flux. Now it approached the untenable.

～

She and Čhetáŋ spent much of their break working at the store. With Kenneth back, there wasn't as much for them to do, yet as with their previous summer days, Mary felt keeping them there protected against "idle minds." Even so, she occasionally took pity on them, observing their huffs and slow feet dragging around Freeman's Grocery.

"It's 'bout to rain, and y'all look so sorry mopin'. Making me sad too. Just go home 'fore the bottom falls out. I can manage," she offered during the apex of their break. "Don't get into nothin'."

They ran from Freeman's as if every opportunity in the world was present within the walls of their bedrooms and arrived just before the floodgates opened. Čhetáŋ played video games in his room, and Lavender tried to master a new acoustic piece Mr. Bynum had given her in hers.

She began going by TB's Music once a week just for pleasantries.

That turned into him allowing her to play around and practice on the electric guitar set up there. He didn't agree to mentor her in the way she previously requested, but he sometimes offered tips and shared music he wanted to challenge her with. This time it was a tape and the tabs for "Is There Anybody Out There?" by Pink Floyd. Titus always had obscure rock or blues songs she had never heard of for her to learn—different from the jazz, R&B, and soul Joshua reared her on. She found the swift changes in lead guitar chords, energy, and focus in Titus's music selections exhilarating.

The house grew quiet once the rainstorm subsided. It was still windy, but Čhetáŋ announced he was going outside to practice anyway. Lavender heard the screen door swing shut and the subsequent thud of the tennis ball against the side of the house. She took a break from her strings and called Cedric, but there was no answer. It left her with only thoughts of his voice which brought a zealous smile to her mouth and quickly evolved into a warm flush down to other parts.

The door to her room was closed, except for a small, inch-wide gap between it and the threshold. Lavender could still hear Čhetáŋ knocking about outside, so she didn't bother rising to close her door completely for privacy. She laid back on the bed and closed her eyes, allowing her hand and fingers to descend again, under her waistband and between her thighs. She noticed the banging of Čhetáŋ's tennis ball subsided for a few seconds but then resumed. Without hearing anything beyond the usual cracks and creaks of the old house, Lavender continued her quest. Her motion was constant; breathing was heavy as she grew detached from all other sounds besides those of her own body until an eventual deep gasp.

When complete, she rested in listlessness for several moments allowing the waves to calm back to her now tumescent shores. Only then did she realize she heard what she believed was stirring from the living room. A door creaked, and the floorboards gave away someone's presence. Or, at least that's what Lavender thought her ears noticed.

She quickly composed herself, jumped from the bed, and moved near the door, wondering if she could hear anyone. There was nothing. Lavender stood and listened, peering through the crack, looking down the long hall until the noticeable silence convinced her of her paranoia. There were still loud and rhythmic thuds against the exterior walls, indicating Čhetáŋ's continued activity outdoors. *If he saw....*

She could only imagine the mortification if Čhetáŋ had seen or heard her. *That ass*, would blackmail her. Lavender grew agitated just thinking about it and slammed her door shut and locked it as though that would guard her against those fears.

April 29th came quickly. Katherine called and sang "Happy Birthday" after mailing Lavender twenty-five dollars in cash.

"You get my card? It's all I got right now," Katherine said.

"Yes. Thank you."

"I'm looking at this place on Taylor Street. It's just two bedrooms, but we can make do if I get it."

Taylor Street was not far from Cypress Grove and wasn't as nice. However, it was superior to anything over on Warren Avenue. Lavender could even reconnect with Nadia and those friends.

"That sounds good. When can we see it," Lavender asked.

"Like I said, gotta get it first, but I'm workin' on it. Gotta talk some stuff over with Momma. Love you." Lavender handed the phone back to her grandmother.

Despite not having Katherine there, Mary worked to make Lavender's day as special as possible. She cooked her favorites—fried chicken, macaroni, and cheese and baked her a yellow cake with chocolate frosting with all fourteen candles on top. She had offered to throw a small party with any friends Lavender wanted. However, there was only one person Lavender could think to invite, and none of the adults necessary to make the union happen were aware it was a relationship that existed, nor how intense—at least for Lavender—it had grown.

Cedric did give her a present at school—a gift bag carrying a teddy bear, balloons, and a Nike skirt. She kissed him on the spot, brandished her items at lunch, then hid them in the bowels of her book bag before she exited the bus and Mary could see. Čhetáŋ caught a glimpse of the paraphernalia, however, and began teasing her with kissing noises until they got to the store.

Her birthday turned into another gathering of just family with one addition, Mr. Bynum. After they'd finished the meal and she blew out the candles on her cake, the family and Titus sat conversing before Lavender opened her other gifts. A pair of gold earrings came from Mary and stockings and ten dollars in cash from Elizabeth and Kenneth. Before Mr. Bynum could give his present, Mary asked Lavender if she had gotten anything from friends at school.

"Pfft..." Čhetáŋ licked his fingers clean of icing. "She doesn't have any friends, just what she got from that boy she likes."

"Oh, she gettin' stuff from boys? You lettin' her see boys, momma?" Elizabeth asked.

"You know better, Lizzy. Just some child I hear her whisperin' on the phone to sometimes."

"Grandma!" Lavender said, surprised and also terrified.

"I don't be listenin' to y'all," Mary said, then turned to Elizabeth, "Just phone talk. She too young to be serious."

"He bought her a dress, though," Čhetáŋ continued while stuffing his face, oblivious that Lavender's acute stare was on him and behind her eyes lay vivid scenes of his execution by her hands.

"A dress?" Mary frowned. "I don't like that now. That seems mannish. Like he wanna see you wearin' it for him."

Lavender almost choked on her soda. "It's not like that. And it was just a skirt anyway."

"A skirt? That's worse! You out here bein' fast!" Elizabeth rolled her eyes.

How a skirt was worse than a dress became an internal quandary

Lavender tried to resolve throughout the evening. The awkward pause in the conversation as everyone looked at her was as if they attempted to discover some new smell or stride about her. Even Kenneth, who didn't have much to say, engaged in this uncomfortable examination.

"We'll talk later," Mary insisted.

Titus cleared his throat to remind everyone of his presence as the outsider in the private matter. "Well, I appreciate you even invitin' an old man to ya party, baby girl." He placed a box on the table. It was wrapped with a ribbon, and he had to use both hands to lift it because of its mass. "This somethin' I know you gon' love. Not sure 'bout Mary, though. Matter fact, Mrs. Freeman you can talk to me later 'bout this if you need."

"Lawd..." Mary exclaimed, clutching her neck.

With a disclaimer like that, Lavender eagerly ripped into the box, curious to discover what it could be. When her unveiling was done, everyone looked down at a black, silver, and mostly reticulated cube. It had a handle and small buttons—an amplifier.

Lavender jumped with excitement and ran and hugged him so tight she pulled the air from them both. "Thank you! Thank you, Mr. Bynum!"

"What is it?" Čhetáŋ asked.

"Somethin' to annoy the piss outta everybody," Elizabeth said.

Chapter 19

Fourteen

"Blackberry Molasses" - Mista

THE ELECTRIC NOTES HUNG IN THE AIR AND ECHOED throughout their home. Ever since Mr. Bynum gifted Lavender a beginner's amplifier, her "shredding" out of musical notes on the strings was incessant. He was right to warn Mary. The first thing Lavender blasted from her electrified Les Paul was Deep Purple's "Smoke on the Water," a song Titus had introduced her to. The rock anthem had simple chords, but she imagined she was the first Black female lead guitarist in a "big hair" band. She would untie her wavy hair, so it fell in her face, and stand on the sofa if no one was home, playing to an imaginary mosh pit.

When she wasn't alone, she tried to be courteous, but her playing still often got out of hand. Mary routinely warned her to turn it down when it was too much for her ears to take. It made little difference, however. The amp was cheap, small, and for novices, but it was mighty. Though Lavender began her journey on electric notes with that single Deep Purple song, she hungrily devoured all manner of rock and heavy metal. Titus could hardly keep up assigning her new chords to master.

Mary, on the other hand, tried nudging Lavender back towards the more melodic tunes of Gospel. At least if she were going to continue to play using the loudspeaker, Mary preferred songs of worship. That had little success, however. The first notes of rock Lavender plucked through the box were a narcotic. She loved the electric chaos.

Whenever the first *snap* and *crackle* of static pumped through the amplifier after she'd plugged it in, Čhetáŋ would cover his ears with his hands or scream, "Oh my God, no!" Sometimes it was a synchronous combination of both.

"You ain't Guns N' Roses! Shut up!" He would bang on their shared wall.

Sometimes she would turn the volume down. Other times, his protests were her cue to "enter" Metallica's "Sandman" with more vigor, laughing as the dips and climbs drowned out her brother's outcries.

Čhetáŋ tried to silence the endeavor in his own way. At first, he hid all the guitar picks he could find. But Lavender had extras, or she would improvise, using coins or any old piece of plastic like the junk mail credit cards that came for Mary. Then he hid the sheet music Titus taught her, which also had minimal effect. Lavender and sheet music were a middling pairing to begin with. She had played mainly by ear and was gifted enough that hearing two passes of a tune, regardless of genre, was enough to sear it to memory. She and Titus would go round and round over what she was actually reading versus what she had remembered. It was one of the reasons he needed to introduce her to new music at a rapid pace and find arcane songs she'd probably be unfamiliar with.

After the sheet music plans failed, Čhetáŋ began to tamper with the settings on the amplifier. That earned him a verbal lashing from Mary once Lavender figured out what was happening.

"Don't go in there messin' with your sister's things no more. I ain't buying one if you break it."

"Yes ma'am," he replied after the tongue-lashing. Though, her words seemed more like an invitation than a threat, to Lavender.

Yet messing with the knobs did not hinder her for long anyway. She learned how to reset and fine-tune them to the sounds she wanted, which often changed anyway. The one thing Titus had warned her against was leaving the amplifier on too long. "It'll blow the tubes," he said. She did not know what that meant in technical terms, but it sounded ominous.

Lavender also couldn't recall how Čhetáŋ figured out about the tubes, maybe she said something in passing, but she soon realized he had purposely begun turning it back on after she would hit the off switch for the night. She gave him one warning over it.

It was late one Thursday evening when she discovered he'd meddled with her device for a second time. Lavender said nothing. She waited until after midnight and quietly walked into the kitchen. She opened the refrigerator door, entered his room carrying the contents she had extracted from the appliance, and poured all sixteen ounces of cold hamburger dill chips onto his torso and face.

He woke up screaming and confused as the sour liquid and large cold chunks of pickled cucumbers assaulted him from above.

"What the...!?!"

"Stay the fuck out of my shit," she issued before stepping back into a fighting stance.

"I'm gonna kill you!" He shouted, lunging towards her with a wet bare chest and wet pajama pants that clung to his legs. But Lavender had several inches and many more pounds over him. She lobbed him away with ease and into his dresser, an effortless task as he was already slick with vinegar. Čhetáŋ slid as though the floor were ice and crashed against the furniture before yelping out in pain. Undeterred, he rose, toppling as he did before chasing her and slipping as he ran.

The noise of breaking lamps and an all-out brawl in the middle of the living room was what awakened Mary, and she made a fast dash toward the commotion.

"What in the world!?" She exclaimed when she emerged from

her boudoir. The stench in the room filled her nose and caused her nostrils to flare.

The fight was rambunctious. Legs flew, fists were thrown, and the occasional spray of pickle juice rose, dispersed, and fell. Mary had to scream at the top of her lungs to get them to stop and notice her at all.

"Stop this! Stop it I said!" Her wet, furious grandson finally calmed, breathing like a bull ready to charge. "Why I'm smelling vinegar?" Mary asked.

"She poured pickles on me! She poured that jar on me!" Lavender wore a broad gloating smile.

"Is that true?"

"He keeps messing with my amp! He keeps turning it on, trying to break it."

As the room settled, everyone donned some remnant of the sour residue, a lamp was broken, and random pickle clumps trailed from his bedroom. Puddles sat in the hall in the shape of footprints. Čhetáŋ had scratches on his cheeks and neck, and Lavender had a knot above her left eye.

The punishment landed as an anvil.

Mary grounded them both and sanctioned all telephone use except for calls from Katherine. Čhetáŋ was held out of his next three games and couldn't play his video games for two weeks. The grounding meant little to Lavender as she didn't go many places anyway. But the punishment over the phone meant weeks without her evening conversations with Cedric. With that being much of their already limited interaction, her stomach dropped at the mandate.

The worst for her was Mary locking away her guitars and Walkman for a time. The nightly gospel duet was Mary's favorite activity for them to do together. Lavender thought she would at least be given that exemption, but the penalty had been absolute.

"You just brought all this on yourself, actin' foolish. Now sit with it," Mary said. "And y'all gettin' up goin' to church early. Startin' with Sunday school this week." Yet another injunction that befell the entire household as a result, as Mary rarely rose before nine A.M. on Sundays herself.

~

Church was never the Adair children's preference, simply based on the lack of it in their lives in Newark. Lavender was thankful that while Mary was a *holy roller*, she was not stringent regarding attendance. Most of that was because she often worked the store half-days on Saturdays when Elizabeth could not. Sunday was her only true day off. They usually walked through the doors of Edgemont Church of Christ about twice a month and never rose for anything earlier than its regular morning service at about eleven o'clock.

Sunday School held a particular form of irritation for Lavender. Besides being *too early*, Edgemont was small, and the few youths there for morning services were all lumped into one class together. She happened to be one of the oldest and had to participate alongside Čhetáŋ and kindergarteners alike.

The very first Sunday of their mandatory attendance, Lavender especially did not care to leave her bed. The sanctions had been depressing. She missed Cedric, her period had started, and she physically struggled to leave her mattress. On top of all that, there was the news of those apartment plans Katherine had in mind on Taylor Street falling through. That endeavor ended with a heated exchange between Katherine and Mary over money.

"I don't know what you doin'," Mary said to Katherine. "All I got is ya word, and that ain't been dependable these last years. Money don't grow on trees, and I got grandkids here I have to help with."

"I'm workin' so my kids can be here... with me, that you ain't gotta worry about. But that won't happen overnight, and this is the start I need."

Mary sent her half of the money she requested. A week later, Katherine called, angry about losing the apartment, and not so subtly blamed Mary for the missed opportunity.

Lavender marched into the Sunday class that morning; her mouth puffed out and demonstrably irritated, avoiding eye contact with everyone.

"Verily, I say unto you, That a rich man shall hardly enter the kingdom of heaven. For it is easier for a camel to go through the eye of a needle than for a rich man to enter the kingdom of God. Matthew 19:23-24." Mrs. Evans, a heavy, round-faced deacon's wife, read loudly to a class of about five students. "What does this tell us?" She asked.

One little girl shyly whispered, "That we shouldn't want money?"

"That's close. We shouldn't love money, is its true meaning. It's like the song they play on the radio, 'Silver and Gold,' by Kirk Franklin. Anyone know those words?" She scanned the room for participation. "Lavender? Happy to see you and Chase here early. You know the words we're talkin' about?"

Lavender shrugged. It was one of the songs she learned to play for Mary.

"Lavender?" Mrs. Evans asked again.

"Yes. I know the words."

"Well then... say them for us."

Lavender sighed, then recited the chorus—that stressed a preference for Jesus over wealth—in a dry, monotonous voice. She allowed the awkward quiet of her expressionless delivery to unsettle the room.

"Well? What do you think?" Mrs. Evans probed.

"Think about what?"

"About the words you were just saying."

"Nothing," Lavender said.

"Come on. That isn't an answer."

What does this woman want? She thought. "Hmm... Ok. What do I think? What do I think?" Lavender's tone sounded sarcastic, and she began rubbing her chin.

Čhetáŋ—who had his head down examining a loose thread of his shirt, looked up after the pitch of his sister's voice shifted.

"I think..." Lavender began. "I think it's mighty funny how the white man took all the silver and gold and then told everybody else 'to have Jesus.' That's what I think."

Čhetáŋ snorted. The other students gasped and snickered, and the coy little girl who had answered earnestly before sat with her forehead scrunched up.

"What white man?" The girl asked.

And just like that, Lavender and Čhetáŋ's obligatory Sunday School attendance ended.

"What's gotten into ya lately? Just being ornery?" Mary demanded after the string of misbehavior and the Sunday School incident by her eldest grandchild.

"No ma'am. My head just in a bad place."

"Your behind gon' be in a bad place too if you don't get right. You lucky I feel sorry for you. I ought not let y'all go nowhere."

"Ma'am? I already can't go anywhere."

"Lizzy and Kenny takin' the kids to the movies Saturday, and your lil cousins wanted y'all to go too," Mary explained.

Spending an outing with her aunt and a trail of elementary school-aged children was not the ideal break from the isolation Lavender considered. However, since Kenneth was going, it could be bearable. There was at least the chance that she would continue her streak of leeching complimentary sips of liquor from him, she considered.

The choices the evening they visited the dollar movie theater were "Honey, I Blew Up the Kid" and "Bebe's Kids." Elizabeth, who often smoked, drank, and cursed in front of her children, was adamant about them not being exposed to the "profanities" she heard were within the PG-13-rated animated production.

"You ain't paying. You don't get to choose." Elizabeth argued as they stood at the ticket window as Lavender championed for the group to see the latter option. "You ought to be glad you even out the house!" She smacked loudly on her gum while deciding between films. "I heard that 'Bebe's Kids' is too grown. Just cause it's a cartoon don't mean shit."

"Babe," Kenneth chimed in, burping cognac as he did. "The girl is 14, she's old enough. Let her go see what she wants. She ain't gotta be with us."

"There you go," Elizabeth fussed. "We came together, we watchin' together. Besides, ain't no way I let her off on her own, and she sneak off or somethin'."

"Sneak off where?" Lavender asked.

"Don't get smart. I been young too. You in yo' lil skirt, like you was dressin' up to go off somewhere." The entire group then glanced down at Lavender's attire.

It was Cedric's gift, Elizabeth referenced, and Lavender had a Nike t-shirt tucked inside of it along with her matching sneakers.

What is it with this lady and this damn skirt? Lavender wondered. "This isn't dressed up," she mumbled. She had only gotten dressed for sneaking off once since she'd been in Montgomery, and Lavender wished she was under those circumstances. Instead, she suffered with this group of *weirdos*.

"Look, I'll go with her then. I really don't wanna see that other movie anyway. How you gonna blow up some kids?" Kenneth suggested.

"That's not what it's about, Uncle Ken," Čhetáŋ laughed. "They're getting blown up... like bigger."

"Whatever. It sounds crazy," Kenneth insisted.

Before they could reach an agreement, Jason bumped Elizabeth as she dug through her coin purse, and quarters flew everywhere. Elizabeth cursed him for not being careful while the attendant at the window grew increasingly impatient at the delay and confusion of the group.

"Two for 'Bebe's Kids.' Four, for 'Honey, I Blew Up the Kid.'" Kenneth said in the middle of the disorder, making a definitive decision.

Running late into the theater, Lavender and Kenneth headed towards the back as the movie had already started. Only a small number of people were inside, which granted them ample room and freedom to partake in the illicit goods they had smuggled in. Kenneth had his flask, as was usual now, plus a box of M&Ms from home which he shared. Lavender pulled out an entire turkey sandwich from her purse that she had made earlier.

"That's flagrant as hell," he whispered, snickering at her contraband. "Now, give me a piece." Kenneth inhaled the entire piece of sandwich she shared in one bite, then washed it down with two long swallows of the brandy.

The lights flickered as the animated children on screen exchanged insults with one another.

Not long into the film, and after both were well into their refreshments, Kenneth's flask fell from his lap onto the floor, making a loud clanging sound.

"Shit," he said, struggling to find it in the dark. He left his seat and squatted in the drabness; patting, fumbling, and appearing disoriented.

Lavender paid no attention at first, but once his awkward crawl on the floor took longer than expected, she looked down to see what the issue was. By this time, he was wedged between her legs and the seats in front, resting his hand on her open thigh for leverage. He paused, then raised his head, looking at her in the dim glare, and gently kissed her where his hand had been. He receded back to his seat with his other hand firmly holding his flask.

Lavender's body tensed from the exchange. Her head spun from the brandy she shared with him, and she attempted to process if she felt what she thought she had.

He returned to an upright position but, before doing so, allowed his hand to settle back on her thigh. Lavender became so stiff it was as if she'd merged with the chair itself. It happened so fast. She still had a mouth full of the M&Ms he had handed her seconds before, and she struggled to say anything.

"What you doing?" She finally got out. Words that stumbled and trembled.

He did not respond, gradually moving his hand higher as the silence grew between them. Lavender muttered again, "What are you doing?" This time a little louder and more forceful.

He leaned in close. Her mind grappled with what was going on, how to end it, and why it was happening at all.

"Nothing. Just playing with you. You know you like that."

What? She thought. She dropped her food and grabbed his hand, trying to push him away. "No... What? Why?" She said. The audience was still sparse, but she swore her voice had echoed throughout the whirling auditorium.

"I know you like this. It's ok if you do." He persisted, still caressing her, applying pressure to that crest. Even while glimpsing away to see if anyone noticed them, he continued with his hands, his fingers.

"I'm... I'm gonna yell if you don't..."

He peered at her with bloodshot, skeptical eyes. His pupils were constricted, and the rest of his face was lifeless. "Ok, I'll stop then." He withdrew his palm but with slow abandon. He kept his gaze focused on her, then lazily slurred, "I hear you sometimes, in your room like the other day. It was just you there. I heard you moaning, breathing.... This what you need?"

That day she thought she was alone at home, but also thought she heard someone else there— *it was him?* She considered other moments. *How many more times were there? Was he watching me?* Embarrassment and confusion cascaded over her. Her head was congested with a cocktail of cognac and betrayal. This man, her own sensations—all duplicitous.

She sat motionless while movie patrons, several rows in front of them, laughed at sequences on the screen. After what felt like a lifetime, he whispered, "I was just wanting to, like, make you feel better, baby girl, my bad."

What?

"Lavender, Lavender," he whispered.

She would not face him. Lavender wondered if she had done something that made it seem like this was what she wanted. Something she did that made him think this was ok for him to do to her. She thought about the alcohol he would sneak her, that she was currently tipsy on, their private conversations, and all the support he'd offered. She wondered if it was all a trick, all lies. Or, if she were wrong for being so simple-minded as to happily indulge in all of that with this grown man.

They both sat in silence for the remainder of the movie.

When his hands had been on her, it felt like time stopped. Now with them removed and the film drawing to a close, the seconds moved too quickly. The aftereffects of this new reality and whatever it meant would be imminent as soon as the credits rolled. The alcohol still hadn't freed her for clear reasoning yet, either.

When the movie ended, she remained seated and only left her chair after Kenny had gotten up and walked away first. When she exited, he sat just outside the theater entrance—waiting.

"Look, now, I'm wrong. Ok? Let's just.... Just you know don't say nothing, ok? Me misreading things."

Misreading? Lavender did not respond. She only stared at the patterns of the carpeting down the hallway. He walked away, and she sat in the arcade area alone. About ten minutes later, Kenneth, Elizabeth, and the others found her there.

On the ride home, everyone except for her and Kenneth, laughed, discussing various parts of their movies. He acted as though he were too preoccupied with the road and watching other traffic as he drove.

"What's wrong with you?" Čhetáŋ asked.

"Nothing," Lavender replied.

"I thought it was supposed to be good," he pressed. "You did all that talkin' trying to go see it too. Aw man, y'all should've come with us then."

"I don't feel good." She rested her head in her hand and leaned against the window.

Once they were home, Lavender escaped from Kenneth's Land Cruiser so fast that she almost tipped Mary over, who stood outside to greet them.

"Wait Lavender!" Mary grabbed her arm. "How was the show? What y'all see?" Mary said as she turned and looked toward the rest of the group. Čhetáŋ slowly exited the vehicle, but Kenneth kept the motor running, virtually flaunting that the rest of them would not tarry.

Elizabeth tried giving her account of the outing. "Well..."

Kenneth cut her off. "We went to two different shows, but they were good," he said from the driver's side.

"Two?"

"Yes ma'am. Chase'll tell you about it, but I gotta make a run," Kenneth continued. Elizabeth looked at him with furled brows, so he added, "Remember I told you I had to help my boy with his car today?"

She shrugged. "I'll talk to you later, Momma." And they drove away.

Kenneth gave one last parting glance towards Lavender, who didn't return his look.

Inside, the house was quiet except for the slow bubbling of streak o' lean in a pot. There was also the low volume of the evening news that played on the screen in the living room that no one paid attention to. Čhetáŋ lay quietly on the sofa with his head bobbing, fighting sleep, and Lavender was still quiet, gazing at the screen.

"Well, y'all," Mary started. "Now that that's done, I might as well tell you." She plopped down in her recliner and took a long sip from a glass filled with iced tea. "Your momma called Friday. I ain't say nothing then cause, well, it took me a minute to swallow it myself."

Fuck. What now? Lavender wondered.

"She back locked up," Mary sighed, playing with the folds of her dress as she awaited their reaction.

Lavender and Čhetáŋ looked at each other, then back at her.

"Everything seemed to be gettin' all better this time, 'least I thought so," she confessed. "She was workin'. Missed out on that apartment and all, but...."

"What was it for this time?" Lavender asked.

Mary cleared her throat. "She say stealing but swear she ain't do it. Not this time at least. Just caught up with some wrong people at the wrong time."

"Why are you being like, dramatic? Not different from the other times. Why didn't you tell us after she called?" Lavender asked in a dull and muffled voice. She rested her sagging head in her palm, obstructing the clarity of her words. Her inquiry was as emotionless as a question about whether venturing outside would require a shield against rain.

"'Cause she sounded more worried. Like this might not be a small thing this time, like the others when she was in and out quick. Even said somebody got hurt around it." Lavender and Čhetáŋ both looked up at the revelation. Mary continued, "But she couldn't talk long. I was gon' tell y'all, when I knew more. Plus, well, I wanted y'all to have fun at the movies and not have it on your mind."

Lavender turned back towards the television, and Čhetáŋ, who was usually inquisitive about matters regarding Katherine, slumped down further into the sofa and said nothing.

"Y'all ok?"

Čhetáŋ grunted.

"I wish you would've told us when you first learned," Lavender said, then she closed her eyes and pretended to seek rest. She didn't know what difference knowing earlier would have made. Maybe they wouldn't have gone to the theater. Or if so, she wouldn't have been persistent about seeing what she wanted and never ended up alone with Kenneth. Perhaps it would have been the jolt of "good sense" she needed to realize that all of this—Joshua dying, Katherine's inability to *get shit together,* the relocation—was just *to be.* Why fight or pretend otherwise? Why imagine some return home or some other hope? All the bad that had happened was fated, maybe deserved, because of some sin she was unaware of. Something Joshua had done, or her mother, or some other ancestor she couldn't name. That as their children, she and Čhetáŋ were penance.

Even with them shut, her eyes stung, and she wiped her face free of the salty stream. She rubbed her calloused fingertips together and thought about how that flesh was once soft and *pitiful* but now felt nothing, no matter how hard she pressed against cold steel strings. That layer was thick and tough. She thought about the amethyst she was partially named after. Katherine chose Lavender because it was not only her favorite flower from Mary's garden. But because it was a color in that birthstone. A beautiful and brilliant birthstone. One that was revered for intuition and love, as Lavender had once learned. Amethyst was called many things in its various forms. She'd heard it called crystal, mineral, and quartz. It was mystifying to her in that way. But it was still solid, hard to permeate. It was still stone.

Chapter 20

Magnolia Tree

"Dirty South" - Goodie Mob, Big Boi, Cool Breeze

"Oh my God, Montgomery is boring as hell!" Kiara stated with loud exasperation after sipping from the "everything-but-the-kitchen-sink" pitcher of alcohol she mixed and shared with Lavender.

"Would you shut the hell up before you wake my Aunt Liz?"

Then *splat!* Lavender smashed a mosquito on her leg.

They were perched on a high branch of the magnolia tree in Elizabeth's front yard in the thick of the July evening's twilight hours. The mosquito repellent had long worn off, and the pests were having a feast on their exposed skin.

"I can't take this shit no more," Lavender whispered, rubbing the blood and smeared mosquito remnants from her skin.

Kiara and Lavender met in ninth-grade Algebra class—the one they both failed. They discovered Kiara had close relatives in Elizabeth's neighborhood whom she would often visit. After that, whenever Mary drug Lavender and Čhetáŋ to Sheridan Heights, Lavender would sneak away to find the skinny redhead whom they simply referred to as "Red," to pass the time with.

It was less than two months before Lavender's sophomore year of high school, and the addition of a new—albeit sometimes "oblivious," as Lavender thought of Kiara—friend in her world could not have been at a better time.

Cedric was gone and had been for over a year. He was a "star" at his new *fancy* school. She would sometimes see him on local sports features on WSKA Channel 11 News or see his picture in the newspaper. She was happy for him even though the way he faded from her life still sometimes crossed her mind. They had the "friend" conversation, and it felt like someone had stolen the air from her.

The added commute time to his school, greater academic and athletic responsibilities, and continued need for discretion all served in the relationship's unraveling. But that wasn't all. Lavender had grown more aloof with him as well. She felt herself doing it. But his touches no longer warmed her, and his lips had stopped enticing in the way they had once before. Another thing Kenneth stole. She understood why these feelings emerged if only she knew how to outwit them.

"You going in?" Kiara asked.

"No.... I don't know."

They lacked anywhere else to be other than outside in the elements if they wanted to continue to talk and covertly intoxicate themselves.

Lavender and Čhetáŋ spent the night with Elizabeth as Mary had driven to Good Hope, Alabama, to attend an old friend's funeral and felt too tired to make the immediate drive back.

"I can't wait until I'm eighteen and get the hell out of here," said Kiara.

"And then where you going?"

"Anywhere. I might join the military."

"Bitch, we're sixteen in tenth grade. You need to be in the ROTC now! And I ain't seen you run nowhere in your life," Lavender said.

"Why you gotta talk about my dreams? And you ain't gotta be in the ROTC, do you?"

Lavender shrugged. "Why don't you like staying at your own house? Why are you always over here?" Lavender randomly switched topics in the way disjointed, inebriated conversations sometimes unfold.

"Jeez-Louise, you want me to leave?"

Lavender laughed, "That came out wrong."

"My momma is aggravating, and too many people there. I'd rather be up here at Grandma's."

"You remind me of my friend I had back in Newark. She was Haitian and had a big family. Never wanted to be home either. She was like, my only real friend up there."

"She speak English?"

"Of course, stupid." Lavender scoffed.

"You don't never talk about Newark."

"Ain't shit to talk about."

"Man, I'd go back there in a heartbeat if I was you," Kiara added before taking another gulp.

But she was not her, and in their fledgling friendship, she had no notion of the void that was there.

It was two A.M. now, and the only noises that had interrupted the orchestra of crickets and owls were the occasional distant ambulance or police sirens. So, the sound of a vehicle slowing to a stop about a block away did not go unnoticed by the two.

The height of the branch and the darkness kept them hidden from Kenneth's view as he exited the passenger's side and walked to the driver's door. Someone lowered the window, and then.... Long strands of hair, untwined and waved from inside, flowing from a woman's head as she leaned forward and gave him a lingering kiss.

"Oh shit," Kiara whispered loudly.

Kenneth and the woman said some words to each other. He laughed and then tried to quiet it once he realized his volume. The woman then drove away, and he paced toward the house.

"Damn. You knew about this?" Kiara asked.

"I knew he wasn't shit, but I ain't know this."

"But he always seemed like good people. He nicer than all the old folks I know, letting us drink and...."

"Shut the fuck up. You don't know shit." Lavender's tone was serious, and Kiara instantly hushed. Lavender didn't mean to be so abrasive, but everybody around her sang Kenneth's praises. "He ain't what he seems."

Kiara left it alone.

Kenneth strolled up the driveway and stopped to light a cigarette a few feet from where they sat, still invisible among the darkness and foliage. A shift in the wind, an overzealous beetle, or some other unexplained supernatural matter drew his gaze directly to where they were, still attempting to go undetected.

"Hey! Who's up there?" He demanded.

The girls descended at a careful pace from the magnolia. He held a defensive stance as though ready to throw a fist or several at whoever was hiding outside his home. But as they came into focus, Kenneth relaxed.

"Nobody but us," Lavender said.

"Why the hell y'all up there?"

Kiara giggled a little and showed him the bottle. "Nothing. Chilling," she said.

He shook his head. "Y'all got nothing better to do than be in a tree drinking?"

They both shrugged. Then he glanced back to where he had just been with the woman and up to where their vantage point was from above. A look of worry and realization showed on his face.

"Well..." he cleared his throat, "it's time for all of us to go home. Right, Red?"

Kiara yawned lazily, "I'll see you later, Lavender," and backed away towards the street.

"I guess you better let me go on in first. In case your aunt's up," he continued. "Then you can sneak on through the window like I know you do."

Lavender nodded in agreement and waited a few moments before easing back around to the side of the house, where she'd left the window unlocked. After crawling back into the guest bedroom, everything grew into an eerie, peculiar silence before the alcohol's effects gently lulled her to sleep.

The next morning when Lavender passed Kenneth sleeping on the sofa, she wondered if his affair was why he hadn't touched or been suggestive with her in his customary way in the last several months. She suspected it had been going on for a while, and it was this secret woman who played a part in keeping him off her. The last time she fought to resist him was before Christmas when he slipped his hands down her spine when they were in the store's storage room alone. Apparently, Kenneth had found some new appalling yet "safer" thrill. An odd feeling grew in her. Gratefulness, fear, and guilt all mixed into a thick nervous sludge that filled her marrow.

Weeks passed after she and Kiara saw Kenneth from the magnolia, and his affair had continued, as far as Lavender could tell. He didn't address it with her or inquire about what he thought she may have known. His occasional tardiness and absences with the family and at the store told the story. He'd also still not tried anything physical with her in that time. All of this filled in the narrative in Lavender's mind. Kenneth still hadn't raised any suspicion from anyone either. The times he was late or missing that would drive Elizabeth toward misgivings, Lavender would cover or outright lie for him. The first time she did it, it came naturally. Kenneth had been a no-show at store closing time, and Elizabeth had wondered aloud where he was.

"He told me he might be late," Lavender said.

"Why you ain't say before?" Elizabeth asked.

"I just forgot."

"Ain't that just like you."

Lavender didn't even immediately understand why she lied for him, but it was easy. Her aunt was always eager to misdirect irritation toward her.

Then another time....

"I'm sorry y'all." Kenneth entered the store right at closing one weeknight belting excuses. "I got caught up working on this transmission with Roger and them."

"Yeah, we know. Lavender told us. Said you was gonna be late when we was 'round here lookin' for you," Mary said.

He turned towards Lavender, who peeked up from mopping near the freezer in the rear of the store. Their eyes met, and then she went back to her task.

"When you was gon' tell me though?" Elizabeth asked him.

He sneered for several seconds. "I hadn't seen you."

He looked dirty enough and smelled like engine oil that it could have been true. But Kenneth had told Lavender nothing about being delayed. They hadn't even seen or spoken to each other.

If he was confused about why she would assist him, he never questioned her about it. It was his lack of inquiry and his disinterest in sexual pursuits with her that Lavender hoped he understood this barter.

She picked up his chores around the store and spun tales about *hearing* "he would be late" or *seeing* him go this way or that. Or she'd draw her aunt and grandmother's attention to other things when the tension simmered in his direction—a dance to quell potential problems and hold what was afoul together for her self-preservation.

There was an unspoken understanding, like a shared glance between the two here or there. Whenever those quiet cues appeared in their interactions, she knew Kenneth was likely meeting his mistress later. And in knowing so, she had agreed to silence and whatever it took to keep everything calm at home. To protect him and this mystery woman's illicit affair that seemed to be the thing shielding her.

Kenneth continued the affair through the rest of the Summer. Only the friction from the occasional sloppy execution of impropriety would arise. Those instances were always explained away by Lavender—his accomplice.

"Lizzy, just ask Lavender," became a common phrase from him during those times. "Lavender, didn't I tell you I was gonna be at *such-and-such....*" A quick glance from both Elizabeth and Kenneth in her direction, and without hesitation, she would issue some form of confirmation.

"Roger" was the prevailing name used in these lies. He was an acquaintance of Kenneth's and someone Elizabeth only vaguely knew and had met once. It was at a party thrown in Roger's honor at his girlfriend's midtown bungalow. Lavender had also only seen the tall, dark, and robust man a couple of times. There was once when he dropped Kenneth off at the store and another time when he came inside. He was talkative and cordial with Mary while waiting on Kenneth.

The ambiguity of that friendship was what maintained the facade. Roger, too, apparently didn't mind having his name tied to Kenneth's affair. Perhaps he was orchestrating his own in a mutual exchange, Lavender wondered but did not know. He was simply an easy alibi to conjure in a pinch. Kenneth, Roger, and Lavender had established a "flow" of all the deceptions.

Lavender felt awkward about her role in it but would remind herself that it was worth it as she enjoyed her freedom away from Kenneth's gaze. She reasoned that if Elizabeth had to be cheated on until she was eighteen and old enough to be away from every single one of them, then so be it. Her aunt was grown and had misled this man for seven years about a boy that turned out not to be his. And well, if Elizabeth wasn't bright enough to pick up on the clues herself, that *ain't my business.*

~

A few weeks into the start of her tenth-grade year, a powerful storm sprung up one afternoon. It sent Lavender and her class-mates into the hallway, giggling and joking as they crouched in their protective positions on the cold floor as tornado sirens sounded outside. The loud horn blasts frightened her when she first moved to the south, but Lavender grew accustomed to them blaring during inclement weather and having no actual twister materialize.

Once school was dismissed, she could see on her bus ride home that while a tornado may not have touched down, a serious squall occurred. Debris was everywhere, and they had to be rerouted more than once due to downed trees and powerlines. The smell of split pine, rain, and steam filled her nose from the open windows on the bus. Her other senses were filled with more oddities as she got closer to home.

"You damn lying nigga!"

Crash!

Glass struck something solid, chairs slid across the floor, and the phrase "You fucking that bitch," was repeated multiple times in various sentence forms—declarative, interrogative, and exclamatory.

Lavender could hear all of this commotion extending from her house through the rolled-down windows of the bus. So could everyone else.

Shit, Lavender thought. Her bus slowed to a halt at her stop only yards from Mary's.

The streets were eerily silent except for a few car horns honking and Elizabeth's yelling. The sight of her aunt's car parked crookedly in the driveway was *wrong* to begin with, Lavender thought. Elizabeth should've been at her own house after picking up Jason and Keshia this time of day.

All the kids who got off at the stop with her could not decide whether to hang around for the show or get to their own homes. Lavender covered her face from shame yet hurried towards the spectacle that was certain to travel the school gossip lines and greet her the next day when she returned to her classes.

She entered to see Mary desperately attempting to hold Elizabeth back from Kenneth, whose forearm was covered in blood and *strawberry jam*? Lavender could not tell.

"Lavender, get out of here!" Mary shouted.

Before she could move or turn her head around after trying to decipher the curious scene, she tasted copper from the blood in her mouth. Then the quiet ringing in her left ear grew louder, and the ceiling tilted and rushed away from her.

She was on the floor. Elizabeth stood over her after just slapping her face with an open hand and the full strength of her body. Kenneth pulled Elizabeth away, and she started swinging at him as well.

Elizabeth caught his right eye with one of those fists before Mary managed to pull her away by the tail of her dress, partially ripping it in the process.

"And you!" Elizabeth's dark eyes and fury focused directly on the girl like radar. "You knew this whole time?!"

It took a moment for all of Lavender's senses to return to working condition and become reoriented. Elizabeth had struck her so hard that one of her favorite, although shoplifted, gold-plated hoop earrings went flying from her ear across the room.

"And why you been lying for him? What he offer you? What y'all doin'? Answer me!" Elizabeth demanded from Lavender.

"Elizabeth...." Mary's feeble and tired voice was just a whisper.

Had this woman lived to only settle disputes? Lavender wondered in a brisk, random moment of lucidity like those that arose and then burst between the clouds of kush she expelled when smoking. Then confusion returned. She looked towards Kenneth, who only stared ahead in a state of drunken depletion.

"Just get out of here Kenny!" Mary pleaded, still having a hold of Elizabeth's skirt.

"Nah, don't leave," Elizabeth said. "Stay! Let's talk!"

She continued to yell other words, and Kenneth slowly tried to respond, but it was all gibberish to Lavender. She remained still on the floor, hoping everyone in the room had forgotten she was there. In all the turmoil, she inched closer and closer to the door. When she was finally able to stand, she first stumbled and then ran from the house, hearing Mary call after her while Elizabeth hurled expletives in her direction like vulgar bolases she hoped would snarl her legs and deal a final blow.

Lavender ran the seven blocks toward TB's Music. Čhetáŋ found her there hours later, telling her to come home, "Grandma outside waiting in the car."

No one spoke a word as they rode the short distance. No explanations unfolded, and no updates on what occurred in those missing hours.

Čhetáŋ finally broke his silence once they got home after they went to their bedrooms.

"Uncle Kenny left," he said in the dark stillness.

Lavender was motionless on top of the covers. She did not even seek clarity on what *left* meant. Was it left the house? Or left altogether?

"So, you knew about this woman this whole time, huh," Čhetáŋ asked.

Her face still ached from the slap Elizabeth dealt, but she managed to get out a few words, wincing with each one.

"I knew something." She took a long deep breath. "What happened?"

"I think you messed up."

She was certain she had without even knowing the context.

"When you were at the store last night, Aunt Liz came and asked you where Kenny was right?"

She had to think back. The instances of her having to recall to Mary or Elizabeth, where Kenneth or even Čhetáŋ was for that matter, all collided. For all the flack she had received for her irresponsibility at times, she had, at that point, been the most reliable of everyone when it came to home chores and store responsibilities, at least.

"I don't remember."

"Yes. You said you saw him with Roger."

"Oh, yeah. And?"

"Uncle Kenny ain't come home last night. Aunt Liz didn't say shit. She went and tried to find that Roger dude early this morning, at his lady house. It was right before she even dropped Jason them at school cause you said you saw them together. Roger wasn't there, but the lady was. Aunt Liz went banging on the door. Man.... Aunt Liz, crazy!" Čhetáŋ paused at the peak of his narration as though wanting to build suspense. "But that lady said she'd dropped Roger off at the airport yesterday evening, same time you said you saw them together. Somebody died in his family. So, this is like, a real thing. So, Aunt Liz went down to The Social this morning, lookin' for him. And she saw some woman dropping Uncle Kenny off at his car."

The Social was one of Kenneth's favorite nightclubs. Elizabeth had driven by several other entertainment venues he frequented but discovered his car in the establishment's desolate parking lot. She saw both the club and vehicle were void of occupants and waited. That's when she witnessed the drop-off.

"Uncle Kenny was still drunk and him and the lady was arguing. But Aunt Liz ain't even say nothing then when she saw it. Grandma had to get Uncle Kenny to come by and help her move some stuff from our 'fridge to the store since the power went out here but not on the store's street. And man, when Aunt Liz caught up with him here, that's when she went crazy."

Lavender listened intently, trying to piece together the day's sequence of events that led to such drama. It still did not make sense to her how she got tied up in it all.

"How do you know all this?" She asked.

"Cause... Grandma picked me up early after the storm. She sent me to my room, but hell, I heard everything."

"I still don't see how I messed up. Like, why that bitch hit me? What if Kenny lied to me too about being with Roger yesterday just like he lied to everybody else?"

"But you said you saw him with Roger. Like with your own eyes.

Not nothing Kenny told you or told you to say. Aunt Liz kept goin' on and on about that part."

It was one word. *Saw.* An absent-minded faux pas. Lavender remembered when she flippantly said it. Elizabeth came by but had to rush away for a last-minute school situation with Jason. She needed Kenneth's help, and he wasn't there. Lavender shot off, "I saw him with Roger." She said it while in the middle of answering a customer, trying to count out the correct change to another, and while yelling at Čhetáŋ to answer the ringing phone. All of that was because Mary was busy speaking with the repairman who came by to see why the AC stopped cooling. A sequence of ill-timed distractions is what led to this.

A *regular* human being would not have even noticed one word like "saw," Lavender imagined. Kenneth not coming home that evening and her one-word mistake caused her to verify something that did not and could not have occurred, and Elizabeth did not miss it.

Kenneth's exposure was probably only a matter of time, though. He had grown so careless at concealing the affair—late nights, heavy drinking. Lavender wondered if keeping it buried was ever his intention at all. The one night he decided not to come home happened to be when his alibi was not even in the state to corroborate the lies.

"Chase. Out." Mary said after entering Lavender's bedroom and discovering the two whispering in the shadows. "Go take a shower. Now."

She sat next to Lavender, who was stretched across her bed and handed her a cold compress for her face. She waited until she heard Čhetáŋ run the water and close the door. Mary got up and shut Lavender's door, then returned to her spot on the bed.

"Why you say you saw Kenny and Roger together?" Mary asked.

"Huh?"

"You said you saw him with his friend yesterday. But you didn't. Why you say that?"

Lavender scrambled for some reasonable answer. "Oh... I don't know. I thought I saw them, but I was wrong. I mean, I saw Kenny. Well, what looked like his car down by our house with some guys inside. I thought it was them. It looked like them from way back by the store. I was just wrong. I didn't pay attention. I wasn't thinking when I said it."

"So, you ain't really see nobody. You just saw two folks in a car and jumped to the conclusion that it's Kenny and Roger?"

When Mary repeated it back, Lavender knew how flimsy it sounded.

"Yes ma'am. I mean, I just looked down that way. Saw what looked like Kenny's truck by the house, same color and everything, and two dudes inside. They looked like, the same size as them. I didn't stare long. I was trying to hurry and get in the store cause I was late."

Mary rubbed her chin, "Hmph.... And you sure? You sure that's all there is? Just misspoke?"

Lavender nodded.

"Kenny promise you something? Or, anything else?"

What was she asking? Lavender wondered. *Yes, he had promised me something. He promised to leave me alone.* But she didn't tell Mary that and did not know how to, if she could or if it was too late to. She swallowed the lump in her throat.

"No, Grandma."

Mary exhaled, "You know you can tell me. I won't get mad."

Lavender smiled, nodded yes again, and thanked her for the compress. "There's nothing."

She could tell Mary had been thinking about this with great attention. But she didn't know how to speak the truth now.

Lavender had been confused and ashamed after the movie theater incident those years before. Wondering if she did something in her moments of drinking with Kenneth that resembled teasing like he said she had.

Kenneth apologized and left her alone for a time after that. Long enough for her to think it was over and done with. But then, another time, when she had to babysit her brother and cousins at Elizabeth's. Jason broke an antique hourglass left by their grandfather, Ernest, and one of the children called Kenneth at his job, terrified over how Elizabeth would react.

Lavender was just as frightened as she knew Elizabeth would blame her as their chaperone. She knew what losing something like that meant, thinking of how she had gone to exhaustive lengths to preserve her father's cassettes.

Lavender didn't realize Kenneth was alerted until he showed up and sent the children outside while the two of them cleaned the mess. But not before telling her he would take responsibility for Ernest's heirloom, then taking liberties with his hands and continuing to explore parts of her.

"Tell who Lavender? I'm just playing around. We're not doing anything," he reassured her.

There would be two more times after that. Worse than that.

Those words, *tell who.... not doing anything*, replayed in her mind often. He was right. She could not prove anything. And, it had "only" been some touching, at least when he said those words. He was convincing. Why jeopardize the little stability she and Čhetáŋ had after everything in Newark over what she couldn't prove anyway?

Perhaps if she said the words then, things would not have progressed. Was that her fault too? The picture he painted over believability and the potential fallout was vivid enough to quiet her. He was beloved by almost everyone as he had once been by her. Even now, with the news that spread throughout the neighborhood over his affair and after his alcoholism grew noticeable, people still found a way to excuse Kenneth.

Y'all know Lizzy crazy was the common assessment among the neighbors. Or, the whispers that Jason wasn't his and therefore Elizabeth was still to blame, also persisted. Had she not known better, Lavender might have faulted her aunt as well.

Is that what they'd say about me? With him? It was my fault?

Lavender wondered if Mary was open to hearing what he tried with her granddaughter in moments where his compulsion met opportunity.

"Nah, Grandma. There's nothing more."

"Well then... I'll tell Lizzy you just made a mistake. Wasn't nothing on purpose. So won't be no tension there. But you need to be careful what you say. And she needs to apologize for hittin' you."

Lavender could not fathom a world in which Mary would think there would never be tension there or her daughter would apologize for anything.

Two weeks passed, and Kenneth still hadn't returned after the fight. Lavender was pleased, but the other minors, especially the boys, lacked their usual buoyant moods. Kenneth called, but Elizabeth would not speak to him. She would not even speak his name. *Ol' bitch-ass* was how she now referred to him on all occasions.

"You can't be saying that in front of Jason," Mary would chastise. But it did not matter. Elizabeth went as far as to change the phone number and the locks.

Lavender admired the tenacity and spitefulness Elizabeth could swiftly adopt. How unfortunate that she was usually on the receiving end of it. What formidable allies they could be without that rift, their shared disdain for Kenneth and their animosity against Katherine.

"The way you get 'em, how you lose them," Mary said. "Lizzy knew what she was gettin' into. He got kicked out the Air Force runnin' round on his first wife with her. She shoulda know'd."

So much grew clearer to Lavender now in such a short time.

After Elizabeth changed their phone number, Kenneth started calling Mary's house.

"Hey, I can't get Lizzy. Can somebody tell her to please call me? She can call me at work."

Delete.

"Hey, this Kenny. Please. I need Lizzy to call. And...."

Delete.

Mary told them not to answer whenever they saw Kenneth calling or some "unknown" number displayed on the caller ID until she said otherwise. But Lavender went further. Not only ignoring those calls but deleting every message he left. Then "forgetting" to tell anyone he called at all.

On the Wednesday afternoon of week three of Kenneth's absence, Lavender walked into her house instead of her fifth-period typing class and gasped at the sight of him sitting at the kitchen table casually reading one of Mary's magazines.

"What... What you doing here?" She stated as the gin she had just shared with Kiara and four other fellow class skippers coursed through her.

"Hey girl," Kenny said, surprised. "I can ask you the same thing." He looked her over. "Hmph," a smirk flashed briefly on his mouth. "You need to slow down."

She rolled her eyes, remembering a verse from a recent church visit about "styes in eyes" or something along those lines about hypocrites. She ignored his observation and tried to steady herself. The euphoric feeling was fresh. She had just taken two full guzzles of the liquid straight from the bottle no less than two minutes before entering.

"I didn't see your car. I didn't know anybody was here," Lavender said.

"You're not supposed to be here either."

"Yeah," she nervously grinned. "I hate typing class so...."

"I parked around the corner a little bit," Kenneth added. "I was hoping to catch your grandmother and I ain't wanna, you know, tip her off, and she keep driving or something. Or call the police. I don't know."

"Right. Ain't this breakin' and entering?" Lavender asked.

He grinned for a moment. "I can't get nobody. Liz has changed the number, the locks. It's like she's crazy. I been leaving messages, but I guess she forgot I had a spare here. I just, I just wanted to see if we could work something out." Lavender shrugged her shoulders and remained quiet. "You know what your aunt been saying?" He continued. "Your grandma say anything about me? Or about trying to talk some sense into Liz for me? She been getting my messages?"

"Nah, I've been deleting your messages," she said with a deadpan stare, and Kenneth frowned. "I mean... I gave her your message the first time, and she cussed me. So, I didn't do that again."

It sounded like something Elizabeth would do. Kenneth let it go. Dejection flooded his face. He was quiet for several moments before turning his attention to her.

"Why are you actin' up like this? Why are you here? Drunk and skippin' school? Your grandma gon' kill you if she finds out."

"Why you worried? Grandma won't find out. By the time she or Chetán get here, I'll be straight again and on my way to the store. I've been sneaking from school like this from time to time since last year. I know you know about that, sneaking."

He narrowed his eyes at her and scratched his brow. "Whatever... I just don't wanna see you get hurt or nothing."

She laughed.

"What's funny? I care about you. Always have. I, I know we've made mistakes..."

Lavender's body tensed. "Nigga, *we*? *We* made mistakes?"

He stuttered a bit. "Aw, aw... come on now, Lavender," he sighed as he tried to put the words together. "You knew what you were doing. I understood it."

"You ain't understand shit! That was all on you!"

"It was all me!?" He bristled, and his tone grew pointed. "Fuck you mean?" He approached her, one fist slapping the inside palm of the other hand. "I don't remember you telling a nigga to stop nothing." He'd gone from calm to furious in seconds.

"What? I did!" Lavender yelled, his shift not deterring her. "I told you to stop the first time, and you didn't. I told you no all the time, and you didn't. And you used to wait until I couldn't fight you or when nobody would know. You knew you was wrong! Nigga you the grown one!"

Tears formed though she tried to submerge them under her surfacing courage. Her knees shook from fear or emotions or the loss of equilibrium from drinking; she did not know. Lavender straightened her legs so they would not buckle completely.

"Lavender, don't try that innocent shit. You were 'round here fucking before me. I knew about that boy. You knew what you were doing. I am a grown man. You knew that. Didn't stop you from stayin' all up on me, trying to be alone with me, wanting to share my same liquor after me, talkin' against your own damn aunt over private, grown shit. Touching me. What does that look like to you?"

Her lungs could not draw oxygen. He was still saying she was the cause. Saying how she moved in her own skin meant she was receptive to being prey. None of those things he mentioned meant anything to her in the moments they were happening. Now in retrospect, she did not know. He muddled her thoughts all over again.

Kenneth stood with a slick feline's countenance, almost strutting. He wore a knowing look that his words had wounded her or at least caused self-doubt; either was a victory. And just as she attempted to mouth some response, he tensed his muscles, clenched his fists, and stood close over her. Her body shrank, and she looked away, becoming a diminutive wilting flower. What little bravado she had was now vapor.

Someone rattled keys in the lock of the door by the kitchen. Mary's voice carried throughout the house as she entered, giving directives to Čhetáŋ.

"You go on in your room, lay down, and put that shirt in the washer. You smell like throw-up all the way here." Mary and Čhetáŋ emerged from the side door entrance into the galley, and everyone's eyes met. The four of them stood as stones, all looking at one another, confused.

"What's going on here?" Mary asked.

"Hey, hey Mrs. Freeman, I... I stopped by hoping to catch you." The smile Kenneth gave was tense as he struggled for the words. "I was hoping to get you to help me talk to Liz."

"Lavender?" Mary turned to her granddaughter, who stood, still shivering from the exchange seconds before. Her eyes were bloodshot, puffy, and watery from crying. "What you doing here? What's going on?"

"I left school."

"Left school?" Mary repeated.

"I wasn't feeling good."

Mary sensed the tension that preceded her entrance. It almost had a taste. Even an ailing, turning-pale-in-the-face Čhetáŋ picked up on it, though he could hardly express himself. A stomach virus had rendered him weak.

"Chase... go lay down. I'll be there in a few," Mary said. She dropped her purse and keys on the table. The house was deathly silent and yet loud with foreboding. Mary breathed heavily.

"Lavender, come here."

Lavender moved forward, and Mary gave her granddaughter a long, investigative gaze. Lavender held her head down.

"Look at me!" Mary demanded. She focused on the teenager's eyes and breathed her all the way in. Lavender trembled and alternated between looking at Kenneth and returning her grandmother's glare. Mary scoffed and squeezed Lavender's hand before turning towards the man.

"My granddaughter might be drunk, Kenny. I'll figure all that out in a bit. I'm old, but I ain't no old fool. Sometimes I'm slow, but I ain't that forever neither." She dropped Lavender's hand and stepped between her and Kenneth. "I don't know everything here," Mary continued. "But I know somethin' in the milk ain't clean. I think it's you."

"Me? What you mean?" He asked.

"I think you need to leave her," she pointed at Lavender, "and my daughter the hell alone now. For good."

Kenneth laughed and swayed about, restless. "For good? Ma-Mary, I don't know what you're talkin' about. This is me. You know me."

Mary's face only grew hard.

He shifted his approach. "Liz would have the last say in that anyway. We been together for years. You can't make her stay away. You can't keep me from Jason."

"That boy ain't yours!" Mary snapped in return.

His face cringed at the words.

"Lizzy is done with you," Mary continued. "I know that. And now that..." She paused to consider her words. "I can finally see just how low a nigga you are, I'm through too. Leave! You ain't welcomed here no more, 'less one of my girls tells me you good, and I don't see that happening no time soon."

Kenneth looked aghast. He peered at Mary, then at Lavender, and back to Mary again as though trying to solve a riddle. "One of your girls? I don't know what you thinking, but it ain't.... Is somebody saying something happened? Because they're lying."

"You doin' all the sayin'," Mary responded.

"I ain't done nothing here!"

Mary turned and faced Lavender. "Did he mess with you, baby?"

"What?!" Kenny shouted, gasping for air like he was drowning. "I ain't... girl, you better say something! Tell this woman what she's thinking is crazy!"

Lavender was mute. Her limbs were immobile, useless accessories. She was a transfixed spectator of her own saga.

Kenneth's face turned into the coils of an electric stove, growing in heat, a hue almost coral. "All y'all are fucking crazy!" He yelled. "Simple country asses!" He paused as though waiting on a final opportunity for a lifeline. Then he grabbed his keys and stormed out, slamming the door behind him.

Lavender was still anchored to the floor. She didn't budge during the entire exchange. She had never seen Mary this way. Her grandmother's small frame and sweet voice concealed a lioness unafraid while protecting a cub.

"Lavender!" Mary yelled, attempting to get her attention. "Did he mess with you?"

"Yes ma'am. I mean, no. I mean, I, I...." Lavender burst into tears. She did not understand why. Her heart pounded in her ears, perspiration trickled down her face, and goosebumps were noticeable on her flesh. All the effects of the ride of emotions the afternoon had wrought.

"Ok, ok, shhh. Shhh..." Mary whispered and patted her back after pulling her into her bosom. "We can talk about it later. Go in my room and lay down." She hugged her close, wiped her tears, and warned her to stay clear of her ailing brother. "You can sleep off that liquor."

Lavender did as she was told. And despite the suggestion that they would speak on the matter later, perhaps when emotions weren't as raw, they never did.

Kenneth stayed away for good. Elizabeth never gave the appearance that his departure was anything other than fortunate. The issue of what did or did not happen quickly drifted into that proverbial closet where all family secrets go to lie dormant.

Chapter 21

Thirty-Six

"This Feeling" - Alabama Shakes

THERE WAS A MUGGY, THICK HEAT IN THE KITCHEN. IT WAS THE end of May, and the thermostat read seventy-two degrees already at ten A.M. The AC hadn't worked for a week, and in addition to that, Elizabeth requested that Lavender help press her hair with the hot comb. The extra heat from the lit eye on the stove drove the temperature up another ten degrees. Lavender attended to the other "kitchen" at the nape of Elizabeth's neck with closeness and precision to not burn her and get her *going*. She made sure Elizabeth took her Lithium and Carbamazepine for the bipolar disorder before she even started on her hair as sort of a bargaining chip, which she hoped would help her mood. Elizabeth hated to take her medications, and Lavender would only do her hair if she did.

"That shit take me out of my head," Elizabeth would say. Which was the point Lavender thought.

For the first time in a while, it did not take much persuading for her to ingest her prescriptions. Her daughter Keshia, at thirty-three, was graduating from an associate degree program near Birmingham as a Medical Assistant, and Elizabeth wanted to make sure she looked good for the commencement.

"Ok. There you go," Lavender said while placing the comb on the stove. Elizabeth got up to check by looking in the small mirror that hung between the sconces on the back wall.

"Yeah, that's good." She turned her radio up so that the new "Uptown Funk" song would boom throughout the residence. "Ooh... I like that lil ol' boy that sing this. He Mexican ain't he?"

"Not at all," Lavender said while scrolling through her phone before placing it on the table. She was looking to see if she'd received any messages from her boss at the bar about her coming in or not, but her inbox was empty. "Now, sit by the fan before you start sweating." Lavender handed Elizabeth a cold beer, her church fan, purse, the house phone, cigarettes, and the TV remote, all in the order of commands she knew would come if she did not take the initiative to provide them.

About twice a month, Lavender would style her aunt's hair. It started with cornrows when Elizabeth was bedridden for a time after her accident. Somehow that expanded beyond braids to other styles and then extended outside of the realm of care one would render for a temporarily impaired individual. Before Lavender knew it, years had passed, and she still found herself doing Elizabeth's hair on a frequent basis, despite her aunt, long being capable of styling it herself. It also did not stop there. Once Keshia moved out, Elizabeth added, "grabbing her meds" and "picking up her food" to these services, even after she had long been cleared to drive. She still avoided getting behind the wheel as much as possible and used her "condition" as the reason why she could not.

Those errands were fine with Lavender originally, but she had been without a vehicle for some time and relied on public transportation now. That inconvenience did not deter Elizabeth from expecting her bi-monthly grooming and delivery services.

It had been about seventeen years since Mary passed away. Lavender was only nineteen then, and Kenneth had already left the family for good. After years of disagreements with Elizabeth, rumors about indiscretions, and that kitchen incident where Mary found him with Lavender, he was just *gone* one morning. Many casual observers were surprised by the abrupt departure. Lavender was not. Relief was her emotion.

He eventually found a wife again, after never extending that title to Elizabeth, and started a new family in Colorado. At least, that was what Lavender knew from Jason. Jason had remained in touch with the man that raised him despite the conditions of his departure. And, on account of his actual father, Jamal, remaining miles away and a virtual stranger. Lavender understood that affinity and even Čhetáŋ's fondness when they spoke of Kenneth. But that understanding came with stirs of nausea in her belly.

After Mary and Kenneth were gone, the five Freeman and Adairs remained tied to the same two square blocks between Freeman's Grocery and Mary's house and also the miles to the north where Elizabeth's sanctuary was. Eventually, Jason left for the military, and when Keshia went off to school, Lavender was the only one left to assist her aunt occasionally. Čhetáŋ was engaged in his own endeavors, most recently raising a four-year-old son and preparing for another baby.

This morning, Elizabeth was in great spirits. Lavender rarely witnessed her this jovial, almost effervescent. There was no ridicule at her expense, no random deviations down memory lane, which always exited at "where Kathy went wrong with her." Part of that was the medication, but also, Elizabeth was ecstatic about her daughter doing something she never had.

"When Chase 'spose to get here to take me?" Elizabeth asked.

"I don't know. You didn't talk to him last night?"

"I wouldn't be askin' if I did. Y'all ain't neva on time and ready for nothin'. Now that Keshia finna be a nurse, she gon' get a big house, and I know I'ma be up there in Birmingham. I ain't gotta fool with y'all asses."

Lavender thought of the thousands of times she had corrected her. Keshia was not graduating as a nurse. She thought about giving Elizabeth the revelation once again that on a Medical Assistant salary, Keshia was no sooner going to buy a big house to accommodate her than *she* was. Keshia was happy an hour and a half away with a man and a baby, and there was a reason she left Montgomery like a bolt as soon as she was old enough. But Lavender didn't correct her on this day. *This nigga got a right to be happy*, Lavender thought, and brag about the children who were purposely never around.

Čhetáŋ arrived, pulling up in his conspicuous automobile. He, too, had recently gotten a degree. One in Sports Management from an online school in Florida. Instead of traveling to attend his convocation, though, he avoided that expense to save money for his son Caleb and the new baby he had on the way with his girlfriend Gloria.

Čhetáŋ exited his royal blue Honda Civic that he nicknamed "Blue Magic." It was wrapped in an advertisement for Railyard Tavern, which everyone made fun of. Gloria particularly hated it. The car wrap visuals were overwhelming. The ugly contrast of royal blue with the company's red, gold, gray, and busy logo design, contact information, and hours of service all came together to be "visual mud," as Lavender put it. The rolling eyesore brought in an additional $200 a month, however, so Čhetáŋ was unconcerned with his sister's thoughts or anyone else's.

"You ain't even got a car. And couldn't legally drive if you did!" His usual rebuttal to Lavender, referring to a recent legal woe of her own creation, which made driving impossible. It was enough to quiet her insults most times.

He stepped out, and all six-plus feet of him unfolded from the small vehicle like a Transformer. He was toned, wearing his cleaned Air Force Ones, navy blue pants, and a button-down short-sleeve shirt. He'd pulled his thick dreadlocks back into a ponytail. Čhetáŋ was a shade darker than his usual desert tone due to hours of tanning under the sun, preparing his baseball field for the season.

"About time," Elizabeth said, slowly making her way down the sidewalk toward him with the help of her cane. "I'll be glad when you do somethin' 'bout this car, Chase. I'm almost embarrassed to ride with your ass."

"You ain't gotta," Čhetáŋ said.

Lavender gave him a sympathetic glance at what he would endure over the next two hours.

"Your ass should be goin'," Elizabeth said, turning to Lavender. "She your cousin too. Doin' what would've made momma proud. Like Jason and your brother. Ere'body else but you."

There it is. Lavender smiled to herself as she held the door for Elizabeth so that she could lift her legs in and pull the cane to rest beside her.

"Whatcha laughing for?" Elizabeth asked.

"Nothing," Lavender said, ending it, ready to pass her off into her brother's hands and out of her concerns. "Y'all be safe."

Čhetáŋ and Elizabeth headed towards Interstate 65 and into the depths of whatever *torturous* conversation her aunt was sure to engage in for the entire journey. Lavender had to work that evening which was the main excuse she gave for not accompanying them. Even if she didn't, she would have found a way to avoid hours of Elizabeth's commentary. "Hotboxing" with her friends before heading over to the bar—which had been a weekend activity of hers for nearly a decade—was more appealing.

Friends, Caesar and Angie, picked Lavender up from Elizabeth's around two o'clock. They had their smoke session and dropped her off at home, which was still Mary's old house. She now shared it with Čhetáŋ, Gloria, and their garrulous son, Caleb Joshua "CJ" Adair.

When Lavender walked in, inebriated, and seeking her bed before working at Club Elite later, she was given little time to cross the threshold before being pummeled with "business" questions.

"You have the money for the month?" A pregnant Gloria inquired while leaning over a steaming pot in the kitchen.

"Yep. Hold on."

Lavender went to the closet in her room, opened a lock box, and took out a roll of money. She counted $1,400 of cash inside. She pulled off four one-hundred-dollar bills and returned to Gloria, who was already demanding more before it was in her hands. "We're gonna need the other $200 for utilities, though. You know this."

"I ain't got it," Lavender responded, wondering if having to listen to Gloria was any less aggravating than what she would be subjected to inside of "Blue Magic" with Elizabeth.

Gloria sighed. The spoon in her hand fell inside the pot and rattled along its rim. "Why must we go through this every month?"

"I don't know. Why *must* we? I get it to you every time, right?"

"Yes. And I have to beg every time as well. If you would just..." Caleb snuck from around the corner of the hallway behind Lavender and nudged her leg just at the perfect moment for an interruption.

"Auntie!" His squeaky voice rang out. "Here I am!"

Lavender turned to greet him and lifted him in the air. "You trying to scare me?"

"Yes! Did I?"

"You did." She kissed his cheek. "Hey, guess what I'm about to do?" The mere presence of the elation he exuded upon seeing her eroded all notions she had of getting immediate sleep. She was now energized to engage in his favorite activity.

He crinkled his deep brown brow upwards, along with a hopeful smirk.

"I'm going to the shed to play. You coming?" She asked.

"Yes!"

Gloria ordered him to clean his play area before he went outside, then she continued her barrage. "When's the last time you cleaned that shed or let it air out? You smell like loud now. You come in here reeking of it. I don't appreciate it," she said while stirring the pot literally and figuratively. Gloria also utilized her best—as Lavender considered it—"fake accent."

Gloria grew up in South Montgomery. But her family was originally from Luverne, which was even smaller and further south. Somewhere along the way, however, she had lost the typical cadence of that pedigree and began to sound like, *whatever this was*. Even Elizabeth agreed with that observation. She and Lavender's mutual distrust of the girl was one of the few things they got along over. Together, they would sit around mocking Gloria's voice with fabricated quotes, evoking what they believed "fun times" in Luverne consisted of. *"Pardon me, would you please pass the jar of pickled pig's feet, my love?"* Then Lavender and her aunt would burst into side-splitting laughter.

Lavender didn't respond to Gloria's question. She only glared at her round, ebony face. She couldn't understand the gall of someone not working or contributing, aside from a bit of cooking, pestering her over rent that was always paid. It shouldn't have mattered what her previous arrangement with Čhetáŋ was. Gloria was essentially living there for free now and had been for over a year between her marketing jobs and pregnancy. By right, Lavender shouldn't have been paying the amount that she was. It was an ongoing point of tension between them—along with several others.

"I'm just asking because the weed smell... I don't want him around it, and it's too much for this house, too, really." Gloria was from a housing project and grew up with five brothers, one of whom was a known weed seller who had dealt to Lavender in the past. Her apparent consternation and aversion to the plant struck Lavender as nothing more than additional sanctimonious performance, like her confusing *Peppa Pig-Southern Belle* inflections.

"Gloria. I ain't smoked in there in days. You think he's gonna get "sixth-hand" smoke inhalation? And as far as *my* house goes, I haven't smoked inside since you got pregnant and never outside of my own room even then. So..."

"Let's go!" Caleb raced back in, and Lavender was more than happy to abandon the current discussion.

When she and her nephew made it outside, she turned towards

him, "Why is your momma so mean?"

Caleb shrugged, "Cause she got that big belly."

"And she's pregnant," Lavender laughed, enjoying the inclusion of him in her mischief. He giggled, oblivious to it all.

They walked out to the backyard and approached the tiny and somewhat shabby wooden storage shed a few yards from Mary's garden. They both carried guitar cases of two drastically different sizes. They passed a long extension cord that ran out near the entrance of the shack, where she would plug in the cord to her amplifier if she were going out to play Joshua's Les Paul. But today, she wanted to relax and fall into a softer moment on her classical with her nephew.

The storage shed was only seven by five feet and had been broken into so many times over the years that they quit storing anything of real value inside, only old Christmas decorations and potting soil. Mainly, it had become Lavender's place where she smoked and played as often and almost as loudly as she wanted. She put a lot of work into soundproofing it with foam, egg crates, heavy curtains, and cushions. It worked. It kept the nearest neighbor from complaining. However, Gloria was somewhat correct. The sound-absorbing materials also soaked in cannabis fumes just as efficiently as they did the acoustics.

Lavender left the door open and sat her nephew near the open air of the entrance.

"Play it," he demanded.

"Nope."

"Yes!"

"Why do you like that song so much?" She asked.

"Because it's fast!"

"Fast? It's country and hillbilly. You wanna be a hillbilly?"

"Yes!" Caleb said with total confidence.

She shook her head. "Plus, you're supposed to play part of it, and you don't know how yet," Lavender gestured towards the little ukulele she had bought him.

"I don't care."

She sighed, and Caleb began to grin in delight as she started the slow build of "Dueling Banjos," letting it get faster and faster. When she reached its apex, he yelled and clapped, then tried to mimic her with his small hands. She knew she was not as fast or as clean as true dueling guitars or techniques she had seen done on a double-neck, but seeing his enthusiasm, always delighted her.

They spent almost an hour playing and talking. Their conversations were effortless and reenergizing. The complete opposite of what was typical of the adults in the house.

"Tee Amášte, you have a good day today? You seem happy."

"I do?" Lavender asked.

It pleased her how he continued to address her by her middle name even though he was a bit older now. When he was born, she felt *Lavender* would be somewhat cumbersome for his developing speech, so she taught him *Amášte* instead. It had become their "special" communication as he was the only person who called her that—something no one had really used since Joshua died.

Caleb's perceptiveness always impressed her. She was high and probably still exhibiting signs of the endorphins from the previous night with a male acquaintance. She laughed almost uncontrollably, thinking of him sleuthing something of that nature from her.

"You're funny," he said as he played with an object in his pocket, which turned out to be an old earring.

"What's that?" Lavender reached for it and, after rubbing her eyes for a bit, recognized the brassy and green, oxidated hooped jewelry.

"How.... Why do you have this?"

"I found it in the kitchen, behind the 'frigerator when I was playin'."

She hadn't seen it in years, not since Elizabeth had knocked it from her ear. Just holding it, she could almost smell the fresh rain of that day and taste the blood again.

Chapter 22

Paper Mache

"Meet Me In the City" - The Black Keys

Lavender perspired, turning portions of her light gray uniform into more of a charcoal shade from the moisture. The combination of dust and the aroma of Pine-Sol in the air as she pushed the mop bucket down the Arts Hall sent her into a sneezing fit. Rosa Parks Magnet high school was usually intact for a place filled with hormonal, rambunctious teenagers. Its orderliness is what annoyed her most. It added pressure to have to do above-mediocre work. The halls and classrooms could not just be a little north of clean. They had to be pristine to look like any work was performed at all.

It had been a long day. The students in a summer art program had apparently started a paper-based sculpture project because that classroom was a task to return to order with leftover paper bits everywhere. By the time Lavender tidied all of that up and entered the music room, the first thing she did was sit and immerse all her senses into the cold carbonation of a Coke-Cola she got from the teacher's lounge. She dropped her head on the desk, attempting to purge her mind and olfactory system of another day of disinfecting.

This was her main job. The one where she had to clock in and clock out, the one that required discipline and professionalism. Her sometimes on-again-off-again work at Club Elite supplemented this. But it was the latter, where she'd been until two A.M., that rendered her so exhausted she lacked both discipline and formality now. Playing guitar with her nephew instead of getting her usual amount of rest before work at the bar was another factor. As was thinking about the tarnished earring, he found while playing. It made her recall the ringing in her ears from the day she lost it. It made her think about her grandmother protecting her in the kitchen. It made her mourn Mary all over again and there was little sleep after that.

Lavender verged on dozing off as she rested on the desk. The thought of the cumbersome trek she had to make just to get back home and repeat again tomorrow added to that depletion. Montgomery's transit system wasn't very expansive, so she had about a mile and a half of walking to the nearest stop from the school. She then had an hour of the route before she was off to walk the seven blocks home. As a pedestrian still thousands of dollars away from even the barest of cars and still barred from a license, she was grateful but cursed the *system* every day.

In the middle of steeling herself for it all, Lavender lifted her head from the desk and was taken aback by something resting unassumingly in the corner of the room. She stared at first as if the Taylor cedar top, grand auditorium, acoustic-electric just behind the teacher's desk were a mirage. Her sluggish eyes widened, and she examined the vision again. *It was really there.* She was in the music room of a school for the arts, but Lavender had cleaned this room at least twice a week for almost two years and not once witnessed any instruments left out, let alone one this expensive. It was still surprising to see it just standing there, almost calling to her.

Her lethargy transformed into bold disregard. The school was virtually empty right before she journeyed down that hallway. The only exception was a couple of administrators still sealed off behind closed doors of the administration offices, way on the opposite end of the building.

I must.

She would certainly be fired if she were caught.

You must. Impish inclinations toward tampering with the device whispered to her.

Speed and silence were imperative. She peaked out the door to get another view down the long hall in both directions. Everything was clear. Lavender shut herself inside, lifted the guitar from its stand with care, and pulled it close to her body. It was the most expensive guitar she had ever held. *Thousands or close to it,* she thought. She understood it was a terrible idea but was also aware she was full of those anyway and pressed forward. Besides, possessing such an instrument in a setting like the auditorium where she sat would likely never happen to her again. She tested the notes. When they came booming forward with clarity.... *Just a few quick minutes.*

Lavender had been in a Junior Kimbrough mood of late and began one of his songs, "Meet Me in the City." The notes bounced off the walls, their echoes sounding foreign, almost as though it were the first time she'd ever heard herself play. She was accustomed to only being inside of her home, or the shed, or at TB's. There may have been a couple of other times she commanded some rickety bar's stage with Titus on a whim. But, hearing her notes back in a manner crafted for a conductor's work was different. It was celestial.

It started with the intention of brevity—*a few quick minutes*—but she couldn't stop. One song flowed into another and another. She wondered how it might sound plugged in but dared not. That would certainly be a bridge too far. Besides that, while the guitar was left exposed to the world, there were no signs of its amplifier, although she assumed it must also be present.

Lavender was so immersed in it all that she didn't notice Chris Daquin watching her for several minutes from just outside the door. Between the two of them, he'd been the only stealthy one. With the classroom door closed and the aerodynamic design of the Nike midsoles on his feet, he didn't make a single sound that alerted her to his approach or presence.

Before she played the opening section of notes from Sting's "Shape of My Heart" for a second time, Chris abruptly swung the door open. It startled her to an instant stop, and the two stared in silence for what seemed an eternity before his voice cut through the chamber.

"Oh, don't stop now after you've shut the door and got it off the stand. Just keep playing like this all good," he said. His scowling face wore stern disapproval but was somehow simultaneously receptive and soft.

"I... I, it was...," she tried to explain but failed. As the words struggled forward, Chris' angry, twisted mouth surrendered to a massive smile that transformed even further into a full belly laugh.

"I'm playing with you," he said. "I mean, I'm not playing. I'm just not.... I left it out. The guitar and..." He spoke in incoherent chunks, attempting to articulate his meaning between breaths and laughter. "No. You still wrong as hell. I'm wrong for forgetting to lock it, but you know you messed up." He sounded almost as undone as she was —trying to be stern but unable to take himself seriously and thereby lacking an understanding of why she was so rattled by him.

Lavender moved with speed and care, rising from the chair to place the guitar back on the stand.

"Nope. Too late for that," he said.

He reached for it and gently removed the guitar from her hands, then walked to the closet and collected its case.

"If somebody else caught you, they would've straight walked you outta here. You know that? Maybe in handcuffs, even. Sorry I scared you, but I was at that door like, four whole minutes. If you're gonna break rules, you gotta be better at it than that."

I usually am, she thought.

Lavender didn't quite know what to make of him. She believed she had seen him before but couldn't remember if it was from school or elsewhere. His accent was confounding. It had a bit of New Orleans flare, as far as she could tell. There weren't many residents from that part of the world who lived in the area, so the sense of familiarity was even more perplexing. He was a deep tawny brown. His manicured, pencil-wide dreadlocks were past his shoulders and pulled back neatly into a low ponytail. He almost reminded her of Čhetáŋ; nearly as tall, just as athletic, except younger. He could have passed for a student under different circumstances, and his deep dimples only added to that youthful radiance. He was something to look at.

"I can't even be mad. I'd be in trouble if the school found out the new guy left their fancy-ass guitar out. Plus, hell, you sounded good. What's your name?" Chris asked.

"Mary."

"Mary?" He squinted his eyes. "That's a lie, but ok."

Even if he could find her name out from other staff if he'd chosen to, Lavender decided not to make it that easy.

"It's not a lie. That's my name. Mary. What's wrong with that?"

"Nothing. Just nobody born after 1990 is named Mary."

"That's presumptuous," Lavender added.

"Which part? The name or the birth...."

"Look," she finally said, frustrated by the back and forth with the stranger and uncertainty of where it was headed. "I apologize. I don't know if you're messing with me, but I'm sorry. I'll never touch anything in here again. Do I need to clean or polish it or something?"

He shook his head no. "It's fine."

"Ok. So, I can leave? You're not telling anyone anything?"

"You're fine." He waited a moment before asking, "How long have you been playing?"

She didn't answer. She rushed to try to escape without further eye contact, interaction, or any other possible punishable behavior.

"Cat got your tongue?" Chris said.

For some reason, the question enthralled her, perhaps the way the old saying sounded in such a foreign and young voice.

"A long time," she responded, moving with purpose to gather all her cleaning materials to depart.

He continued watching her escape. "Well, it was nice meeting...," Chris started, but before he could finish, she had fled. The squeaking wheels of her rolling cleaning cart moved fast as she proceeded down the hall.

This was her fourth year with the school system and would be her second disciplinary mark if he reported anything. It wasn't illustrious work, but it was manageable, steady income, and she was happy to have the job with her lack of experience in most things and the couple of misdemeanors that peppered her file.

Lavender worried for days following the encounter, but after two weeks passed and there was no mention of it from her superiors, she relaxed.

She felt free then to plan and budget finances with Gloria over Čhetáŋ's much-belated graduation celebration. It was a long, arduous eight-year journey to complete his degree. He paused his education to play for a 2A Minor League team for a while, paused again when Caleb was born, and paused once more for a stint with a 1A+ team. He finally realized he was delaying the wrong pursuit. Having never been called up to the Majors, Čhetáŋ made more money at his current job as the Sports Coordinator for the Aaron Avenue Youth Center—his old youth baseball club's center. It was full circle. Through all those twists and turns, Lavender kept a roof over them after Mary passed, kept them both fed and mostly out of trouble. She felt his degree was just as much hers. It should've been a celebration reflective of all that struggle as far as she was concerned. A "blowout."

"We not doing a party. We're just having a nice dinner." Gloria insisted when Lavender pressed her for the details of the celebration.

"This is a big deal. My brother gonna want more than a dinner."

"I'm telling you what he wants. We're not redoing the last party."

Lavender sucked her teeth, wondering when they would let that go.

At a previous house party they threw for Čhetán's birthday, Lavender had gotten such a cocaine high that she randomly began playing guitar for the attendees, tried to fight the hired DJ over that, and with occupied bathrooms, "discreetly" urinated out in the yard which happened to be anything but discreet at all. The final trimming on the evening was taking, without asking, "Blue Magic" for a store run, being pulled over, and ending up arrested for driving without a license and operating a vehicle under the influence. A sober Čhetán, who did not drink, smoke, or engage in any of the sorts, had to leave his own party to post bail. It was how she'd ended up with a suspended license. Lavender rarely ventured beyond the self-medication of alcohol, marijuana, or the occasional "roll of ecstasy." Her lack of control was one reason. Veering too close to being Katherine-adjacent was the other.

"I don't understand why we can't have a party, though. What about all the other years where nothing happened?" Lavender asked.

Gloria rolled her eyes and proceeded with plans for, Nexus, an upscale restaurant with menu items Lavender could barely pronounce and no listed prices on its online menu.

Lavender let it go but approached Čhetán a while later about it. He was brooding and quiet and busy organizing baseball items in the trunk of his car.

"Nexus?" She asked as she approached.

"Huh?"

"Nexus fool?" Lavender repeated.

"Man... chill out. I ain't worried over that. If she planning, let her plan it," he said. He yawned with exhaustion from the work at the youth center and from his moonlighting job. His friend and coworker, Ian, had started a lawn service business and had brought Čhetán into it.

He smelled like grass to Lavender and not the "fun" kind.

"But it's your party. At least have a kickback at the house."

"That's what you want. Gloria wants dinner. I don't want anything, really." He grew quiet again.

"What's wrong with your face? And please don't say it," Lavender said.

"Ok, I won't."

He'd spoken with Katherine earlier and it seemed to weigh on him. He'd attempted to give his sister the details of their discussion, but Lavender, as usual, waved him away, indicating she wanted nothing to do with anything Katherine had to say. She never asked him about it but had an inkling it must be the thing bringing down his mood.

"Bro... quit worrying about her."

"Who else will?"

Lavender waved a dismissive hand.

"I think she's sick," he continued. "She sounds tired and short of breath. Waiting on test results, but she up there on her own with the parole. We're still the only family she has if some shit happens."

Since Mary's death, he had stepped in as the bridge between Katherine and the rest of the family—a link rarely traversed by either side but a branch still extended and present.

Out of all the years and promises of a homecoming, Katherine managed the trip home just once, during a Thanksgiving holiday. He'd visited her twice in Newark—both times at a correctional facility.

"You mean, *you're*, the only family she has. Ain't nothing wrong with that woman either," Lavender insisted. "She playing you like she played Grandma. She's out again, broke, and probably trying to get money. She'll be right back in there. Like always."

Čhetáŋ stared at her with a blank expression. "You ever think you play a role in that?" He asked.

"How?"

"Cause, if you keep treating her shitty, why would she do better? She might as well stay where she is if you gonna keep her where she's at. You feel me?"

Lavender rolled her eyes. "Ok HOV," she responded in a sarcastic tone implying that he'd spoken with a rapper's cadence and flare like the popular Brooklyn lyricist turn mogul. "You're just a fool. She's never changing, and I'm not stressing."

"Y'all more alike than you think."

The suggestion was almost enough to make her walk away. "Enough with this," Lavender said. "I ain't with Gloria's ol' bougie mess."

"Then don't come."

After Gloria's dinner for Čhetáŋ, Lavender joined several of her friends at a restaurant and oyster bar called Ivan's. His celebration was just as she expected, an *Ambien feast*. A bore. It was mainly Gloria's college friends rattling off their accomplishments and plans, surrounded by "Reserved" cabernets, merlots, and ryes.

"You know, *fancy* drinks," Lavender said, using air quotes as she recounted the dining experience with Kiara, Angie, and Renée as they sat in Ivan's. "All they do is talk about resorts, their 'brand,' and real estate. Niggas do one all-inclusive to Jamaica and think they're Dos Equis."

Montgomery was a sleepy, conservative city, and Ivan's, on a Sunday night, was one of the few places with any activity. It was usually crowded for this reason and popular for its live music showcase. One had to be there early to procure a chair or be subjected to a standing position along the walls until a patron left.

Lavender was the first person to exit Čhetáŋ's celebration, catching a ride with Renée over to Ivan's so she was there in time to join the others, hungrily devouring food and gossip at their table.

"I swear to God," Lavender laughed. "You know Jermaine… black, long as hell, it was like… I felt like I was playing a goddamn clarinet." She raised her hands, cupped, and positioned them, one behind the other, twisting in a back-and-forth motion towards her mouth.

"No!"

"Girl, shut up!"

Kiara and Angie howled loudly with laughter at the reenactment of a sexual activity she had recently engaged in with a mutual acquaintance. Renée screwed her face, repulsed by the entire discussion.

"Renée, we sit and listen to you talk about toppin' off chicks all day. Don't be like that," Kiara giggled.

Lavender and Kiara had remained friends over the years, adding Renée and Angie into the mix. Kiara now lived with her boyfriend and the father of her only child, a daughter, in the midtown area. Renée had once worked with Kiara at Walmart and held the reputation of being able to load and lift nearly as much inventory as any of the men on her shift. She was tall, stocky but fit and kept her hair cut short. Out of everyone in the group, she and Lavender were the least connected, albeit friendly.

Angie was from Elizabeth's Sheridan Heights neighborhood. She wore conspicuous lace front wigs that fell against her golden bronze skin and kept long ornate acrylic nails. She had two boys of her own. Lavender had known of Angie in passing, but they did not become good friends until they happened to spend time together at the municipal jail once years before. Angie was there for check fraud and Lavender for shoplifting. That chance encounter not only established their friendship but directly led Lavender to two more misdemeanors: one for check fraud and the infamous "birthday DUI" from Chetán's party since it was Angie who'd supplied the cocaine that evening.

Angie also introduced Lavender to her cousin, Caesar. He was originally from Memphis and a former football player for a local university who ended his career in injury. Alpine, brawny and covered in tattoos, he and Lavender frequently shared a bed within days of meeting. They still carried on in that casual carnal fashion. Caesar was also regularly involved in quick money schemes, the kind that had ensnarled both her and Angie in those fraudulent check situations.

Čhetán despised him.

Lavender knew Caesar nor Angie were good company for positive outcomes, but they were fun and manifested escapism, things she needed, especially during the years when they came into her world.

It was rare that all four women were together in a single moment, but when they were, their conversations were the height of obscenity and coarseness, with one attempting to outdo the other in shock value.

It was ten-thirty P.M., and the band was setting up in front. Lavender, still giddy with girl talk, ignored the ensemble. It was congested and loud, so the crowd drowned out the band's introduction. However, the room quieted once they began playing tracks from D'Angelo's "Voodoo" album, and the lead singer and pianist broke into song.

All eyes and ears were fixated on the performers as the people settled at their tables. Lavender raised her head and caught a glimpse of the musicians on stage. They were a quintet; a man on drums, one on saxophone, a lead guitarist, another on bass, and then, the pianist.

"Oh," Lavender's mouth involuntarily fell open upon seeing him.

"Oh? Oh what?" Kiara asked.

"I know him," she said.

"Who? The singer?"

"Yeah." It was the music teacher from weeks before, the one who had most likely spared her job by remaining silent over the guitar incident.

His voice was a warm and inviting tenor, a little raspy with the same dash of New Orleans she had picked up on before. He reminded her of a milder-sounding Otis Redding if he was from some parish of Louisiana. It was a lovely juxtaposition, to her ears at least. He was engaging, and when he smiled, those deep dimples beamed like it was his own music he gleefully crooned.

On stage, he looked like a grown man, not some fifth-year senior as he did in their first meeting. His locs were still pulled back neatly but had a more intricate styling pattern. He wore a crisp white untucked button-down shirt with sleeves rolled to his elbows. His navy-blue fitted pants stopped perfectly at the top of spotless white Chuck Taylors as though tailor-made.

She remembered now why he'd looked familiar to her that afternoon in the classroom. It was no illusion she had conjured. He had played at her club some years back. He was just beginning to grow his hair long then, but it was unmistakably the same young man.

The band completed one song and moved into the next. It was all R&B or old soul—music that resonated with the crowd of late twenties to forty-something-year-olds. By the time they wrapped up to take a break, they had the entire place dancing and singing. He led most of the vocals until he moved from the piano to pick up a soprano saxophone, where he was just as skilled and commanding. Lavender did not move from the moment she recognized him.

"Where ya at! Y'all good?" He asked over the mic while the bass player and drummer carried on the melody in the background.

The crowd replied in unison, "Yeah!"

"I'm Chris Daquin, and we're Basin Street. We're gon' keep this going after a few minutes," he said. Then he spoke about tipping, being good to the bartenders, and what their next set might entail. He was full of charisma, laughing while conversing with individuals up front. Then Chris wrapped their final song before an intermission to a cascading close, and he and the rest of the band exited the small makeshift stage.

"I'll be back," Lavender said, stepping over Angie and heading towards the bar.

She saw him standing there, drinking and laughing with four other men. He was caught in a furious discussion about defensive backs, wide receivers, Alabama football, and the odds of titles and records with the approaching season. Chris dove into the conversation with excitement, endorsing Louisiana State's program and its prospects. They issued phrases like "spread offense" and "running routes." It was all talk Lavender had no interest in or understanding of beyond knowing that college football was the blood of this state.

Chris' back was to her as she made it to the counter, and she positioned herself behind him. Lavender wore jean leggings, a white cropped tank top accentuating her bosom, and open-toe stilettos that made her almost as tall as him. Even with that display, none of the men noticed her. They were too submerged in gridiron disputes.

She waited and waited and, after several moments, decided she looked the, "silly tower," just standing there. They paused their chatter for several seconds, which offered an opportunity for her to step forward and say something, but she hesitated.

Lavender looked this group over. Chris' apparel appeared so polished that it could have been tailored. His company of friends wore fedoras and newsboy caps, seersucker pants, Polo shirts, and Guess loafers. They all looked no older than twenty-seven or twenty-eight, which was still almost ten years her junior. They referenced homecomings and the like from large SEC schools they had attended. It was almost a repeat of Chetán's dinner, which she had just run from, except this gathering felt inexplicably more intimidating.

Her usual seductive confidence was gone. The longer she stood observing them, the more she bowed to self-doubt. Lavender thought about their initial interaction and how she must have looked, caked in dust and sweat. Every impulse now said, "ma'am, leave this *boy* alone."

Lavender abandoned the idea of speaking to him and decided to try again later or forget about it completely. She turned to walk away, and as she did, he also swung around towards the bar. Their eyes met for a microsecond with Lavender whisking past. He paused as though the fleeting glance held some modicum of recognition. Then the circle pulled him back into their debate, and Lavender was lost to the sea of other patrons.

The following week, she walked Chris' hallway at the school again. Ever since her sprint away from him at the bar, she hoped to see him but had had no luck. It was mere chance that the guitar incident happened, and she'd encountered him that first time. It was still Summer break, and despite one or two specialized programs hosted at the school, most teacher sightings in the evenings when she worked were sparse. As she passed his classroom, she noticed the door was open, but it was empty and dark.

Lavender was unsure why she had this compulsion to see him. Perhaps it was to thank him for not turning her in. Or maybe to reset the tone of how they had first met. She then wondered what the point of that would amount to and regretted not taking advantage of the moments at Ivan's while she was all made up.

When her shift was done, Lavender walked across the empty school parking lot to her bus stop over a mile away. She placed earbuds in her ear and hit play on the old model Walkman cassette player she still owned. Although it continued to serve the purpose of playing Joshua's tapes, the outdated equipment was embarrassing, and she usually carried it hidden in the book bag she slung over her shoulder, allowing only the wires to show.

Her father's tapes still more or less occupied the same spaces in Mary's yard and under her bed. She had done audits on them over the years—excavating to check for broken seals or moisture the way Cedric taught her. They were always as they were when she meticulously put them in the Earth. She once performed the tedious task of duplicating them on all new tape and burying them away again.

She had once bought a cassette player that was also an MP3 converter and expensive at the time of her purchase. She managed to switch some of Joshua's tapes to the digital format when she had a working computer. But the finished sound quality was not the best, and the device quit on her after the first sixty or so conversions anyway.

After all that time, she still hadn't found a more affordable or practical method that fit her budget for preserving his recordings better than what Cedric instructed. Every time she did an audit utilizing his methods, Joshua's music was still in pristine condition. Cedric was her first and, as she considered, only love. But it was so green and transitory. How could that quantify as love at all? She sometimes wondered if the universe had sent him to her for the singular purpose of saving Joshua's voice.

Loud guitar riffs blasted through the earbuds placed firmly in her ear. That was probably why she didn't hear the car approaching or yelling.

"Yo, Mary! Yoooo, Mary!!"

A voice hollered from the driver's side window of a blue SUV. She heard the second shout and yanked one of the earbuds free. *It was him.*

"How are you doing? You ain't hear me calling?" Chris asked.

She turned her music player off, pleasantly surprised but trying to suppress the smile her mouth so eagerly wanted to flash. "Hey. No, I didn't hear you. What's up?" She said, attempting to sound indifferent. Lavender had heard someone scream for "Mary" but forgot she had given him that name.

"That's a good way to get your ass hit. Walking with earphones in the street."

He parked the car and shut off the engine. His demeanor and smile were disarming, so she responded as playfully and crassly as he had.

"Oh? Is this the street? Normally, motherfuckers don't come flying through empty school parking lots, surprising me either."

"Touché," he smiled. Chris exited his vehicle, then leaned against it with folded arms. He looked her up and down with a strange smirk. "But then I was just sort of returning the favor."

She tightened her face, confused by his meaning.

Chris's beard was tapered, and his hair was pulled up into a "man bun" with defined sections and smooth edges like he had recently left the barbershop. He wore sweat shorts, some form of retro Jordans, and a sleeveless t-shirt as though headed to a pick-up basketball game or leaving one. This was the most casual she'd seen him.

Still fine. Her eyes ran the length of his body.

"Last time I saw you... Well, you surprised me," Chris continued. "You sorta just popped up, then you looked me dead in the face at the bar and couldn't even speak."

Her cheeks were flushed. He had seen her that night. She stared at the ground like the words to circumvent embarrassment were beneath her feet. Lavender realized while glaring at asphalt that as fleeting as their initial encounters had been, they were still noteworthy in his mind. Chris had even known and remembered her in that ephemeral second at the bar when there had not been much reason to.

"Oh?" She reached for her composure again. "Well... I mean, I wasn't really paying attention, so..." She casually shrugged, gesturing as though she didn't notice him that evening.

"Stop it," he said. "You knew that was me."

I damn sure did. "Maybe I did, but you were all caught up with your boys. I didn't think you knew who I was anyway," Lavender said, allowing her eyes to focus on his.

"I mean, it took me a minute. You did look... different. But in a good way. I definitely knew you."

They stood silently for a moment before Lavender remembered the reason for her hard press across the parking lot.

"Well, I gotta go catch this bus before it leaves me."

"You catching the bus?"

"Yes."

"Where you going?" He asked.

"Uh... home. It's after five, what you think?"

Chris grinned, finding her bravado amusing. Then he inquired where exactly "home" was. She explained her long commute to the south side, then abruptly ended her response.

"You holding me up, sir," Lavender said as flirtatious and as serious as she could.

"Oh, I am? You want a ride?"

God, yes. "For real?"

"No, for play," he taunted. "Yes, a ride. What's wrong with that, Mary?"

"Nothing. Just, you know. I appreciate it."

"I'm just trying to be nice, Mary. That alright, Mary?" He winked and repeated the false name with deliberate inflection. Lavender searched his face, and they both laughed.

"I can't with you," he smiled. "Yeah... 'Mary.' Who's that?" He walked over to the passenger side and opened the door for her. She allowed that gentleman's gesture to only impress her momentarily before hopping in and getting comfortable in her seat. He made his way back around to the driver's side, got in, and slammed the door shut. The vehicle was junky inside, full of crates and music books, and smelled of musk and cedar. Old blankets were piled high in the back to conceal whatever was beneath them.

Lavender couldn't help but wonder what he was doing there again during the desolate week.

"What you doing up here anyway?" She asked.

He picked up the laptop that sat on his armrest and gave it a little wave.

"I forgot and left this."

"Dude, again? Nigga how you get this job?" She said, remembering how they had first met, with him leaving the guitar out. He covered his eyes and grinned.

"Look, I'm new and still trying to get used to everything. I'm trying to get this room together, and they had me come in for this two-week music program the school hosted when I left that guitar that other day."

"I see."

"Yeah, so after you were in my room and did the drive-by at the club, I did ask about you a couple of times. Took me a while, too, seeing as though I'm the dumbass going around asking folks about *Mary?*"

"Oh, so you asking about me?"

"I mean... yeah. I had to find out who the crazy lady was who was just violating my room and stalking me at the oyster spot. So yes, I asked about you."

"Hmm...." She rubbed her chin. "My real name is Lavender."

"I know that now."

"And I wasn't stalking you. I wasn't sure if you'd say anything about the other day, with the guitar. So, I was checking. I wanted to thank you. I mean, if you hadn't told on me."

"You know I hadn't, but I get that. My name is Chris, Chris Daquin." He extended his hand for an official greeting.

They rode off, and unlike her normal hour-and-a-half journey home via the bus, she was in front of her home in fifteen minutes. The ride over was quiet, besides him talking about getting ready for the school year and upcoming shows with his band Basin Street.

His quintet had a show out of town nearly every weekend for the rest of the summer. But that schedule would settle down in August because he had to save time for the school band and their shows once it was back in session. He also played for his church choir some Sundays, and it had all been extremely tiring yet "worth it," she learned.

He parked on the curb in front of Mary's, and Lavender thanked him. Before she got out, he touched her arm.

"So, can I drop you off again? Like after I take you out? Nothing major, just you know we keep bumping into each other, might as well throw some food or drinks in. Right?" He said. His smile was bright and inviting. "Plus, I'm interested in hearing you play more if you don't mind."

Lavender cleared her throat. "We can probably do that."

He pulled out his phone and handed it to her so she could add her number. "Don't put Mary in there," he laughed. "Your real name is different. It's pretty, but different. There some story behind it?"

"Yep, my parents gave it to me."

He sighed, shaking his head. "I see me and you gonna have issues."

"No, we're not," she said, slamming the door shut behind her and peeking back through the passenger window. "I just got a bit of a mouth on me. You should probably know that." She smiled, enjoying the tease, imagining its effect on him.

Chapter 23

Beignets and Jackson Pollocks

"Spottieottiedopaliscious" - Outkast

CHRIS DID NOT WASTE TIME CALLING HER. HE ALSO LET HER know that was an aberration for him. "I don't want you thinking I'm thirsty or nothing, but I told you my crazy schedule and wondered if you'd be interested in rolling with me this Thursday someplace? I have a quick practice session with my band, and we can grab food after?"

She agreed. They then spent the next hour and a half talking about music—new and old— and learning a bit about their respective backgrounds.

Lavender only disclosed fragments of hers in short bursts of disjointed, nonlinear exposition, like Jackson Pollock engaging a canvas. If her discussion was a Pollock, then his was a Tommy G. Thompson. He was quite content to dominate the conversation with long colorful strokes and accounts from his upbringing in New Orleans, painting animated scenes with his words so vivid she could almost hear the horns and taste the powdered beignets.

When she asked if he named his band Basin Street because he was a Louis Armstrong fan or if it was from the street in his hometown, Lavender could hear him gasp.

"Oh my God, girl, who the hell are you? I'm impressed."

"I know a few things," she insisted.

He crafted an answer that lasted nearly thirty minutes. He spoke of New Orleans before Katrina. How he and his family moved around after the storm but settled in Montgomery, and he had been there for six years. He recently finished his master's degree in music when the high school hired him. Chris named the band "Basin Street" as an homage to home. He said he was a so-so player on several other instruments. However, he was a trained pianist but still revered Louis' trumpet. Ultimately, he wanted to be a songwriter but understood making a living from it was a long shot, so he formed the band. He believed it would help him make connections and build a following. Chris was a talker, and she didn't mind it. It fit perfectly with her aversion for that kind of intimacy.

"It took me a while to get used to Montgomery, though," he admitted. "I hated it at first. It's small and nothing to do. But I'm used to it now, I guess. It has a growing art scene. Downtown is getting nice."

"I still don't know if I'm used to it. At least you were from the South. It was a complete culture shock for me. Damn loud ass crickets, flying roaches. The roaches fly, man! And are big for no reason! First time I saw one, I almost gave my grandma a heart attack! I was screaming and running through the house."

He snickered. "You definitely couldn't make it in Louisiana then. That's swamp land. Everything bigger. We got catfish as big as men. But baby, the food? Best you'll ever eat, and I've been everywhere."

She loved the inflections in his voice when he spoke certain words and sounds — especially the "A's." She could listen to the accent all day, she thought. She wondered how *Amášte*, with its arcs and bends of the "a" pronunciation, would sound rolling from his lips.

"So, you moved here when you were twelve?" He asked. "So, you what? Like twenty-eight, twenty-nine?"

She cleared her throat. "You off by like seven."

There was a pause.

"Wait? You're thirty-five?!"

"Thirty-six."

"No way," he said. "You don't look it. You look so young."

"I am young!"

"You know what I mean," he laughed. She could hear he was flustered.

"Is that an issue?" Lavender asked.

"Not at all. You may have a few things to teach me then."

"I'm sure I do."

They continued their conversation for almost another hour before ending.

A few days later, Lavender feverishly went about her bedroom throwing clothes everywhere, looking for her most revealing yet comfortable sundress. Chris didn't say much more about where they would possibly end up after the band's practice, but she wanted to be ready for anything and didn't have a lot of versatile clothing options of that nature, save for the solitary item.

The yellow-ochre, billowy gown was short and accentuated her legs. It tied just below her breast and fell off the shoulder, revealing the top of her single but elaborate tattoo. It ran the length of the right side of her torso and part of her back, from the top of her shoulder down the side of her ribcage, and continued until it ended just above her pelvis. It was a labyrinth of musical lines, notes, and symbols that swirled and extended, some just near her breast and playfully jutted in and out as they wrapped around a depiction of Joshua's Les Paul. There were clefs and resets, and ornaments like the glissando. The body of the guitar was the largest part of the artwork. It traversed her back and some of her side. At the base of the guitar's body and along her lower abdomen, "Amášte" was written in calligraphic script. Above that, the Oglala Sioux Tribe flag. The entire illustration stopped just at her waist.

It had taken three years and several hundred dollars she could not justifiably afford to spend to get the tattoo just as she wanted. When it was new, she enjoyed the gazes it drew, especially from men when she was daring enough to show much of it. But, as the years passed, she eventually grew tired of having to retell its meaning to them. Tired of the attention. Tired of explaining the actual musicianship behind it. That, it wasn't for decoration only. That she was part Lakota even if so much of that knowledge was stolen from her. Having to explain that she could actually play the thing depicted and probably better than most anyone they'd heard. A chronicle told again and again only to understand they didn't care about any of that, only how the flesh underneath it could satiate them.

Chris was punctual and pulled in front of the corner house minutes before his stated arrival time. When he stepped from his truck, he smiled brightly upon seeing her. He was dressed casually—sweatpants, Jordans, and a black Muhammed Ali graphic tee that defined his chest and arms.

"Don't worry," he said when he reached the porch. "This is just my practice gear. I ain't gon' take you nowhere in J's and sweatpants."

She examined him as he advanced and decided nothing he said was logical. He looked tempting in anything he wore.

"You ready?" He asked politely and stretched his hand forward to help her down the steps, placing his hand on her lower back as she met him at ground level. He walked ahead to open the car door for her. Everything about Chris' mannerisms, courtesies, and even his perfectly aligned, white teeth, which said "braces" and "orthodontics," made Lavender feel he was from *better* stock than most of her circle and old flames. It was the same sort of recognition that had left her speechless at Ivan's and caused her to sweat now.

Basin Street held most of its practices in an old warehouse downtown. It was a communal space that several other bands, dance troupes, and a variety of other entertainers and artists rented out. Old leaflets, trash, glitter, and fabric scraps were scattered about, remnants of the other building-mates. Nothing existed within its walls besides a stage, storage closets, a bathroom, and a few folding chairs.

Lavender's thighs stuck to one of the metal seats as she listened to them run through what she learned was their warm-up and one of their filler songs—"Spottieottiedopaliscious," by Outkast. It was the kind of crowd-pleaser they'd quickly bring out if gigs ran longer than expected. Chris sang the opening verse in an easy high tenor, and Emmanuel, the band's trumpet player, delivered the iconic horn riff. The other three band members were Quinton, Travis, and Eli, who were on drums, lead, and bass, respectively. They were a small but skilled group, and this practice was a tune-up for a performance they had in Columbus, Georgia, the coming weekend.

The hour-long session was an abbreviated one. Chris stated as much in his introduction of Lavender to the other members and how they owed the coming briskness of the evening's practice to his date. Once it was over and everyone cleared, only the two of them remained, and Lavender waited while he searched for sheet music and did a final lock-up of the facility.

"When I find these pages for this lesson plan I'm working on, I'll change, and we can bounce," he yelled out from a storage room across the building. "Sorry for the holdup!"

She yelled in return, "It's cool."

"What!?"

Lavender departed the metal chair that tried clinging to her and walked over to where he was. "I said it's cool."

"Oh," he smiled, scavenging through a locker near the back of the room.

"You need some help?" She asked as she began making her way closer to him.

"Yes and... no. I mean, we got so much stuff in here, I couldn't even tell you what to look for."

The closet was a confined and dusty space, made even more so by the four lockers inside and years' worth of items that artists had left behind and no one had bothered to remove. Lavender stood, pressed against the door, as Chris scanned through more music books, squatting to pick through those that had fallen to the floor.

"Well," he sort of groaned, "I don't wanna hold us up any longer. I don't think I'ma find it tonight, plus we need to bounce if we're going to make the movie. Maybe Riverwalk after?" He gave her an inquisitive glance.

"You sure I can't help, though?" The semi-disingenuous offer of assistance slipped from her mouth in a near whisper. It was something she felt she needed to ask, even if she didn't want to rummage through old, grubby papers and debris the way he was. She looked down at him as he knelt on the floor, trying to collect everything and return the items to their place. He didn't answer but stood and stepped to face her, allowing his gaze to linger for a bit. It was a different look he gave, as if he was studying her for the first time, peering from her feet to her calves and then stopping where her eyes peered back. Her relaxed position against the door and whispery offer of futile assistance made her sound vulnerable.

"I don't want you to get your dress dirty," he said, playfully tugging at the fabric portion around her navel. The gentle confidence of the motion almost made her moan, but she caught herself. Lavender relaxed into the cool metal door where she stood, allowing her head to tilt back and her arms to go limp beside her.

"You let me worry about how dirty I get, ok?" She said, smiling, then looking down at his lips.

Chris returned the suggestive grin, then reached forward, wrapped his arm around her waist, and pulled her close. Then, he leaned in and placed his lips on hers. They were soft and inviting and felt good. She raised her arm and began playing in his dreadlocks, twisting one that had fallen to his shoulders. Her body hummed with the touch, and she couldn't fathom stopping. This turn towards more sexual exertions in the shabby closet was sudden but a transition she had wanted since examining him at Ivan's. They did not make it to their second location.

During the twenty-minute drive across town to his east-side abode, she'd continued with her kisses, working her hands slowly up his thigh, tugging and twisting the bottom of his shirt and waistband of his pants, teasing him as he tried to focus on driving. Every several minutes or so, he'd whisper a low surrendering moan which only encouraged her further.

When they arrived at his home, she led him with assurance by the hand to his own front door as if she had been there before and knew the landscape. Inside, Lavender looked around for only a moment, making small observations of the arched entryway into the kitchen, and vaulted ceiling of the living room, and the long hallway that led to multiple bedrooms. Everything from the appliances to the crown molding seemed fresh and expensive. But the three seconds it took to make note of those things were all she could dedicate to the interior design of the home in the cul-de-sac.

Chris watched her from the foyer. She kept her eyes on him as she untied the front of her perfect yellow-ochre sundress she'd fretted over finding and let it fall to the floor, revealing she wore nothing underneath but her elaborate tattoo. Lavender watched as his eyes went up and down her body and followed the art as it dipped underneath and around the curves of her breast and down to her waistline. He made his way towards her with urgency, pulling off his shirt, and grabbed and lifted her a few inches as he continued walking toward his bedroom.

~

The sex was how she enjoyed it. She'd straddled him, despite his protests to take control, working him until she panted and perspired, but not before he exhaled and shuttered. He gathered himself and, with an abashed face, steadied to service her another way. But she stopped him, lifted his eyes to hers while perched on top of him, and pleasured herself, never averting her gaze. His face changed from deep reds of awkwardness to delight in the process.

When she was done, she rolled her weed and made fun of how hard his bedroom "tried to seem important" with all its books and musical decor on the shelves of two large bookcases.

"Yeah, I'm feelin' this old-nigga-feng shui you got. Cute."

He countered the sarcastic remark by claiming her elaborate guitar tattoo, and that evening in his classroom was all a ruse. That she was only posing and couldn't be the virtuoso she led him to believe. He meant it as light taunting. She took it another way. Along with the other items that decorated his room was an unassuming classical guitar resting on the window seat at the bay window. It looked as though it was more for decoration but after examination, Lavender knew it was also functional.

"May I?" She asked. He consented, and she picked it up and performed her tuning regimen.

"This is *Sonata number 1, G Minor, Presto, BWV 1001*. That's Bach for you laymen," she said as she stuffed the joint back between her lips. She took a long breath and made sure of her finger positions before starting. Her eyes remained focused on the fretboard in the beginning. Then, gradually her gaze alternated from it, back to being closed, then back to her hands as the melody fluttered against her bare midsection. Chris' eyes were vast, and he covered his agape mouth with his hand trying to conceal the chasm. Her fingers moved up and down the strings like swift, smooth, pulsating waves. The only word that came to him in the moment as he devoured it was, "Exquisite."

Then she got him aroused again, but this time he didn't allow her to have her way. He used his mouth until her body trembled. It wasn't until the weed was gone and until they realized the hour was getting late for food that their date began.

~

Roadhouse Grill was open and still busy with patrons dining, drinking, and watching any number of baseball games or preseason NFL news. It was far from fine dining, as the empty peanut shells on the floor cracking beneath Lavender's feet indicated. However, as far as restaurant options went in the city, it wasn't a cheap offering either. She was pleased that on a late, last-minute, post-copulation food run, he'd driven her for steak versus more mediocre fare.

"So, Ms. Adair, how come you can play like that?" He chomped down on a roll as she sipped tea and then spread butter on her bread.

"I told you."

"You said your daddy played and taught you, but there had to have been something more. I'm just saying. It takes a long time and continuous play for what you do. People really train, especially classical."

"I mean... it's nothing." She bit into her bread again, not engaging him fully. "After he died, we ended up here. This old man named Titus taught me some too. He taught me electric and sheet music. That's pretty much it."

He gestured with his palms up, imploring for more information. She exhaled and crinkled her lips.

"Who was Titus then? Was he your music teacher or something?"

"Nah."

"Ok, so...?" Chris continued to pry.

It dawned on her that she had never thought about Mr. Bynum as her music teacher, really. He was a friend who shared ideas. And just as confounding, until then, she never thought of him as a *friend* either. He was all of that. None of that. More.

Just like all their previous conversations, this one was one-sided, with Chris disseminating the most and her interjecting here or there. It was ideal. He led a far more interesting and accomplished life than she had. Nobody wanted to hear about her unappealing sob story.

"Oh my God," Lavender blurted, dry and monotone. "He was just a guy who owned a music shop in the neighborhood and was, you know, happy being nice to a neighborhood kid." She peeked around for their waitress as she squirmed about in her chair.

"Well, that's dope then, I guess," said Chris. "Not many people willing to do that and for nothing in return."

"I just had a lot going on back then," she added. "He liked my playing. Tried to make me a stronger music reader. I picked up on a lot on my own. I mostly played by ear before then. That Bach, I learned by ear after a few runs."

"Bullshit," Chris said, dubious of the claim.

"Nah, for real." She smiled. "But Titus did make me a better reader, though. I owe him that." She sipped her beverage again. "I was a lonely, strange, and sad girl. He probably just felt sorry for me." She realized her last words were thoughts that almost made her leery of the man across from her—his opinions and accomplishments and his intentions. "Why you so pressed about it?"

"Not pressed, it's just, you flow through styles real easy. Like you were on classical fingerstyle tonight but acoustic and playing blues when I caught you in my classroom. Just not many can do that. Wondering where all that came from. And like, shit, with all that skill, you just was sort of chilling in my classroom all nonchalant. Like you're unfazed by any of that."

She shrugged. *I am, unfazed.*

"You got a favorite? Style, I mean?"

Lavender had to think for a moment. "My daddy was mostly jazz. But he kind of liked it all, and so I ended up that way too. I gravitate towards the rock and blues side, though."

"Interesting. Most people blessed enough to nail down that hard-ass fingering in classical just stay there. It's refined but, like, delicate. I don't know."

"Two things I am right? Refined and delicate?"

They both laughed.

"Classical's cool," Lavender continued. "Just not a lot of room for improvisation. And to me, that's the heart. I like the transitions of rock and the energy and going off course, just cause. I love the pain in early blues. Like that I'ma die if I don't have you' shit."

He laughed.

"I feel that. For me, it's sorta opposite. I like the structure of soul and R&B. I like knowing where it's going. The patterns. But even in that, there's feeling. There's pain and love. It just flows from a different place, I guess."

She weighed how she hadn't spoken with this much depth around music to anyone since Titus, or maybe even before that when she was just beginning to learn the craft with Joshua. Perhaps not ever.

"You were clowning my room before, but you must have a dope ass instrument collection. Of guitars from over the years and from your dad?"

"Nah. We lost a lot from then. I only have his electric." Then she grew reserved.

They both remained silent for a while, the noise from the activity in the restaurant making those voids less conspicuous, but only by a degree.

"I like you, Lavender, for real. I want to get to know you better. If you'll let me."

"How's that supposed to work, really? The twenty-seven-year-old pianist and music teacher with the thirty-six-year-old janitor who picks up the trash and shit at his little special school?"

"I think you're overthinking it."

Lavender rolled her eyes and grinned. "You're young. You ain't thinking at all."

"So why are we here? Why'd you agree to this date?" Chris asked, looking around, then leaning closer to discretely add, "Was all this just...."

"To fuck you? Yes, absolutely." Her words were not discrete.

He snorted loudly for all in the restaurant within earshot to hear, and Lavender almost choked from the uncouth outburst.

All she could see was an educated, accomplished, *proper* man, whom she was beginning to enjoy, but who would soon lose interest despite his words. "You're a nerd. You know that?" Lavender said as she watched his face turn red again.

Their waitress arrived. "Ok... medium-well ribeye, potato, and salad. For you, sir, prime rib, sautéed mushrooms, and steak fries."

"Thank you," Chris replied, and the server departed. He returned his attention to his date. "Now, what's that? A 'nerd.' Is that something you old folks say?"

He smiled and carved into his steak as Lavender did the same. They didn't broach the subject of just what it was they were interested in from each other for the remainder of the course. They only people-watched and remarked on some of the other patrons, making up humorous anecdotes of what they believed the couples said to each other at their booths.

Once they'd consumed their meals and waited on the check, Chris sipped from the glass of Merlot he'd been holding since before dinner came. The restaurant was quieter now. It was a late week-night, and there were few lingering pairings left, excluding themselves.

"Despite what you think, Ms. Adair," he stroked his beard, "I don't give a damn what you do. I don't give a damn where you live or how old you are, or where you're from. None of that." He slid around next to her and placed his fingers near the nape of her neck to fix two curls of hair that were out of place. She looked down at her plate as though disregarding his actions but also allowed his fingers to play where they landed. "I thought you were sexy the first day I saw you in your baggy janitor's dicky suit—super dirty, sweating, looking silly pretending you were giving a concert in an empty ass room. You can play all hard and act like I'm too this or that. That's cool. I'll do what you want. If you just wanna lay up and smash, you ain't gotta do shit but call." He moved his hand down to her thigh, and she turned towards him, arching her back. "Or, if you just want to play some music sometimes. It's really all on you. But know, ain't no judging with me. I like you as you are, and I wanna explore that some more."

She did not expect that poised declaration of reassurance nor how it caused her body to react.

He brought his hand up and extended it towards hers, "Is that ok?" He asked.

She placed her hand inside of his, sipped from her glass again, then responded, "We'll see."

Their night ended with him driving her home and a departing kiss. She sailed inside her house, and Čhetán was still up.

"Who was that?"

Her sanguine expression faded, and she found her typical mellowness again, which Chris had stripped away momentarily. "Nobody," she said in a dull pitch.

"Right," Čhetán responded. "Talked to momma tonight, and..."

"Not now Čhetáŋ." He had pulled her down from the clouds with that one statement. "I just walked in the door."

"Aight, fine."

Lying across her bed, she replayed the evening, smiling occasionally. She looked across her disarrayed room. Piled, unfolded laundry was everywhere, including atop her amplifier. It rested near the dresser where she had left it after playing with CJ again in the shed that afternoon. It made her recall Chris' inquiries about Mr. Bynum and how she had developed musically. Titus had given her her first amp and taught her about effects and other tools that stretched her playing, like distortions, whammy bars, and fuzz pedals.

She remembered the time Titus let her seize his work office at the shop for almost an entire day without question. It was the afternoon Kenneth reached the apex of the tilling he had done of her.

She grew to casually accept his touches as an odious price for getting along. They were infrequent, after all, and she avoided conditions that left them alone together most times. Yet, with all of that, twice, he went beyond just touch.

The first time it was soft and disguised as giving. It had come in the shadows of the night in a reticent guest room in Sheridan Heights, in a home occupied by her aunt, her brother, and her cousins. Mary was in Newark over more of their legal affairs. Elizabeth snored from her bed. The arrogance, Lavender thought, even then. The games. It was "selfless," "only to serve her." He covered her mouth. She was half asleep and her body forsook her, which was another kind of torment—a betrayal. And he would exploit that treachery later to sanction deeper exploits.

That final time, alone in her home, he smelled of rum and tobacco at noon and fell upon her as she lay on the sofa. Mary and Čhetán had left her there undisturbed while they went on some escapade. How he sensed she was accessible mystified her.

"No," she spat out in protest. "My... period..."

"Uh uh, liar. I know your cycle, and that don't matter anyway," he said in a raspy voice.

He was not soft and patient that time. There were no whispers dripping with manipulation to cast fear and docility. He smothered her under the dense weight of sweat, foul breath, and coercion. And once the culmination of those acts was met, he sloppily removed himself from her and left.

She ran the seven blocks to Titus' shop, bursting into its interior, wild and perspiring. The few customers there were jolted by the rowdy entrance and the "bizarre" girl who'd erupted inside and barged past the "Employees Only" sign without apprehension. Titus jumped at her appearance as well but did not bring attention to it. He simply reminded those there to "not worry 'bout his granddaughter" and then returned to the sale he was making. By the time Titus made it to her, Lavender was done weeping and wiping Kenneth off. She sat, reviewing the sheet music and playing the notes on the guitar she and Mr. Bynum were working on. She knew she must have looked frazzled and lost because, upon seeing her face, Titus hushed any questions he may have had and gave her leave. She played until Mary came looking for her, then played for another three hours.

Titus fed her, ignored her when necessary, tutored her, and allowed her to play freely, use his shop, use his equipment, and sometimes use his money. She didn't know why he'd done any of it.

Once Parkinson's accelerated beyond his ability to care for himself, he moved to Fort Lauderdale to live with his brother and his family. She visited him once. He was taken care of and seemed happy, but he could not communicate with her much anymore. Lavender had traveled with an acoustic guitar he had given her and played some notes as they'd once done together. She could tell he appreciated it even if he could not say so.

She kissed his forehead and decided she couldn't see him like that anymore and never went back. Knowing he was cared for was all that she'd wanted to have right in her mind.

Chapter 24

Train in the Vestibule
"Baby Please Don't Leave Me" - Buddy Guy

THE FULL MOON REFLECTED ON HER HAIR AS THE WIND FROM the car's rolled-down window lifted and cast curls across her face. She was so untamed, beyond what the mason jars of moonshine they'd consumed from the hole-in-the-wall club would've caused. Lavender was wild and free, the tilt of her neck, the way her loose-fitting skirt rode high, flaunting her thighs. *Fuck.*

Chris had never known anyone like her, like how'd she been on stage destroying his expectations when she played that Strat like a *man would.* But not just any man. Some man pouring years of agony and remorse into the thing. Lavender could be that but then revert to the quiet, modest, and almost adolescent disposition that she now had as they rode back to his home. The juxtaposition of it all. *Fuck.* The vision tangled with her sweet smell and the thoughts of her copious lips against his. All of his senses were inflamed. Yet, Lavender sat quietly, staring off into the distance, enjoying the breeze of the night air against her face, oblivious that she'd subjugated him at so many turns.

She pivoted and noticed him staring at her and smiled. Chris felt perhaps she was embarrassed, not expecting the evening to go the way it had. But her modesty served only to fuel his curiosity and excitement.

When he asked the previous night where she wanted to go on his evening off, Lavender suggested a somewhat distant "juke joint" called Tammy's. It was in the city of Wetumpka and deep into the woods. So obscure and tiny was the location that in all his musical performances and travels around the area, he had never heard of it.

"How do you know about this spot?" He asked her upon arriving in front of it. The only way to access the establishment from the highway was down a long gravel road. Oak trees and moss rose on both sides of the trail, covering it like a shadowy awning. When they reached their destination, an open grassy space served as the parking area. A few sedans were parked, but it was mostly pick-up trucks and motorcycles as far as he could see. A spattering of custom license plates with insignia of the Confederate army was visible and dispersed throughout the lot. This was not *his* crowd, he knew.

Once inside, he felt like they were the youngest patrons there, as everyone else seemed well into their fifties or sixties. Some were even older. Men with heads of white hair upheld by red, leathery necks and bellies that fell over their belts. Chris was relieved that they weren't the only guests of color, at least. Maybe a third of the crowd was Black. *Old* still, but at least that eased his mind some.

"Um... why you got us out here with the Ghosts of the Confederacy Past," he murmured. She laughed, touching his hand.

The place was a chimney stack. Almost everyone blew smoke from their cigarette, cigar, or pipe. Even Chris' nose, one well accustomed to the exhaust of nightclubs, burned from the stench.

"I've been coming here off and on since high school," Lavender said. "You made me think about it the other day, talking about Titus. I haven't been back in years, though."

"High school?" He asked, surprised by that information. He

didn't doubt her though. The old man collecting the modest price for entry at the door knew her. So did the bartender.

"Oh my word... Lavender!" An older white woman squealed from behind the bar, raising her hands up as though a spirit of praise had filled her.

"How are you doing, Mrs. Gayle," Lavender asked with a slight smile.

"Lemme look at you!" The woman shouted.

Mrs. Gayle came from behind the bar and gave Lavender a swinging embrace. "Ya still look the same. Whatcha been up to?"

"Nothing much. Just working." Lavender said, appearing uncomfortable with the woman's quick rush to a renewed familiarity.

"Been almost 'bout ten years? Since we had the little shindig for Titus. Oh, how I miss him so. You know how he's doin'?"

"He's fine, last I checked. His brother takes good care of him." Lavender said.

"Ain't that a blessing."

They carried on for several seconds then Lavender introduced her to Chris. The woman handed him a greasy menu to look at, though he couldn't understand why. All they served was cheap beer, boxed wine, a couple of cocktails, batches of the owner's home-brew, and for food, hot dogs, burgers, and chips. It was hardly the type of evening he'd pictured when he dressed in his Brooks Brothers' slim fit and Polo button-down before picking her up.

They took a seat about midway towards the stage, and despite himself, Chris broke down and ordered two franks and a beer while Lavender got a mason jar of the hooch. There was an opening band performing a slow dragging blues number. Occasionally, someone from the audience would hop on stage carrying an instrument case, pull out a horn or a guitar and join in where they could. Apparently, it was something of an "Open Mic" night for musicians.

It was tight, loud, rowdy, and they blasted southern rock, blues, and a bit of country. None of which were the staples of any soundtrack of any era of his life. However, the drinks were strong, everything was cheap, and Lavender seemed at home, so he tried to be open about it all.

A little while later, the band left the stage, and B.B. King filled the air from an old jukebox before the next act set up. In walked a short, portly, old gray-haired Black man. He was ushered in surrounded by three other gentlemen, all carrying instruments and assisting him with each hunched-over step.

"Oh shit..." Lavender said when she saw the audience part for him and his convoy like he was divinity and moved towards them. She rose from her seat and stepped forward. "Mr. Pugh!" She touched the man on his shoulder as he passed near her.

"Who that, baby? Who that?" He asked, seeking the source of the gentle nudge. He faced her and squinted hard. "Oh my... I know this face. Look who it is! This Titus' baby!" He laughed gruffly, pulling her closer to him for a hug. He swung her so hard she almost tipped over. "Gal, how you doing!? Ain't seen you in a month o' Sundays! How Titus? I miss dat boy there. You doin' aight? You gon' get up there wit' us ain't cha? I know you is. It's been too long." His voice rang throughout, managing even to breach through the other loud chatter and music. He ran all his sentences and questions together so that Lavender could hardly respond. She still reeled from the brew and the barrage of excitable ranting that poured from Pugh like a geyser and couldn't fully comprehend what he had asked.

"Look, this my last time playing here," Mr. Pugh continued. "Might be my last time playin' at all. Got that sugar, you know. Can't hardly see. Only God knows the day and time." He was limping and pointed to his foot. "Can't hardly walk neither." He pulled his arm from around one of the young men who assisted him and flashed his harp. "But I bet you what..." he leaned in towards her, in a *whisper* that was not. "I can still make this sang like pussy!"

Chris chuckled, overhearing him, and Lavender shook her head, laughing hysterically. "Still the same, Mr. Pugh," she said.

"Ima look for ya! Ima look for ya! Alright now! Good seeing you girl!"

He staggered towards the stage with the other musicians. A few moments later, they secured him a place on a stool in front of a microphone while he barked orders as they set up.

Chris was stupefied. "Did we cross some dimensional plain when we drove down that country ass road or something?"

"What?"

"How the hell do you know all these old people? Like, is this real?"

Lavender grinned. "I told you. I used to come with Mr. Bynum sometimes, and everybody knew Titus. He'd play open mics and drag me up there. So, everyone knew me too."

He rubbed his temple, then a sly grin spread across his face. "Ok. So, you going up?"

"Huh?" She threw back the last of her moonshine and playfully rolled the jar in her hand.

"I heard him," Chris insisted. "Get your ass up there."

"Hell no," she scoffed. "Last time I did something like that was over ten years ago. Plus, did you see me bring a guitar up in here? You think I got one up my ass?" She lifted her wrap skirt at that moment as she sat across from him, angling her legs to tease a peep show. Lavender smirked and reined it all back in. "Mr. Pugh is crazy," Lavender continued. "He's sweet, but he talks so much, he forgets half of anything he says to you, even back then. I know he gotta be worse now."

The two consumed several more drinks and verged on drunkenness while watching Pugh's performance. They applauded and whistled, and despite his age and physical ailments, he'd been honest in his self-assessment. He could make the harp sing. He blew it with energy and fire, and grit. It was a faculty that managed to elude what time had stolen away from so many other traits he once possessed. Everyone in "Tammy's" whooped and hollered.

As Pugh went on performing, a couple of souls from the crowd wandered on stage with their instruments to jump into the groove as well. One was a young white man who strolled up and hopped in on rhythm guitar during one number.

It was likely that action that had recalled Lavender to Pugh's thoughts because even as the band started a new song in the medley, Pugh was heard off-mic asking, "Where she at? Where she at?"

Lavender had a mouth full of a Ball Park frank attempting to soak up all the alcohol in her gut when she heard him, mouth closer to the mic again. "Where she at? Y'all see her?"

The keyboardist who was next to him looked around, found her in the crowd, and pointed her out.

"Damn," Lavender said.

"Uh oh," Chris sneered. "Your boy is callin' on you."

She shot Chris a cutting glance.

The keyboardist beckoned for her, and while she was in the initial stages of shaking her head to protest, Pugh spoke into the microphone, much louder now.

"I want y'all to meet this here young lady I ain't seen in a long, long time. My good friend's daughter. My friend Titus always let her play when she was just a little somethin'." He squinted in her direction, appearing to struggle to make out her features. When he found her, he extended his hand towards her. "Now I tell ya, God is good. I was just thinking 'bout my ol' partners. You don't know how long ya got. And God done bless me to see Titus' daughter here again since he don' left for Georgia. Come on up, baby!"

The lack of factual information that accompanied his introduction made Lavender cringe. But the loud proclamation had cornered her into some form of response either way.

Chris was overcome with amusement as Lavender's face turned red, and he fell into a deep, fierce fit of laughter. The kind of laughter that brought tears to his eyes, without a single sound emerging from his throat. Lavender flipped him off.

She took a big gulp of beer and walked to the stage. Her pace was slow and methodical. Chris couldn't tell if she stepped in such a manner to avoid slipping from intoxication or if she was using it to buy time to decline the request.

"I didn't come here to play. I didn't bring a guitar," she said, leaning in and whispering to the pianist. But before he could relay that message, Pugh was already gesturing for the young white gentleman who'd just taken the stage.

"Let her see your Strat, boy."

The young man hesitated for a moment but then passed it to her.

"You know this?" The bass player asked. They were at the outset of the first few notes of a Buddy Guy number. Lavender nodded in affirmation.

Of course, she knew it. She knew all of Guy's vibrato, bends, and extension of single notes, she thought. For a brief period, she'd consumed everything that was Guy's like a lost orphan, just discovering her parentage. And before she could process what happened, she went from the jaunty position of eating, drinking, and whispering suggestive thoughts to her escort to standing in front of forty people with a Strat in her hands.

Lavender looked over at Mr. Pugh, who wasn't paying her much attention. He was readjusting his microphone and chair as he prepared to sing, placing his harp in his pocket. The snare kicked out the rhythm of a song that sounded like drummers leading soldiers marching into battle. The bass player jumped in, and the young white gentleman who had hopped on stage continued to keep the rhythm going with another guitar he'd managed to confiscate from someone in the audience. She looked at him briefly, and he nodded as if saying *You got it from here.*

Lavender turned and took in the crowd, most of whom were drunk and unconcerned about the preciseness of what she was about to play as long as it sounded good and helped keep the time and booze flowing. She saw Chris smiling with his deep dimples and resting on the edge of his seat. Part of her wanted to step down from the stage right then. Another part was consumed with nostalgia and the heat and *thump* of the bass booming in her chest like her heart beating.

Lavender hadn't played in a group of musicians like this since before Titus left. And the few times she'd been on stage before then, it was in this very arena. She wondered what type of spectacle she was about to make of herself but proceeded anyway. She pulled up her long billowy skirt and tied two ends of it into a knot, high to the middle of her thigh so that she wouldn't accidentally trip. She picked a couple of strings on the guitar, testing the tone and volume. Then, she closed her eyes, breathed in, exhaled, and opened them again. She swallowed hard and then made the Strat scream and plead for "its woman" to never leave. The floorboards, the wall, and the ceiling rumbled from the stomping and yelling that reverberated throughout the congregation.

There was a freight train speeding through the vestibule, or at least that's what it felt like to her from the pounding feet and thunderous applause that left her ears ringing when she finished.

<h1 style="text-align:center">Chapter 25</h1>

<h1 style="text-align:center">Nineteen</h1>

<h2 style="text-align:center">"So Many Tears" - 2Pac</h2>

NINETEEN. I'M JUST NINETEEN AND NO ONE. NO DADDY, NO *momma. Now, no heart*. Lavender thought to herself the morning of Mary's funeral. She was still in her simple black dress, pantyhose, and black flats as she knelt in the dirt in the backyard. Runs and small holes were in the knees of her stockings, which didn't matter to her. She hated them. It was only to shut Elizabeth up that she even agreed to put them on. Now that the service was over, Lavender wanted to ruin as much of the nylon as possible simply out of spite.

So many people were inside talking and sharing their stories of Mary. Lavender even heard her name a few times as guests wondered aloud where she might be. Hidden among the tall floppy elephant ears that grew near Mary's garden was where she had gone to disappear. Mary loved those plants, how large they got, and pretty and green they could be when attended to properly. They were still thriving.

Off to the side, perpendicular to the back porch, were the flowers of Lavender's namesake. Based on the small corner they occupied, one may have never guessed they were Mary's favorite. But they constantly needed attention. They needed lots of sun, and that was the side of the house they gave the most. "The more care you give 'em, the more you love 'em. Even when they don't love you back" was something Lavender heard her say about the flower once. And they often didn't love back. Alabama's soil and climate made it a struggle for them at times. But Mary had made them healthy and bold in appearance.

One of the noticeable voices missing from inside the house was that of Katherine—absent from her own mother's funeral.

She had been out of prison and at a halfway house for almost a year and had been speaking with Čhetáŋ and Mary regularly during that time. She made promises to travel down after she worked some things out in Newark and was in the process of that when they got the news of Mary's cancer diagnosis. When it took a turn for the worst, Katherine's calls were a routine occurrence. She communicated faithfully, even managing to soften Lavender, who began speaking to her again.

"You coming?" Lavender asked during their last conversation after the funeral arrangements were made.

"Yes baby, I'ma make it down there. I already got my fare. I just wish.... I should've been there sooner." Her voice was already hoarse, but it cracked. Lavender could hear the deep breathing in the phone and knew she was sobbing. All the same, Lavender's only thought was *yeah, you should've*. "Should've" been here years ago. But, she kept a receptive tone and bid Katherine a warm farewell. "Guess we'll see you soon," and hung up.

There were so many regrets and so much that wouldn't have happened if there was anything behind Katherine's words. But Lavender also considered that things happen as they do. She probably would have missed out on the relationship with her grandmother and with Titus.

Then—in typical Katherine fashion—a few days before she was to arrive, silence. The vanishing act was how it had always unfolded when she was in the process of reversing course. Or, when she found she could not fulfill the terms around some promise, and would rather avoid conflict about that by playing the ghost. When Čhetáŋ called the transitional housing facility where she lived, no one had seen her that entire week. At best, it meant she had violated her parole and would soon be back behind bars. At worst, it could be anything. It was usually some stage of relapse, however. Once again, Lavender found herself seething for being gullible enough to trust and foolish enough to think her grandmother's death would change that woman. The "final time," she vowed. *A coward.*

Lavender watched the hope drain from her brother and turn into disappointment over Katherine again. *Hopefully, he learned,* she thought. Čhetáŋ was devastated that even now, his mother could not keep her word. Grandma Mary was dead, Katherine's only time to say goodbye, and it still did not matter. It didn't steady and direct her home.

Lavender prepared to suture this reopened wound with all the alcohol, sex, intoxicants, and any other "balms" she enjoyed indulging in. She knew her forays into numbness would be some of her worst. She planned on it. Her grandmother had left her. One of the only people she knew who loved her despite all her flaws was gone—one who, maybe, loved her more because of them.

She stared at Mary's garden, smelling the rain approach as the wind stirred. The sorrow once again rose in her chest and threatened to choke the breath from her before she opened her mouth and let a deep sob burst forward. She held it together well throughout the service, feeling as the oldest of the grandchildren, she couldn't allow herself to mourn freely. She was the one who had to keep an eye out for Elizabeth's antics and help comfort Jason and Keshia. But out in the garden—their garden—alone, she let her pain pour down like the falling rain.

Čhetáŋ saw her through the kitchen window. "Look like it's

about to storm," he said as he came out to the garden. He kneeled and put his arm around her shoulders, comforting her in silence for several minutes.

"Well, what now?" He finally broke the hush. "We by ourselves again."

He had just turned fifteen. Lavender was still underage but had been bartending at Club Elite ever since she graduated high school despite not legally being eligible to hold the position. She'd lied and flirted her way into it and lied, flirted, and more to keep it.

"I'm gonna work," she said.

"I don't wanna live with Aunt Liz for real," Čhetáŋ continued with a look of worry.

She laughed at his genuine panic over the prospect because she had no intention of allowing it to happen. She wiped the tears from her cheeks. "I'm gonna do what's necessary so that doesn't happen. You might have to work a little too. But I have to show Liz we can keep this house."

"Keep the house?" He seemed unconvinced about this proposal.

"Yes. It's gonna be a fight, though. She doesn't want me keeping it, I'm sure. I heard her and Grandma talkin' about selling it once. Guess she could still do that, but that bitch a lot of things, stupid about money isn't really one of them."

Čhetáŋ raised his eyebrows, intrigued by her meaning.

"The block's shit. She wouldn't get a lot for it right now. I heard her say she wanted to hold on to it longer to see if she could get a lot more later for it, after white folks start coming in. Funny acting as she is, she'd probably rather it be empty. But I guess she could tolerate our asses there renting if we're paying and paying on time. Nobody outside the family would put up with her as a landlord for long." She rubbed the side of her face. "You're the key, though."

"Me? How you figure?"

"Cause it kills two birds. Y'all get along better than we do, but she doesn't want to be your guardian for real. Have you living with them and be responsible for you. Renting to me gets you out of her house and this house cared for. You just need to stay in her ear about it."

He nodded in agreement, smiling as he began to understand.

On to less agreeable topics, she thought, "And *your* momma?" She said, with intense emphasis on the "your."

He sighed, and his smile evaporated.

"Don't tell me another damn thing she has to say," she said.

He shook his head, acknowledging, for the first time ever, that Lavender's aggravation and rigidness there may have always been appropriate.

"How you do five years, get to a halfway house, be maybe six months from freedom, and piss it away? And you miss your own momma's funeral! For what?" Lavender asked to the clouds or the pending rain or to the grass beneath them, certainly not to Čhetáŋ, who was just as confounded as she was.

"Well, it wasn't her fault she was there the last time, at least," he said.

"Boy, stop. What about before? She didn't have to do any stealing or hurt anybody. She was caught with the niggas who did. Why is she even around all of that? How'd she end up in that circle? Stop excusing it." Lavender didn't tarry much longer on the subject or the I-told-you-so's. "And that's what I try to tell you about who you hang around, too. You're gonna graduate. You're gonna get your grades. You're gonna still do your baseball. You're gonna work if you can. You're gonna wear condoms..."

Čhetáŋ frowned, turning red before grinning to himself.

"I'm dead serious, Čhetáŋ. I'm not playing. You can't be out here raw dogging these girls. It's just me and you, and we can barely take care of us."

He cleared his face of amusement and grew serious again. Lavender was delivering her manifesto in Mary's garden of how they would carry on without the matriarch, without Katherine, with no one but themselves.

Remaining in the only home they'd had after leaving Newark did not become the battle Lavender anticipated. She remembered Mary describing the way Elizabeth took care of her father, Ernest, in his final days. *Give 'til she 'bout spent* were her exact words.

The time between Mary first having symptoms, to her passing was rapid. Pancreatic cancer began to ravish her system, and a "switch" came on for Elizabeth.

She woke in the mornings, drove to Mary's, and prepared her breakfast and medication regimen. Then she'd work a full shift at the bank. In the evenings, she was back in her Buick fighting rush hour traffic to be at Mary's and ensure dinner was made. Then Elizabeth helped bathe Mary and get her ready for bed. She routinely put in sixteen-hour days before making it home to deal with her own children and personal obligations. This drill was repeated every day for six months before Mary got so ill that hospice was necessary.

The only recess Elizabeth had was in the fact that they'd closed the grocery store after Mary's diagnosis. Even then, she could not seem to find much rest. She passed the empty building every day. It was destined to be yet one more eyesore on a block of several other corroding structures. The once vibrant neighborhood had succumbed to interstate encroachment, families relocating, and urban sprawl.

"It wasn't much, but it was Daddy's. We could've kept it if I had more help," Elizabeth said in frustration the day she announced its end. After thirty years, the doors of Freeman's Grocery would be shut for good. No one had to say the words concerning the "help" Elizabeth mentioned.

Lavender knew and agreed. A family that was whole, with effort, could have managed. Instead, they had Katherine. There was no wholeness there and certainly no help.

Mary still had enough energy then to continue playing the peacemaker when Lavender would enter some tirade over Katherine.

"That's your momma. I don't want my last days to be this between y'all. Her and Lizzy still at odds is enough as it is."

"Stop talking about last days, Grandma. You're gonna outlive everybody except for Čhetáŋ's ol' 'stay in the gym' ass," Lavender would joke. But she understood she was witnessing the dimming light of a woman who'd been just a casual visitor in her world only seven years before. What would direction be without its center now?

Elizabeth's hands were in everything during Mary's decline. Lavender and Čhetáŋ assisted as much as they could or as much as their aunt would allow. They cooked meals, aided Mary's movement about the house, and cleaned her when required. Lavender was there during the day, and Čhetáŋ helped when she bartended at night. They wanted to do more but....

"Y'all's helping, getting in my way," Elizabeth would say.

If they didn't make the food just right, or if the medication wasn't given at the precise time, to the second, every evening, or if Mary's clothes for doctor appointments weren't what Elizabeth would've laid out, or how she would've ironed them, it was a problem. Then Elizabeth would spend hours correcting their alleged mistakes. She cooked in the wee hours of the morning, preparing meals to store, re-washing just laundered clothes, and setting them in a specific order, obsessively cleaning Mary's room and lavatory.

"What's wrong with her?" Keshia asked Lavender late one Sunday night. It was after midnight, and they listened from Lavender's bedroom as Elizabeth cooked and packed food to stuff in a freezer that they already could barely close from her performing the same ritual the day before.

The week hospice arrived, all of it came to an abrupt and paradoxical end. Elizabeth went from a restless caregiver to a listless recluse who didn't venture from her house. She couldn't even get out of bed. Everyone assumed it was grief and gave her the time and space she needed. Yet, even on the morning of the funeral, she was still dormant and fastened to her room.

"You gotta get up. You have to get ready," Lavender told her. "You know your sorry ass sister ain't here, and you need to be the daughter Grandma raised."

Lavender left for an hour to help Keshia with Jason and greet some distant family and church friends who'd gathered to line up. When she came back, Elizabeth was dressed and combing her hair.

"Put some goddamn pantyhose on, Lavender. Of all days, show some respect!" Elizabeth said to her when she returned. Lavender thought that was the end of it. She felt she had steered her back to her old self.

The following Friday, in the dead of night, with her children long asleep, Elizabeth left them, got in her car, and sped down Northern Boulevard toward downtown. She told everyone it was because she could not reach her niece and nephew on the phone and thought she'd left the gas stove on at her mother's place. Elizabeth had been at Mary's earlier but made no such calls to Lavender or Čhetáŋ. Nor had anyone used the stove there at all that day.

The authorities said she was going upwards of eighty-five miles per hour. Lavender wondered if she intended to crash the car into the reputed, vile waters of the Alabama River just off the highway and cede this world to them all. If so, she never made it to that target. Instead, Elizabeth lost control of her car just before the Rail Yard. She careened down an embankment and into a thicket before the trunk of a Cottonwood halted the car's momentum. The crash left her with a concussion, lacerations, and several fractures, the most severe being that of her femoral shaft.

Physicians observed her mental state and determined she needed a psychological evaluation, which Elizabeth objected to. It wasn't until someone mentioned "The Department of Family and Child

Services" that she agreed. A long journey of interviews, more observations, surgeries, diagnoses, and physical therapy ensued.

With the question of what to do with Mary's house looming amid it all, Elizabeth was almost eager to pass along the concerns of it to Lavender, who had been dedicated to Elizabeth's care during the entire ordeal.

Mary's old Lincoln Town Car still ran then, and Lavender drove back and forth, completing errands, taking Elizabeth to her appointments, doing her hair, helping with her cousins, and cooking.

"You sick?" Čhetân asked during this period. "I mean, I know she needs help, but you're over there almost more than you're home."

"You wanna have to move out? I'll be twenty. She could say I'm grown and wanna get whatever money for this place and kick us out at any moment. I'm trying to keep her happy."

It was true. But so was the fact that the accident had frightened her.

Lavender had grown immune to the jagged nature of her relationship with Elizabeth, but if her aunt had perished in the accident, she had no idea what she'd do. Lavender almost found herself ill again, considering the upheaval it would cause. When she received the call from Keshia, sobbing the morning of the car crash, Lavender's throat filled with salivation, then burned with acid. She fell into a fetal position attempting to prevent her stomach's undigested sustenance from heaving into her chest.

That was on purpose. Lavender felt it in her gut.

She needed her aunt to regain that old cantankerous will to live.

Elizabeth never offered much expressed gratitude for everything Lavender did after the accident, said for a stray "'preciate it" and the eventual extension of her childhood home. Lavender had no idea what the mortgage was then, but she understood that with its age and history, it couldn't have been much less than what they were paying and still cheaper than any rent for a comparable size. Elizabeth was far from growing wealthy from them, so they reached an equilibrium of sorts.

"Long as y'all keep up the payments, y'all can stay. The minute y'all don't, I'm selling. I ain't keeping no grown folks, and I don't wanna be bothered trying to hold it, neither."

Lavender was grateful and understood her aunt's grace only extended so far. She knew that the edict was law.

She was armed with a general high school diploma and a bartending job that met ends most months depending on tips. Lavender worked hard for those, keeping a queue of the club's regular patrons happy and confident that they could access the long, sienna-toned, sensual woman. She called them her "friends." They called her "Doll" due to her youthful appearance and the dark spirals of hair that caressed her face. The moniker conjured a juvenility that made her cringe which she veiled with tempting smiles whenever men whispered the name in her direction. When she knew the rent would come up short, she modeled that smile more intently and batted full dark lashes until gratuity covered the difference.

Sometimes the home and car repairs or concerns like Čhetân's prom or cleats and hundreds of dollars of more baseball equipment made the financial shortcomings steeper. In those times, she snuck a more acquainted "friend" home under the concealment of the dim pre-dawn stars while Čhetân slept—later having the money she needed for her aunt.

Sometimes she needed extra ounces of Kentucky whiskey after. Sometimes she wasn't certain if her prudence was enough. Or if anything was discovered or discernible in the aftermath of those liaisons. Or what visions that might project into the world about her story. It did not matter at the end of the day. As long as they could pay, they could remain in their home.

Chapter 26

A Hurricane

"Sorry" - Beyoncé

WHEN LAVENDER WALKED INTO HER HOME WITH CHRIS IN TOW well after midnight, they were greeted by the vision of Čhetáŋ and Gloria stationed at the kitchen table holding grim postures. Arriving home at this hour was typical for Lavender any day of the week. Yet when she did, it was usually to pitch darkness and the pulse of slumbering deep breathing from every other inhabitant. Čhetáŋ's cognizance and focused eyes at the late hour in the middle of a workweek made her wince.

"What's wrong with y'all? Why y'all up?" She asked. Lavender's heels clapped hard against the marble foyer entryway, echoing throughout the otherwise stilled house. It was a further irritant to Gloria's ears as her jaws tensed with each of Lavender's steps.

"We just got back from Kindred South Emergency Room with CJ," Čhetáŋ explained.

"Why!? What happened?"

"We don't know. He had..."

"What y'all do in the shed?" Gloria cut in before Čhetáŋ could finish. "What did you let him get into this time?"

Lavender looked at her with surprise. She and CJ were out in their outdoor sanctuary playing the Les Paul with the amplifier earlier that day. They had gone at it for hours, but it was something they did twice a week or more as routine anyway.

"What you mean? Same thing we've done a million times in the shed. He ain't get in nothing. What happened?"

"I told you about taking him out there! I told you about all the smoking and whatever you into and him getting exposed to it," Gloria said.

"What are you even talking about? You're not telling me anything right now." The mysterious news and random accusation confounded Lavender.

"He got sick," Čhetáŋ added. "Had this rash and screaming in pain about his leg. I never seen him like that."

"His leg? What?" Lavender covered her mouth, gazing between Čhetáŋ and Gloria, and Chris stepped aside, preparing to leave. "Wait," she whispered to him, surprising even herself.

They'd been together almost every night that past week, at his place, or out late at Sous La Terre, a basement jazz club listening to other bands. And despite that pace, she found she still desired his presence. She turned to Čhetáŋ. "Now, what about CJ's leg? I'm confused."

"None of this happened until after y'all were out there today. It came out of nowhere, hours after y'all came in. Like a reaction to something, and we for damn sure didn't do nothing out the ordinary," Gloria volunteered.

"Well, I didn't either... whatever this is." Lavender swayed from consuming the largest portion of a beverage she'd shared with Chris earlier. Although a bartender, she wasn't a wine drinker and still hadn't appreciated the difference in strength between port wine and regular red. It left her more intoxicated than she had intended. That and the lack of detail from her two housemates began to feel like subterfuge. "Where is he now?"

"Finally asleep after they gave him something," Čhetáŋ said.

Lavender's drunkenness was apparent. So was the categorical

shift in the inflections of Gloria's voice as it slipped from the "proper" English Lavender and Elizabeth mocked. It was now a deep south Montgomery cadence—often the only notice of her rising temper.

Čhetáŋ knowing both women well, tried a conciliatory tone. "We really don't know much more than we said. Was he good with you earlier?"

"Yeah, everything was good. I mean, I didn't notice anything."

Gloria rolled her eyes, huffing, before jumping in again. "Was you high? Drunk like you is now? Would you even know if something was wrong?"

Lavender bit her lip to suppress the obscenities she wanted to cast in response, and it ached her mouth to abort the words. Chris saw her face and rubbed her lower back. She ignored Gloria, instead responding only to Čhetáŋ. "If he wasn't feeling good, he didn't say nothing. But you know how he is when we're out there playing."

"No, we really don't," Gloria interjected once more.

"Why didn't y'all call me?"

"We did. Seven damn times," Gloria spat. "We ain't know what was happening, how long it would be! We blew you up! We had that happening, and the man coming to fix this water heater was gon' be here today, the only time he could."

That man was an old friend of Gloria's who had offered to do the work at a discounted rate in his off time. It was the only kind of rate they could afford, and it meant it had to be done around his schedule. They had one window of opportunity after being without proper hot water for two days and had to delay it to deal with Caleb's emergency since Lavender was unavailable to assist.

Lavender reached into her pocket to find her phone was dead. She'd been so engaged with music at Chris', drinking and in his bed, that she hadn't noticed it was no longer buzzing with activity. She tried to shake her head sober.

"Right." Gloria said, reacting to Lavender's realization of the lifeless device.

"Well, I'm sorry. Guess I wasn't paying attention."

"Hell, do you ever?" Gloria mumbled under her breath.

"What?" Lavender began to reach her limit. "Nah, say it with your big, bougie ass voice."

"Hey, can you, whoever you are, leave? This a private matter," Gloria said to Chris before returning to Lavender. "Once again, you're in here high as a kite with niggas like you do, when we got real shit going on."

The tension in Lavender's face intensified. *The audacity*, she thought, speaking to Chris this way and implying certain things in front of him. What she did or the friends she entertained and how she entertained them in her own home that didn't involve Gloria in any way, was not *this bitch's* concern.

"You talking hella reckless right now and don't even know what you saying. I haven't been smoking and can have and do what I want in my own damn house!" Lavender clutched Chris' arm. "You need to apologize to him."

"I ain't apologizing shit," Gloria responded, bucking her eyes and stretching her neck for emphasis.

"Lavender," Chris began, "I'm good. She doesn't need to..."

"And, your damn house?" Gloria scoffed. "It's Chase's name on the contract with your crazy aunt. My money helped contribute on y'all mortgage and fix this raggedy shit up. Still, every month I gotta beg and plead for your half of the rent. A house you barely at between being in these streets or at that club? Or with these... niggas. This ain't hardly your house, really. That's your raggedy shed, though."

Čhetáŋ was silent throughout the rant, as though his companion's thoughts reflected his own, Lavender observed.

Gloria stood inches from the pair during her tirade, flailing her animated arms about. Her limbs orbited her bulging belly like satellites as she emoted. She came close to hitting Chris in the process of expressing her thoughts.

"You better calm the fuck down," Lavender said.

"Or what?" Gloria stepped closer. "You ain't gon' do shit. If I wasn't pregnant, my bougie ass would've washed you."

Lavender smirked and stepped away. "Nah *you* better be glad you're pregnant. Čhetáŋ, get your bitch."

"Bitch? What?!" Gloria's eyes were fire.

"Ok, y'all," Chris said, forcing his way between them, unable to remain a bystander any longer. He pulled Lavender to him and held her arm. "Hey, be cool." Then held her face. "I'm not trying to add tension here, so I'm going to go. You going to be ok if I do?"

"Of course she will," Čhetáŋ finally spoke. "Who you supposed to be anyway?"

"Chris."

"Ok Chris. You can go. I got this."

Now you speak? The thought flashed in Lavender's mind.

Chris smiled and looked at her, stroking her cheek. "You good?" He whispered and kissed her.

"Yeah, I'm good. This is little shit."

"Pfft," Gloria huffed from the corner.

Lavender walked him out. As Chris departed, only the thin layer of mesh from the screen door served as a barrier between the powder keg inside and his escape. Čhetáŋ's voice carried past the yard, complaining about her "bringing dudes in all times of night" like she "used to."

"We're a family in here now," Čhetáŋ said.

"He ain't just some dude," Lavender responded. "You're acting like I have folks in and out of here."

"Didn't you have Caesar over like last week or so? It was somebody else you was hanging with before then. Now him? You know I don't like Caesar anyway. It ain't a good look," he said.

She quietly waited to watch Chris drive away.

Once his car was out of sight, Lavender made her way to the hallway toward Caleb's room.

"Where you going?" Gloria barked.

She was still in her heels, still clouded by the wine's influence, still a bit louder for Gloria's liking.

Lavender opened his door and got close enough to his bedside to see the anti-inflammatory medication and ice pack on the nightstand with the medical identification band still wrapped around his wrist.

Gloria pulled her away by the arm. It wasn't a harsh tug but had enough force that Lavender tumbled through the doorway. Her pointed heels and wine caused most of the fall, but Gloria had given the necessary momentum for it to all work together toward Lavender's plunge.

Čhetáŋ immediately stepped between them as Lavender grasped at anything close to prevent her spill. She found a hand full of Gloria's shirt in the process, and the propulsion sent Gloria back into the wall with a loud *thump*. Lavender lifted herself from the floor. Then the three backed out of the room in an awkward dance of bodies, pushing and threshing while trying to maintain footing and not disturb the sick child.

An exhausted semi-sedated Caleb moaned momentarily, then turned back over and never woke from the ruckus. Čhetáŋ remained a blockade between the two and managed to shut Caleb's door. The promenade carried on into the hallway and then the living room.

"She hit me! She pushed me!" Gloria howled, irate, referencing the incidental contact Lavender made with her. "Hell no. She has to go Chase! She needs to be out our house!"

"Nobody tried to hit you. You pulled me down. Hell, your ass hit me!" Lavender disputed. Her face was flushed and sweaty. Her dress hung partially off her shoulders from where Gloria had almost pulled her to the floor.

"I was trying to keep your drunk ass from going in there and waking my baby! And then you put your hands on me?"

"I ain't put no goddamn hands on you! I was trying to not fucking fall."

"A lie! I know what I felt. You pushed me into the wall!" Gloria clung to her lover. Looking at him as though seeking a champion for her cause. "Chase?" Her eyes, once a hurricane, now peered at him as soft and alluring as the shores susceptible to those storms. He'd been void of all sound, and Gloria awaited the confirmation she needed.

Lavender awaited her longtime advocate. In all the chaos, Čhetáŋ's reticence was the most vociferous matter that had occurred the entire evening.

Lavender retreated, rubbing her temples as a throbbing headache emerged. She looked at him, still awaiting supporting words. Awaiting "it was an accident, Gloria," or anything of the sort and received nothing.

"Bet. I'm gone," Lavender said. She grabbed her purse, keys, a few items of clothing from her room and the dead phone. Then, she stopped and snatched a charger from the wall before exiting, slamming the door behind her. Lavender remained on the porch, vaped nicotine, and waited for her phone to gain just enough power to make a call. When it did, she reached out to the accommodating and familiar body she knew best and ended up in the last place she imagined her night culminating—Caesar's bed.

Chapter 27

Fruitless

"Get Up, Git Out" - Outkast, Goodie Mob

It was after three A.M. when the fight with Gloria and the turbulent night concluded. Lavender resisted calling Chris back to rescue her after everything, especially knowing he had a four-hour drive ahead of him in the afternoon. Basin Street landed a last-minute show in Gulfport that would have him in the Magnolia State for a couple of days. He had invited her, but she couldn't get off work with such short notice.

He texted her to say he made it home and to ensure she was fine. Chris' text flooded into her phone's messages the moment it regained power, along with several other texts she missed, including a flurry from Čhetáŋ and Gloria over CJ. Then there was another message that preceded Chris'. It only read, "*WYD?*"

If anyone was inclined to still be up and nearby and unrestrained by the obligations of work or family like Angie, Kiara, and Renée were at that hour, it would've been Caesar. She only needed a few hours of rest, a place to change clothes, and a way to make it to work later. Lavender told him as much when he answered the phone in a dry sleepy voice, and she disclosed her predicament.

"My brother over here. You can sleep in my room," Caesar said.

"And that's all I'm doing," she insisted.

"Uh huh."

She spent the next two nights there, then another at Angie's while Chris was away. It was as if time had reverted to the days when the bulk of her moments were between the club, home, and with these two cousins, meandering in the streets. The days they enjoyed partying from Montgomery to Memphis, Birmingham, and Atlanta. It was days of cheap hotels, empty liquor bottles, codeine, ashes, and a thick haze. The kind of fog Lavender sought after Mary died.

Lavender returned home, but waited until a time of day she knew both Čhetáŋ and Gloria would be away. She found her home as expected, as though a massive argument between them where she was essentially told to vacate, hadn't occurred just days prior. That was until she reached her bedroom. Someone had replaced the standard interior doorknob with a keyed lock.

"The hell?" she hissed.

Lavender was three-and-a-half days into rewashed clothes and was eager to shower, swap those garbs for something fresh and sleep in her own bed.

"What the hell is this?" She texted Čhetáŋ along with an image of the door. He did not respond, so she sat idly in the dark living room, waiting, burning. Each minute with no response or without his arrival was additional tinder. Lavender played a continuous loop in her mind of how she would curse Čhetáŋ and would've punched Gloria had it not been for the baby she carried. And how she should be given credit for that seeing as how they'd grown up in neighborhoods surrounded by *ladies* who wouldn't have cared about Gloria's circumstances.

The deadbolt turned, the door creaked open, and Čhetáŋ entered. He was alone and appeared tense.

"Lavender?" He called. He finally made her out in the dark and turned on a lamp.

She stared at him, with her head resting in one hand, scratching at the upholstery on the arm of her chair with the other.

"I know you pissed," he began. "We just need you to like know, we're for real about this."

"Oh? You're *for real* about this? What does that mean?"

"It means, until the baby is born, we think you just stay at Angie's or Kiara's or something. That's just a few months. I can't have all this stress around Gloria, especially with what we don't know going on with CJ. She ain't comfortable with you and everything right now. That's just more stress." He could not make eye contact with her during this broadcast. He only drew circles and other patterns on the carpet with his foot.

"I'm not causing stress. I'm living my life like I always have."

He rolled his eyes.

"Your girl causes stress," she added.

"Ok, whatever. But she's the pregnant one, and our son is sick, so."

"So, what I gotta do to get my own shit? Get permission from my guard? That you? And then what? You gotta ask your warden? You couldn't call and tell me this was what y'all were doing?" Gloria had really gotten into his head this time, she thought. None of this sounded like him.

"Pffft, why call?" He asked. "You ain't called in three days either, not even to check on your nephew. To see if he was fine, if he needed anything. Nothing." He stuffed his hands into his pockets with a forceful tuck. "CJ was sick again yesterday, and we had to take him back to Kindred. We hear from you? No. Probably laid up with somebody, laid up with that one you brought here the other night. CJ was askin' for you too."

"What you want me to do? Y'all was trippin'," she said.

However, he was right about Caleb; now that she had learned it happened again and CJ asked about her, she almost felt ill herself.

"And you still should have checked on him." Čhetáŋ went and unlocked the door to her room. "This is just temporary—a few months. Gloria will have the baby and we'll know what's going on with CJ. And you and Gloria would've cooled off. You'll probably be back before then anyway, when she's had time to chill."

"And what you got to say? Why are you agreeing to this? This is our house? You can't seriously believe I tried to hit that damn girl."

"I don't know that. You were drunk. I saw both y'all grabbing at each other and her hitting the wall. Maybe it was an accident but y'all always beefin'. She ain't comfortable, and she's carrying my child. Gloria was upset that night and yeah, shit got out of hand. You ain't see CJ like we did. Meanwhile, you're grown, and was gonna have to figure out living arrangements in the next year anyway once the baby gets bigger."

Lavender sucked her teeth. "Yeah. But that's a year from now. Not today."

"And you got time. Your stuff is here, ain't it? It's just you need to be mostly away right now while we figure this out." He sighed, "Give it time. She might even reconsider, and, you might end up finding somewhere else you want to be anyway. This almost like... a jump-start."

"This ain't no goddamn 'jump-start'. This is you kicking me out my house, no matter how you frame it."

Lavender understood that remaining together with his growing family was untenable. Mary's home hadn't magically expanded from its original three-bedroom design. They'd planned to partition off part of the master bedroom for the arriving infant, conceding that space to the baby for the first year at least.

Lavender had warily agreed to make the move. Seeing as she only had herself, that seemed the easiest. She was supposed to be searching for someplace else but hadn't started yet, believing she had a while longer. There was more money to be saved, her license to restore. She'd even had thoughts on trying to find some affordable used vehicle before facing that chore. A part of her hadn't accepted she would actually have to exit her grandmother's home—the one she'd worked so hard to have. But, she supposed it was Čhetáŋ and his family's now. She was the one on the outskirts.

"How is CJ?" Her mind drifted back to Caleb and the news of his second spell.

"He's better now, but it was just like before. He had more swelling this time, though. We should have test results back soon, they say."

"Hmph," Lavender paused, "That bitch somewhere trying to blame yesterday on me too, huh."

Čhetáŋ swung the door to her room open. "You know what, get what you need. When you need more call me and I'll come let you in, until this all ironed out," he said.

"I hope y'all know I'm not paying rent here in these *few months*, if my things are here are not, since I gotta be 'mostly gone.'"

"We don't. We talked about it."

"And this flimsy ass lock," she said, laughing. "What's to stop me from coming in here and carding this shit when I want or kicking it in? It's my room. My door. My name that got this for us in the first place."

"I don't know. Changing all the locks might be next. Guess we'll see. This really some shit you should've already been thinking about."

"Don't talk to me like my damn daddy. This illegal, you know," Lavender added. "Ain't you supposed to give a thirty-day notice or something?"

"What you gon' do? Take us to court?" He laughed.

"I might."

"With what money?"

"I can ask Aunt Liz and..."

He laughed even harder then.

Lavender gathered a few of her belongings; clothes for the club, the uniform for the custodial job, and some toiletries. Then she called around until she reached Angie and waited on the porch. Three hours later she arrived in her compact Ford, blasting "Trap Queen," with her sons on the back seat.

~

"I came looking for you the other day," Chris said, touching her shoulder from behind. Lavender stood in the doorway of the Janitor's closet with her earphones on. She pulled them away, and Chris repeated, "I said I looked for you the other day. The other janitor lady said you called in sick. Everything good?"

For the first time, she'd hoped she wouldn't run into him.

"Yeah. Everything is cool." She found Chris' feet, tracing the lines of the Nike patterns, and let her eyes linger there a moment. Linger anywhere but his face.

"I hadn't heard from you most of the weekend and most of the week," he said. "Shit at your place got crazy. I was kinda worried, really."

"Yeah, sorry about all of that. I've been back and forth a lot these last few days and couldn't really talk too much. How was Gulfport?"

"It was chill, you know. Hit up the casinos down there. I probably lost half of my cut."

She could not relate to that in any way, at least not blowing earnings on gambling. When she squandered a paycheck, it was only on what she could taste, devour, and asphyxiate underneath. She finally lifted her eyes to his. They were warm as usual but cast a dubious expression when peering back.

"Your brother and everything...."

"It's fine. We're good. The stuff with my nephew had everybody heated. I'm sorry about that."

"How is he? Your nephew? They figure out what the problem was?"

"They still don't know for sure. They have to do more tests but, he's better."

It's what she hoped, at least. Lavender had not been home or had spoken with Čhetáŋ since she left all those afternoons ago with Angie. She didn't know any specifics of her nephew and gave the answer she hoped for most, clinging to the idea of *no news is good news*.

"I should know more soon, but actually... I moved out that night. I've been trying to get settled. That's why I've been MIA."

"Oh?"

"Yeah, I finally got tired of Čhetáŋ's baby momma. I decided that was it, how she was talking to you. Really, I've been working on this for a while. But that night really jumped-started it."

"Hmph," he paused. "I'm sorry to hear that. Where'd you move to?"

Here... there... with a dude I get high with and fuck sometimes. "Just one of my homegirls right now," Lavender said.

"Bet. Can I see you soon? No pressure. Maybe when stuff ain't so hectic."

"Yeah, that's cool."

He tugged at her shirt a little, then hurried off in the opposite direction.

Watching him walk away, she was relieved that he did not make this the awkward encounter she thought it would be. Relieved he didn't acknowledge anything Gloria or Čhetáŋ shouted in his presence. Relieved, he still seemed ok with the mess that she was. However, she wondered how long that would last.

She lay wrapped in Caesar's sheets again that night. Lavender was unsure of what she and Chris were involved in or how he felt, but her thoughts kept drifting toward him. Even now, with the vow of abstinence she'd pledged to Caesar after he took her in, entirely evaporated.

She was between his and Angie's cramped apartment that entire week, and Caesar's body felt like home. She did not worry about his opinions of her because there was an unspoken understanding that they were the same type of pernicious.

Caesar came to his bed and climbed on top of her, waking her from a dream. In it, she was back in New Jersey, but somehow not in their old apartment. Čhetáŋ and her mother were there, and they ate food on a pallet, but it was also out in her grandmother's garden simultaneously. The lavender was tall and purple but intermingled with Mary's elephant ears. She didn't see her father, but she still felt his presence. Then the door burst open, and it was him. He smiled and hummed a song from his diaphragm. "My Amášte!"

Lavender frowned as she emerged from her tranced visions, annoyed. She hadn't dreamed about Joshua in years, and now someone shook her from it by planting deep, bitter, kisses on her mouth, numbing her lips.

Oh.

As the residue of cocaine settled and dulled the feeling in the places of her mouth his tongue explored, she remembered how easy it was to fall back into this. Yet, it felt hollow this time. It somehow managed to feel less authentic than her dream—an imposter when her mind had filled her with genuine affection. Maybe it was always this empty, and she just realized it.

The next morning was a Saturday, and lacking any purpose at all, she drug herself from Caesar's bed and onto Elizabeth's doorstep like a bewildered stray cat. It was early, just past sunrise, the earliest bus she could catch. She sat under Elizabeth's small awning that left her legs unprotected for almost two hours and sunburned.

Elizabeth later emerged from inside her cave, aggravated. "Why you out here girl?"

I really don't know, was Lavender's primary thought.

"Shirley come calling me saying you been sitting out on the steps all morning," Elizabeth said.

"I came to," Lavender thought quickly, "...braid your hair. Isn't that today?"

Her aunt was confused but soon returned to her usual caustic manner. "Crazy ass girl, you just did it last week. Why you ain't call, then?"

"I don't know. I just, got it wrong, I guess."

"You guess? And why you ain't knock?" Elizabeth went on complaining.

"Knock for what? So, you could curse me earlier than right now? I wouldn't have to do none of that if I had a key by now anyway." Lavender said, then spewed the excuse that she was on the phone under the awning all morning and lost track of time.

"Hmph," Elizabeth grunted. "Well come on. You gon' redo my hair? Since you over here like you ain't got sense."

"Sure."

"And you know why I won't give you no key. So, you and them guhls from 'round the corner, um, Angie 'nem, can be in and out of here and come in all times of night. Smelling like niggas and reefer like you be at your place?"

Well, there goes that. The thought had crossed Lavender's mind to inquire about letting her board there until she could find something.

She loosened every row of Elizabeth's braids and gently scratched her head. Her aunt hummed in satisfaction. Lavender washed her mostly gray coils under the kitchen faucet, massaging her scalp as she went. She parted and greased each section, then clamped tightly to fashion new rows. The entire endeavor took about two hours that Lavender stretched out as long as possible. Hours that, for the first time since she'd been helping Elizabeth with her hair, didn't seem like a tiresome chore. The mundane and monotonous routine of it was familiar territory, one of the few dependable excursions of the last two weeks.

"What's wrong with you? I asked you about the baby."

Lavender's thoughts had drifted, and she didn't hear Elizabeth bring up Caleb.

"I guess he's doing ok."

"You guess? Why you guessing? I heard you and Chase was fighting. Y'all stay fighting ever since that girl. You know I can't stand her," Elizabeth continued. "She more high-saditty than even you was."

Lavender grinned, "Yeah, I guess you can say we're fighting. I ain't living there right now."

"What you mean?" She asked, grabbing Lavender's hand to pause the hair styling.

"I mean, I'm not living there now."

Elizabeth breathed heavily. "I know you ain't let that heifer run you outcha own house."

Her aunt's thoughts were a labyrinth of contradiction and concession—as they'd always been on her good days. To Elizabeth, Lavender was displeasing because she was "high-saditty" due to her fairer skin, hair texture, and origins as a northerner. Those traits didn't make her "better" than anyone else. In the same vein, however, Gloria annoyed Elizabeth for being "high-saditty" when she did not—unlike Lavender—have the right to be because she was dark and country. She should have been humble. Only Elizabeth's mind could reconcile those opposing sentiments into a single harmonious idea.

Lavender also noted her aunt's declaration of the house being "hers." Elizabeth never missed an opportunity to remind her niece and nephew that the house was not theirs but hers through Mary. And wouldn't be theirs until the ink was dry on the deed of the lease-to-own. It didn't matter that it was almost paid off or that they'd been paying the note for nearly twenty years. It still wasn't "theirs." It was never "theirs" until Elizabeth needed to win some debate or some repair was needed. Then it was "theirs." This was all an ironic clue that she had taken her medication and was thinking clearly.

"Well, I just didn't want any drama. She's pregnant, CJ's sick, and I was gonna need to leave eventually," Lavender offered.

"You a good one then. I might've had to move, but I be damned if they make me cause they say so. You should've never took your name off that lease."

"Yeah, well, when I did.... Wait, you was the reason I did. When we switched from lease, to lease-to-own, when Čhetáŋ was in the 2A league and you thought that was going somewhere. You said he looked 'better on paper' than me."

"I did didn't I. Well, you was stupid for doing that. All the time and money you put in."

"I didn't think about all that then. Hell, I was glad to be off and not have my name legally tied to shit with you."

"I see that too."

"Turn your head," Lavender said, as she worked Elizabeth's hair from another angle.

They grew quiet, then Elizabeth asked, "So, where you staying?"

The question was partially why Lavender was there. She didn't have a stable solution and if her aunt couldn't be an option, perhaps the visit would offer a "Liz" perspective.

"I haven't decided. I'm with friends right now."

"Friends? Ain't none of your friends worth shit. You been doing good lately. Holding this job steady, ain't been in jail since the car thing. But your old ass back with your friends?" Elizabeth sucked her teeth.

It was a rare positive acknowledgment from her aunt. Lavender almost thanked her.

Elizabeth yawned. "Well, like I said, you can't stay here. I don't 'llow fornication, and partying, and guitar playin'. Better get your own."

"Gotta have money for that. In this town, a car for that too. I was saving when all this happened."

"Well, you messed up the car thing. And you shoulda been had money if you ain't waste so much of it playing around and drawing on yourself," Elizabeth added, referring to her tattoo.

Lavender wondered how all of these people discarded all she'd done to keep the house up and keep Mary's car going all those years. Or on Čhetáŋ's needs outside of what his scholarship covered to only focus on what she could've done better.

"Y'all act like I wasn't supposed to live and be happy where I could. Y'all act like I ain't have shit I needed to forget sometimes." Lavender said.

"And now you by yourself and homeless. What you got to show for it?"

Chapter 28

Let It Burn

"Bitch Better Have My Money" - Rihanna

EIGHTY DOLLARS AND FIFTY-SEVEN CENTS. ČHETÁŊ LOOKED AT the receipt for the Methotrexate again and passed it to Ian. The medicine was a chemotherapy drug used to treat various types of cancers, lymphomas, and arthritis. He was never happier to be picking it up, though. Happy it was *only* for the juvenile arthritis they'd diagnosed Caleb with and not for those far more scarier things. Systematic Juvenile Rheumatoid Arthritis or JRA or "Still's Disease" was frightening enough. *What a long-ass scary name for something that attacks kids*, Čhetáŋ thought. It was foreign to him. He'd never known anyone with it, had never heard of it before, and didn't know if it ran in his family since there was little he knew of Joshua's side. But, here it was, showing up randomly one day, nasty and cruel. He wondered about the baby still growing in Gloria's belly.

It took the doctors weeks of testing to figure out what it was. When he and Gloria first heard the diagnosis, they were relieved it wasn't cancer. However, when they learned of all the possible complications and issues Caleb might face, they were almost over-come with the same level of anxiety. The brochure they received mentioned flare-ups of rashes, fever, and swelling. That was bad enough to them, but then there was also the potential inflammation of the lining of his lungs, heart, lymph nodes, and liver. He may grow and develop slower than normal. It was waves of potentially horrible outcomes for them to worry over.

"And that's just one of the prescriptions," he said as Ian looked it over.

Ian was a director at Čhetáŋ's youth center. When Čhetáŋ discovered their mutual affinity for the New York Yankees, as they pondered over the roster and reminisced over 2009—the team's last good season—Čhetáŋ knew he'd found a friend. Ian even included him in the fledgling lawn service business he operated on the side.

"That's a lot for lil man," Ian said. "But you still got some money coming in, and now that you got that paper," a reference to Čhetáŋ's degree, "The youth center gonna get you that big raise!" Ian stretched his arms up, suggesting a large sum of cash. They laughed at the assertion of higher wages from their employer. "We got these yards, too," he added, reiterating the lawn service. "And, I mean, you still got family to help."

Čhetáŋ wasn't even certain if he could work much on the lawns for extra money with everything else going on. *And family?* Čhetáŋ thought while reaching for the Newport Ian smoked. He supposed that would be the sister he had just kicked out. Or maybe, it was his paroled mother who had been ringing his phone lately—certainly needing something. *Which of those would be help? He must mean Gloria's family.*

Čhetáŋ coughed as the sensation of burning exhaust filled his chest. His eyes watered, and he considered throwing the cigarette at Ian.

"You know better, lightweight," his friend laughed.

As if the situations with Lavender and Caleb weren't enough, he had been missing Katherine's calls. She had left messages stating she needed to discuss her results and "some other things" with him. If he was unavailable when she called, Katherine was often difficult to track down afterward, with all the rules surrounding phone use at the transitional house. Plus, she had a job now. "Working at a bakery," she told him. Her voice chimed like a shopkeeper's bell with that announcement over the phone. *She sounds happy, at least.*

A sudden loud bang sounded behind them as Angie pushed open the screen door to the backyard with enough force that it ricocheted from the wall.

"Your money or your life, hoe!" She yelled upon stepping out on the back patio.

"The hell wrong with you!?" Ian shouted, startled.

"My bad," Angie laughed. "Y'all just standing outchea, gazing, lookin' like 'Brokeback Mountain.'" She snorted at her own joke as they stared blankly, unamused.

Lavender emerged from behind her, wearing gardening gloves and carrying a plastic bin under her arm. She walked towards a specific location in the yard but stopped next to Ian and reached for a draw of his cigarette also. She twisted her face after inhaling. "I don't miss that taste and smell, but it'll do at least until I get through this yard work. Then me and that 'gas' got a date."

"Yard work?" Ian looked at Čhetáŋ for clarity. "We gon' add her to the business?" He laughed.

Čhetáŋ didn't smile. He rolled his eyes and shook his head.

Lavender walked towards her intended destination, sat the bin on the ground, pulled her gloves tighter around her hands, and began digging with the shovel she'd left there days before. Čhetáŋ leaned against the wall. *This was the depths of insanity*, he thought.

"Dude, what she doing?" Ian asked.

"Some stupid shit," Čhetáŋ said.

Lavender continued digging until her shovel hit the hard exterior of one submerged bin. The outside covering read "Joshua tapes" handwritten with a sharpie on torn paper that was adhered to the lid and covered by clear packing tape. She dug until she had exposed most of it, then lifted it from its hole.

The congregation of Čhetáŋ, Angie, and Ian alternated between suspended silence and murmured mocking declarations about her.

When she finished, she returned to partake of the cigarette once more, breathing heavily and sweating.

"Angie, I got one more from out here to get. I'ma wrap the dirty ones in plastic before we get in the car."

Angie blurted out a confused "Okay?"

Čhetáŋ could take it no longer. "That's so dumb. Don't make no sense at all. What you trying to prove? You ain't been back here looking at these bins in years."

"It's dumb to you, maybe," Lavender shouted back.

"It's dumb to everyone. Ain't that dumb y'all?" He turned towards his fellow observers.

"I don't even know what this girl doing," Ian added, and Angie only raised her hands in indifference.

"She copying buried tapes or checking on them or burying them or... I don't know. Something with these old cassettes my daddy had," Čhetáŋ said.

"Tapes?" Ian frowned. "Yep, that's crazy. Why she doing that?"

"Cause *she*," Lavender interjected, "wanna make sure all the music she got left of his gets saved, and there's a bunch of backups in case some shit happen. That's why. And clearly, I'm not burying anything right now. You saw me pull this out the ground. Right, dumbass?"

"I'm the dumbass?" Čhetáŋ laughed. "Look at you! Digging like an idiot! You ain't thought about them things in years, but you out here today, just having to get them," he used his fingers as air quotes, "when you knew I'd be here, be here alone. Hoping I'd see and feel sorry for you and let you back I guess."

"You ain't alone. Your chubby friend right there," said Lavender.

"Hey!" Ian blinked, sucking in his stomach.

"You didn't know he was gonna be here. You just knew CJ and Gloria were away, and I was letting you get in the room."

Lavender rested her foot at the base of the bins. "I'm getting my stuff and moving some of these to my new place. Cause I don't know what plans your baby momma got now that I'm gone."

"Right," he scoffed, then asked, "So you got a new place? Where at?"

She nodded affirmatively, and Angie gave her a glowering side glance but said nothing.

"Don't you worry about it."

"I'm really not. And why would we mess with any of that? Why would we need to dig back here? Even if we did, I'd let you know first."

"How I know that? You didn't let me know before you locked me out. You taking her orders and that's cool."

Čhetáŋ sucked his teeth as she continued her project, now refilling the holes.

"Is this supposed to move me or something?" He asked.

She kept shoveling and pouring.

"Am I supposed to feel bad?" He probed once more. "That you're out here, sweating, like you just gotta move all this stuff too? We didn't ask you to do that."

Shovel and pour. Lavender had developed a rhythm. Čhetáŋ heard the melody of "I've Been Working on the Railroad," buzzing in his ear and chuckled.

"Something funny?"

"Yes. You're certifiable," he said.

"Really? You do remember helping me with this, right?" She pulled her gloves off and stuffed them in her pockets.

"Yes, when we were children. Children, keyword. I never understood why you didn't do something better with them by now, like a safe, or..."

"How these gonna fit in a safe?" Lavender interrupted. "Where would I put it if I had one that big? I'd need a unit down at some climate-controlled storage facility, and how long was I supposed to pay for that, month after month, year after year?"

She had a point he considered, but still, this was insanity.

"I don't know, but you been doing this digging routine for years and ain't come up with a better way yet. You claim you so attached to Daddy's recordings, but you haven't invested anything into saving them for real. Just like you go on about music, be in that shed, but you ain't gonna do shit with them guitars either." *Waste. All waste. All nonsense.*

"All you do is talk, smoke, and come home with anybody," he continued. "Like you did the night we put you out. Like you been doing since I was in high school. Like I couldn't hear your ass. That's you, wasting time, wilding out. Not growing none." He squinted his eyes and rubbed his goatee. "By the way, your nephew is doing fine. Thanks for asking."

Lavender grimaced, tightening her grip on the rusty spade she held. She glanced at the other witnesses. Angie wore a smirk while Ian avoided eye contact. She didn't respond to the last part of Čhetáŋ's appraisal.

"He wasn't just my damn daddy," she huffed. "I shouldn't be the only one bothered to wanna keep up with his things. Whenever you ready to hand me the money to convert approximately 2,800 cassette tapes plus some old ass 8-tracks to the damn cloud or whatever or however I'm supposed to do it, I'm ready. I don't even have a computer. Piece of shit I did have, quit working years ago. You got one though—schoolboy. We could've been doing this together if you wanted. But you know, I ain't shit. Guess this wasn't worth your time." She hesitated and punctuated her sermon with the same sarcastic tone that he had. "By the way, how it feel to have a house to sleep in, food to eat, and clothes, all while taking you damn near a decade to finish one basic ass degree. You're welcome, though. Thanks for the appreciation."

Čhetáŋ fumed. Every muscle in his jaw and throat tightened, and an Arctic wind cut through the Summer evening.

"Yeah," Ian uncomfortably chimed in. "I think we can go inside for a minute, miss lady," he said, gesturing towards Angie.

"Hell nah! I ain't going nowhere," Angie snickered as she sat down on the patio step for a more comfortable view. "This good!"

"How you figure I ain't appreciate it? How long are you gon' hold on to that? It's what you wanted to do," Čhetáŋ growled. "I ain't ask you for that. That's gon' be the one thing you ever did for the rest of your life? You gonna hold that over me forever? Begging for worship? Whining forever about, *what you did*? Hell, do something else. Anything."

"I ain't never whined or begged your ass for nothing, Čhetáŋ," Lavender countered. "Or asked you to return them favors. But now that you're *on*, you ain't gotta shit on me either. If it wasn't for me, you and your whole ass family wouldn't even have the house y'all kicked me out of."

She articulated her last sentence just as the world around them seemed to waver between two song beats. Between the cascade of car motors and the 808s of subwoofers on their street. Her words were spoken emphatically and free into that brief quiet—echoing—therefore demanded a response.

"So what you looked out for a while," Čhetáŋ fired back. "You still did that for you. Or... used that as an excuse to do what you wanted. I had somewhere to go. I could've lived with Liz if I had too. I ain't the one she couldn't stand. Plus, it ain't like I didn't start bringing in money. I could've brought in more. I had my own hustles."

"All I hear is 'could've.'" Lavender said. "Between them times you made money playing ball and then classes and then knocking up Gloria, that didn't amount to shit," she added. "You was committed to making ball work and was glad I was there holding everything down. That's fine, but don't act like it was something different."

"Whatever, Lavender. All this time, and this janitor job the only and longest real job you've had I can remember, even in those years you were, *taking care of me*. Wasn't nothing but messing around with club niggas. That's what you wanted to do. I ain't ask you for that. Look like you had a great time to me. I was covering for us and in school and playing ball and starting a family when you was in and out of trouble and barely holding a job. That's why it took my ass a decade for my basic ass degree."

Lavender scoffed and wiped her brow. She grew quiet and returned her focus to restoring the yard to a tidy state.

Čhetáŋ was still hot at the insinuation that he'd apparently been little more than a leech; that he was the single reason she hadn't done or attained more. *Those were choices*. She was adamant about things like him pursuing his baseball like "Daddy would've wanted" and getting a degree as Mary had discussed. Now she stood here chastising him for doing those exact things; things that had nothing to do with how she'd chosen to live her life.

"You waste time, treat people bad and be in mess," Čhetáŋ continued. "From Momma to Gloria to Liz, to... Kenny. Hell, you found some way to be in the middle of Kenny leaving us. How that happen?" His mind returned to that time Elizabeth had bloodied Lavender's mouth over lying for his uncle. The time he had regurgitated his morning away at school to finally be rescued by Mary and come home to find Lavender there with Kenneth in the middle of the school day. That, being the last time he'd see Kenneth at all.

"You was like fourteen," Čhetáŋ continued. "You was wilding even then. Messy. Always in drama. But I'm done covering for you now."

Lavender's eyes filled, and she pressed her lips together before looking away from him. "What are you talking about? Covering?" She said virtually no louder than a breath.

Čhetáŋ on the other hand had found his voice and was as strident as he'd ever been. "I'm saying, CJ is sick. I got a family to consider and worry about, and it's time you grow the hell up."

Chapter 29

Open House

"I'll Take Care of You" - Bobby "Blue" Bland

WHEN LAVENDER SHOWED UP ON CHRIS' STEPS A FEW HOURS later with two dirty plastic bins, his perplexed look did all of the communicating for him. She knew she sounded desperate on the phone, especially after being somewhat distant with him for nearly two weeks.

"Don't laugh at me," Lavender pleaded, sweaty and disheveled from digging.

"Laugh? Why?" Chris asked, peering down at her and the crates.

"Couple things from the house," she said.

"Yeah, I figured that when you called, but...."

"These are my daddy's tapes. Well, some of them. I had these buried with some others."

"Buried?" He asked, rubbing his face.

"Yeah... You want the long story or the short?" she asked.

"Long."

Lavender sighed.

"When we'd just gotten here, my dad's bandmate sent down all his cassettes and stuff. We didn't have anywhere to store them. But of course, duh, it's my dad's stuff, so I wanted to keep them all, you

244

know. I buried them to keep them safe and out of the way." She shrugged her shoulders. "I used to make copies, put 'em back in their cases, wrap the shit out of them in plastic, wrap those in like two garbage bags real tight, then put them all down in these bins." She pointed at the containers. "Duct tape the shit out of them. Put those bins in another garbage bag sometimes. Bury the whole thing. This was fourteen-year-old me who came up with this. Well really, it wasn't me. I had a little geeky ass boyfriend then, he told me about frost lines, and steel wool and insulation and...."

Chris' brows furled, and he squinted his eyes in befuddlement as she led him through this maze of a tale.

"Anyway. It was cheap, and it worked. Nobody thought about them. I didn't worry about thieves, fires, storms, nothing. And they still play, as good as day one. I thought it was real smart at the time." She laughed as a clunk of dirt fell from one of the boxes and landed on his pressure-washed, painted, and pristine garage floor. "Shit used to take me weeks to recopy, to keep on fresh tape. I did that every few years. But, it's been a while now, and..."

The adrenaline and emotion from her blowup with Čhetáŋ raced through her system. She heard herself rambling on and on and knew she sounded as ridiculous as Čhetáŋ had accused her of being.

Chris smiled and picked at the exterior of the bins a moment. "How many of them do you have like this?"

"Oh..." she laughed. "There are like another four, same size, buried in the backyard by what was my grandma's garden."

"Damn. How many tapes he have?"

"Almost three thousand. Including some eight tracks."

He lifted one of the bins into his arms, laughing in disbelief. "Three thousand?"

"Yes. You talking about a man who recorded most of his shows for almost twenty years."

"Guess there wasn't any mp3 then, huh. That was a lot of damn work," Chris said.

Lavender smiled bashfully, knowing how it all sounded. She

should've changed strategies away from this antiquated approach decades ago. Her face turned serious then, reflecting on things Čhetáŋ had said.

"I have an interior closet close to the garage," Chris offered. "I can put these in there, and they'll be safe." He walked back inside, and she followed like an abandoned puppy. "I guess... well, are you bringing the rest, or what are you gonna do with the others you mentioned?"

She looked towards the ceiling with coy eyes and flushed cheeks. "Leave them there? I don't know. I didn't have a plan. I was just trying to piss him off, my brother I mean, when I dug these up. To sort of guilt trip him into letting me come back, since, we never really argued like this before," she exhaled. "Didn't work. I only took these two so even if he said no, it wouldn't be a big deal to keep with me or go back later and put them where they were but..." her voice tapered off. After the way Čhetáŋ spoke to her, she didn't want to return at all. For any reason. "But... well, I don't wanna haul these from place to place if I can help it. I'm not going back there."

Chris' expression was sympathetic but strained like he felt embarrassed listening to her attempting to explain this.

"Like I said," Lavender brought her story to its feeble close. "I ain't really have a plan."

"Interesting," Chris said. He'd lowered the bin back to the floor and stood with his hand under his chin, projecting the profile of a sleuth.

Then Lavender remembered that what she had just disclosed wasn't quite the story she'd spun for Chris originally about how she'd ended up out of her home. She hoped he had forgotten, and she tried to smooth the edges of her narrative as best as she could. "I really just went by thinking we could work something out. That's all." *This man has me not thinking straight.*

"And I'm guessing y'all couldn't work anything out?" Chris asked.

"Huh? Oh. Nah. My brother just kinda went off. So no. Had me trying to defend old shit he doesn't even really know shit about."

Chris was quiet as he moved about arranging things and reorganizing space within the closet. "I'm listening," he said.

"I don't even get a thank you. Just what I ain't get right. When I didn't do this or that. And then like..." She paused a moment to compose herself. "Some stuff happened with my aunt's old man a long time ago. He brought that shit up. I was only fourteen years old, like, the fuck? What's that got to do with anything? Čhetáŋ don't even know about that. I kept all that. He ain't got a right to talk on it."

Lavender didn't reveal much in those few words, but it was more than she'd ever said to anyone regarding Kenneth. Not even to Mary.

Chris paused, wincing a bit after the words "only fourteen years old," but said nothing. Lavender never even noticed his trepidation. She just rambled on, stopping only a passing moment to thwart the rising tears.

He continued allowing her words and feelings to flood into the empty peace. It seemed necessary. When it felt like she had nothing else to pour, he handed her a key.

In the time she'd been talking, he moved a third of his belongings from the closet into another room, creating ample space for every possible bin or belonging of Joshua's she may have. He twisted the lock to the door and then closed it.

"See, you're good to go," he smiled. "If that's not enough, just let me know. I can move more."

"Wait? So, all that's mine?"

"Yeah. You can bring whatever tapes you need to if you feel like it and access it however you like. I'll help you go get them if you want, too."

"I don't want to put you out like this, like...." Lavender stammered.

"Stop that shit. It's whatever you need."

It almost sounded as if he was offering more to her. *A fool. A complete fool.* That's what she thought of him even as she felt other places on her body excited, disagreeing with the assessment. *Who opens their home to someone else's literal dirt?* Thinking of the other muddy bins that remained.

This was a failed ploy against Čhetáŋ, not some tactic to allow a man she'd didn't know very well further inroads into her already mass of confused feelings.

"Thank you," she muttered softly and grabbed his hands as she kissed him on the lips. "I'll let you know about the others."

"Let me know if there's anything else you need. For real, anything," he added and gave her an examining stare.

She wrapped his arms around her waist then slid her hands down the front of his sweatpants, but he stopped her. Chris brought her in close to him. His breaths were light flutters on her neck, giving her goosebumps. His swaddling embrace disarmed her into a posture of almost crying, so she buried her eyes into his chest until the sensation was gone.

Chapter 30

A Likely Story

"Basin Street Blues" - Louis Armstrong &
His Hot Five

IT WAS A COUPLE OF WEEKS SINCE THEY'D RECONNECTED AND she'd dumped her father's music at his place. In that time, he'd taken her out on several occasions and conned her into auditioning for his band.

The treachery began with what was to be a typical date. She met him at the warehouse, and at the time, she believed they would leave for their outing after practice was over. When she stepped from Kiara's car and into the building, she discovered that practice was still moving along with high energy. It was also loud with the chatter of groups of other people she hadn't seen before, sitting along the wall. Most were men varying in age and all either cradling saxophones or guitars. Chris was on stage, directing and yelling instructions, and far from detaching himself from the chaos to get ready for a date.

She was a bit surprised by the vision. Chris was punctual and formulated in all things. Getting places was more of a chore now with her being from "pillar-to-post," as Mary would've called her living situation. And no Čhetáŋ to drop her off places. Going through the effort of getting rides for a particular time, only to have to wait, was

249

not part of her calculus for the evening. She was irritated when she locked eyes with Chris who approached carrying a guitar.

"Hey..." he began. She saw the hesitation and her gears started to turn. "I forgot that we were doing open calls today. Looking for a couple rotations, or backups, maybe even permanents."

So, what. Her eyes read.

"I'm still taking you out after, but... I thought you might wanna give this a try." He lifted the guitar and nodded towards the stage. "For the hell of it."

"You can't be for real," said Lavender.

He shrugged and waited as if giving her a moment to consider it.

"Oh, this your girl right here?" Eli, the current guitarist, inquired in a volume loud enough to echo across the room,

Her eyes grew sharp in Chris' direction. "I swear I ain't set this up," he pleaded.

"Then what's he talking about?"

"Yes, I talk about you. I've told them you play. I didn't say you were auditioning... definitely."

Lavender rolled her eyes.

"Look," he continued. "This is like the final call. These dudes over here," he waved towards the men just feet away along the wall. "Most already practiced with us, and we're narrowing it down. I just thought since you were here..." He tried to nudge the guitar into her hands, but she stepped back.

"Yeah, I'm good on that," she said flatly, then stood along the same wall with the candidates.

"Cool," said Chris. "I'll just, you know, sit this with you, just in case." He leaned the instrument against the wall beside her. "We shouldn't be too much longer, anyway."

He retreated to his piano bench on the stage, and she sunk as far back into the wall as she could. She picked at her fingernails and showed as little interest as possible.

One candidate nearby approached her with the chair he'd been sitting in. He was an older, heavyset, Black man, perhaps in his late fifties. He sat the chair down. "Miss, you can have this seat," he said.

"Thank you," she whispered without looking his way.

"Man, these young bloods, they don't know how to treat no lady," he said, scanning the length of her body. "He could've offered you a chair. You auditioning too? What's your name?"

She was dressed in a halter top, heels, and a skirt with a high split and had stepped in late and absent any instrument. Nothing about her said "auditioning." She ignored him and stared into space, believing his question was disingenuous from the start.

Her disinterest didn't dissuade him. His face perspired and the dubious grin spreading from cheek to cheek revealed a chipped tooth on his top left incisor. "Cause I was like," he droned on, scratching his scruffy face. "I saw him bring you that Strat, but... I ain't trying to sound bad, you'd be the prettiest lady guitar player I don' seen if you was one."

She turned and looked at him with a creased brow. "Can you leave me alone?"

He lifted his arms in surrender and retreated, muttering something inaudible to her but loud enough that others along the wall laughed in unison.

A few moments later, one of those men went up with his saxophone and blew his way through an Earth, Wind and Fire cover. Then another several minutes later. This time, he carried a guitar and played an uninspiring rendition of Lauryn Hill's "Ex-Factor."

They should've been well into their date, but instead, it was this tedium. Her feet started to hurt, so she finally took the seat the older man offered. Coincidentally, he was the next candidate to approach the stage with his guitar.

He was *ok*, plucking his way through the notes of a blues song she was familiar with. He made a few technical mistakes even if he didn't attempt more involved flourishes.

Zero creativity, she thought. No added bends or vibrato, no trills, no ascending legato where she knew she would've played. She found herself ghost-playing those embellishments on her upper thigh instead.

All in all, from what she'd heard, they were all fine. Fine enough for anything a cover band that would rarely need a true lead guitarist could justify.

Quinton twirled his drumstick around between his fingers and yelled, "Anyone else?" Several band members' eyes drifted over toward her.

I swear I ain't set this up. Pfft.

"You trying out, Miss Lady?" Eli asked.

"No, nih," a voiced stated. It was her stout, chipped-toothed frenemy. His ego was still bruised from her earlier dismissal. A couple of faint sneers followed. "Y'all think she gon' do something with that Strat," he added in a low voice only meant for those near him, but she'd overheard.

Heat is what she felt. Her mind shot back to several of Čhetáŋ's last words to her. Those being, "you ain't gonna do shit with them guitars" and her not having something to show for anything she's supposedly done.

Lavender grabbed the guitar and approached the platform. As soon as she saw the wah and fuzz pedals, she knew what she would do. She squatted by the amplifier, which lifted her skirt just to the cusp of brandishing the entire room and adjusted several settings. She plugged in the pedals and made changes as well.

Chris smiled like a proud conspirator, waiting to watch his plan unfold.

"How you wanna do this mama? Solo?" Eli suggested.

"Um..." she paused for a moment. "You know 'Maggot Brain'?"

His eyes widened, and a slow smile spread over his face. "Yeah, I know 'Maggot Brain.'"

"Bet." She placed the Strat over her head.

Lavender had played the Hazel solo so many times she felt confident that despite not being able to play in the weeks of being a nomad, the muscle memory was all there. Even if it wasn't perfect, the E minor pentatonic scale it fell on, allowed her some grace to freestyle with the feel as she chose. She fiddled with a few warmup strings.

The warehouse had calmed since she got there due to candidates gradually departing but it slowly started to wake with chatter when those who remained noticed her taking her place on stage.

Once the first few somber introductory notes of the song slipped from Eli's strings and Quinton came in with light percussion, the warehouse became quiet and still.

Then she picked those first two strings—flat 7 bends, to the 1... and it grew quieter still. She rode the emotion. Her eyes closed most of the time, not needing to see the fretboard. She was in the song.

George told Eddie to play the melody as though his mother died. Lavender knew how to lay that type of loss on strings. She only made a few concerted glances at the frets and looked up once to face the audience when it came to an intricate trilling moment. She wanted her fingerwork examined by all in the room. And then she turned and locked eyes with Chris, who was on his piano stool, motionless.

She didn't do the full ten-minute solo. Or maybe she had. Maybe it was longer. She was on another plane. It wasn't until her descent that she could hear the nothingness in the room.

She didn't know if they thought she was good. She forgot a couple of parts, and wasn't as clean in other places. The song was emotional, she knew, and maybe the void of noise was a reaction to that element.

When she opened her eyes, there were smiles. Then there was clapping, with her biggest detractor being the loudest. There was also Chris' face—calm and stoic as ever, staring and dreaming. She unplugged and slid the Strat off her shoulder and handed it back to him.

"Come on, stop being a punk! Eat it!"

Lavender and Chris lay splayed across the bed. He attempted to feed her a crawfish he pulled from the étouffée, which room service had just brought to their French Quarter hotel room.

"That's nasty!" She protested adamantly.

"Oh my God... you're 'forty years old' and never had a crawfish?" He sneered.

"I'm not damn forty, asshole!"

He laughed. "Ok, ok. But we teach rounding up after a number that ends in five where I'm from, and you're on six so..." He twisted the tail, peeled off the shell, and dropped the morsel of meat into his mouth. Then he placed the head of the carcass to his lips and sucked hard. Lavender twisted her face into a monstrous composition and mimicked the act of vomiting.

"Gross."

"You don't be complaining no other time," he said with a wily grin. Then, her mind flashed back to their previous evening in that bed in front of the open curtains overlooking Jackson Square—being an exhibition for that block themselves.

This was their second night in the Crescent City for a Jazz festival where Basin Street performed. Unlike before, Lavender made sure she could travel with him this time. The band had their set the previous afternoon, but Chris wanted to stay an extra day to show her a bit of his hometown and the ward where he grew up. Then after the performances and landmarks and succulent cuisine they returned to St. Ann Street and he kissed her in front of that window.

He was firm and caring. He gripped and held her with intention, directing her with and without his words. His touch was delicate, his kisses on her mouth and body were warm and lush. It was a combination of hard suasion and wanting, wielded with soft urging, almost like pleading to be within her. She was loud. He controlled her and Lavender had not always liked that. But his domination also emitted a vulnerability that he was the one at the mercy of her anatomy. It had been only minutes into the intimacy in front of that window before her deep and protracted eruption caused her entire body to constrict, surprising even her. She became warm, recalling it again.

Chris continued eating his food, oblivious as to how his words had just sent her thoughts racing.

"I can't believe you ain't never been down here," he said.

"I haven't been a lot of places," Lavender stated, refocusing on her steak and eggs.

"Yeah, but you're a 'forty-year-old' musician. Kind of like being a swimmer who ain't never seen the ocean in real life."

She rolled her eyes, "I wish you'd quit calling me that."

"What? Musician or forty?"

"Both."

He hadn't shut up in the days that had passed since her "audition." Despite her repeatedly telling him it was all for show, to hush doubters in that room.

"I just think you'd like it a lot," he said about her joining his band in some capacity. "It would be good for you."

They collected their belongings for check out at the hotel.

She didn't know how she felt about constantly being in his orbit, first at the school and potentially with his band. There was also the contact he tried to put her in touch with who lived in Prattville, a suburb of Montgomery that had donned itself the "Preferred Community." Chris described the contact, Patrick, as a middle-aged white man with two sons who lived in Old Ridge. They were interested in classical and jazz guitar respectively, and seeking a tutor with experience in both, hadn't been as easy to find. She stuffed the man's number in her pocket and never called. She couldn't fathom how she would relate to anyone with enough disposable wealth to spend on classical and jazz guitar on fickle teenage boys. Nor did she have a way to get to Prattville even if she wanted. Montgomery's transit system barely serviced Montgomery, let alone accommodating ten miles north of its borders. She almost laughed in Chris' face when he delivered the details of that "opportunity."

When it came to Basin Street, however, she was leery of the commitment. She also disliked the assertion that somehow it was all *good for her*, as though he knew best. "Y'all barely need the lead guitarist y'all have now with the kinda sets you play. I got a lot going on, and I just wanna sit back and not get caught up in all that."

Chris left it alone. Instead, he moved on to another matter. "What's up with your living situation? You still working stuff out with your folks or staying with friends or what?"

"Oh, um, a bit of both, I guess."

"So, I was thinking, you already got all that shit at my place," he laughed. "What if like you stay with me until you know, things better with your brother or you have some other arrangement?"

"Uh..." she stuttered.

"No pressure to answer now. Just thought I'd offer." He smiled graciously and continued dressing and packing.

They made their way down to the hotel lobby and stood in line waiting to close out their lodging when Chris was recognized by an old friend. They embraced and howled, and Lavender took a couple of steps back to allow room for the raucous reunion; securing his long keyboard case and other bags while his attention was diverted.

She allowed his cohabitation invite to settle in and contemplated the decision. She never lived with a man before, and with his age, she doubted he had much experience there either. Yet as with youth, what else did he know but to leap first and think second?

But she was also growing weary of the vagabond lifestyle. She was sure the rotation between her friends—at least for Angie and Kiara—was exhausting them as well. She accepted living with Angie's rambunctious pre-teen boys invading her corners of the cramped apartment when she was there. It was rightfully theirs. When they would look through her purse or "accidentally" come upon her leaving the shower, it annoyed her, but there wasn't much she could say.

Kiara was her longest friend, but sleeping on the sofa at her place with her daughter and boyfriend there felt more of an invasion than at Angie's. She didn't bunk there as often.

Elizabeth had ruled her out already. She thought about asking Renée for accommodations for a while, but they weren't that close, and Renée lived the furthest away, below the airport. That left her with Caesar, where—after Angie—she slept the most.

He was often away anyway, still roaming and rollicking at the pace they kept in their twenties. He came home drunk, sometimes with other women. He'd do lines and offer them to her and expected her legs to part as always. She resisted the former with frequency, still recalling the birthday incident. The latter, not as much. *I just need to buy time.*

The last couple of years had seen ill-timed events deplete chunks of her cache. She had to go in with Čhetáŋ to patch the roof and fix a burst pipe in the foundation. Things often broke in the old house, and they were responsible. Repairs were, in fact, one of the few times they could always count on Elizabeth to insist it was "their house," "it's in y'all contract" of the lease-to-own. These were all expensive necessities that Lavender believed were an investment into something that would be theirs outright soon. It wasn't until she argued with Čhetáŋ that she'd learned he'd been, in fact, "covering" for her, and none of it mattered.

She envisioned the slack-jawed looks on her brother and Gloria's face when they discovered she was shacked up with a real professional man on the east side of town in a large house in a gated community. The thought kept tempting her mouth with a spiteful grin.

She was so immersed in the clouds she didn't notice Chris had paused his reunion and pointed at her as an introduction to his friend.

"Oh, hey. I'm sorry," she realized.

"Lavender, this my boy Adam. We grew up together in Pontchartrain Park."

"How you doing, Miss Lady?" He enveloped her hand between both of his.

"I'm good," Lavender smiled with coyness.

"I see you carrying that piano case too. You look like you serious with it like Chris's ass always was."

"Hell yeah, she's more serious than me," Chris interrupted before she could correct him. "But it's with them strings, though. Phenomenal."

"Oh? Lady guitar player. You in the band too?"

"She works at the school with me, and she's... working with the band some," Chris replied, still answering for her,

"That's what's up then. A pleasure to meet you."

They had an entire discussion all around her. She hadn't responded to one inquiry of his, just stood there smiling, like an idiotic attendant for Chris' keyboard.

She supposed her truth wasn't *sexy* enough to disclose, especially in front of a childhood friend. Homecomings were supposed to be celebratory and self-congratulatory after all, she reasoned. Chris' answers came so naturally and with such ease; like he had practiced how he'd introduce her and mastered the narrative. A "phenomenal guitarist and school instructor who moonlights with a traveling cover band throughout the country," as he had led this man to believe did sound much better than her life. *I sound like I got my shit together*, she thought.

Lavender wondered when the best day would be to return to her house and collect the rest of her things so Čhetáŋ and Gloria could watch.

Chapter 31

The Fast Song

"You're Next in Line for a Miracle" - Shirley Caesar

"HEY MOMMA," A TIRED ČHETÁŋ SPOKE INTO HIS MOBILE phone. "You gon' have to keep this brief, I can't add too many more minutes to your phone this month."

"I understand. Just wanted to know 'bout my grand baby." Katherine sounded depleted, but still in good spirits.

"That boy mostly back to himself. Running his mouth, playing. He's doing good. The doctor's prognosis sounded good too. Just gotta keep him on these meds a while."

"Praise God! I can't wait to see him!"

"Yeah, me too."

"And the other thing?" Katherine asked.

The other "thing" was the tension between him and Lavender. She had been out of the house for almost two months, and the only communication he'd received from her since their big argument were a few texts asking about Caleb's progress.

"Everything gonna be just fine," Katherine went on after he didn't answer. "Don't worry yourself. God's got you. When I get down there, I will do anything y'all need me to, to help out."

The idea of her coming home was such an abstract thought for so long, he pondered how real this was. They discussed it over the past year, but nothing was concrete. It was aspirational talk the same way it had been countless times before. It wasn't until the last ninety days or so that she'd relayed definitive plans to him. He knew this because sixty of those days were full of anxiety over CJ and medical bills and refills.

Čhetáŋ chuckled into the phone with a bit of apprehension. "I don't know. You really still trying to do this? Now, I mean?"

In their previous conversations, she discussed the details of her affairs. The time she could reside in the transitional facility was nearing an end, and she needed arrangements afterward. Usually, that was boarding with a friend or finding space in some low-income housing. "I'm fifty-nine. I'm done tryna piece stuff together first. I got this heart thing, too, and I been a fool long enough. Should've left... a long time ago. Only thing I wanna see of this 'Garden State' is in a rearview mirror now."

"I mean, that sounds good and all," Čhetáŋ interjected. "Different from how you've spoken before. Which is cool, I guess. If you set on this, it ain't gonna be easy. You have to commit. Ain't no do-overs this time. No coming with your old mindset."

It had to be said, he thought. He had a son and baby on the way. And while Gloria would eventually return to work and his new academic credentials would offer opportunities, the road to that future was still rife with the impediments of the present. The last thing he wanted to do was add to his current full plate.

"I know. I've come to terms with all my twisted thinking," said Katherine. "Hell... some of that is why I never came before. 'Cause why would I bring my troubles there? But I want a clean slate. I don't wanna see these same streets, these same people. Before, even with my clearest head, trying to get it together here, it just ended the same. I can't promise perfection, and I ain't. That's part of what was fuckin' me up, 'cuse my language—needing perfection. Shit had to be 'perfect' 'fore I thought I could do anything. But the first step of making stuff right, or better, is leaving here."

She sounded sincere, but he also had his own family now to consider as much as he wanted to help.

"I'm not gon' be no burden on you," Katherine continued. "I'm working on getting in this program beforehand, and I wouldn't have to be at y'all's house no longer than a few weeks. I already got ICAOS working out with the courtesy supervision program and all."

That sounded fine to Čhetáŋ, but he knew until those doors were opened, she would essentially be another dependent for him no matter what utterances to the contrary she spoke. He already had to help her pay for the fees and applications for the transfer, and history wasn't on her side. She'd had a previous transfer request denied. It was all an exercise of faith.

"I'm grateful for everything y'all have done so far. Proving my new residence and the support and all," Katherine added.

He thought about how the word "y'all" suggested Gloria was in full support. Only he knew that to be thin at best. He was not forthcoming with his concerns to her about it all. He painted it in rose-colored terms. Only mentioning that if Katherine came at all, it would be a brief stay and that with Lavender gone, the baby on the way, and CJ still needing some monitoring over his condition, the additional adult in the house would be helpful.

Katherine continued to speak on programs, potential employment, and a sponsor she already had in place.

"You really been working on this. And what about your heart valve stuff?" He asked.

"I gotta treat myself better, and, well, I got Medicaid."

It was a lot to digest at once. It would've been helpful if his sister were open enough to help smooth this process. *She may never come to a day to be that open to momma*, he thought. But her absence this time was partially his fault. Another thing he'd have to eat.

"Look, we gotta go. I was tryna get off this phone before now," Katherine said as her voice went hoarse. "Gotta save minutes. But I can't wait to see you, baby." They said their goodbyes and ended the call.

With Katherine re-entering their lives seeming more imminent than ever before, he tried reaching Lavender again to no avail. A couple of initial times he called, she was unavailable—like she hadn't paid her bill. Not unheard of for her, but annoying, nonetheless. Later, the calls went directly to her voicemail. He couldn't figure out if she was having phone issues or just avoiding him. He wasn't going to go out of his way. He'd committed to that notion the evening he'd returned home to find all her things were gone. She or someone had carded the lock to her room, and everything was emptied except the furniture. The never submerged sets of his father's music, her guitars, clothes, the record player, all gone. There were even several patches in the backyard that looked as though they'd been disturbed—excavated. She was *gone, gone.*

He felt bad, but didn't. He'd heard folks say they saw her leave with some guy they didn't know, which was as much as he expected from her. He was a bit surprised at the level of severance she'd committed to. He figured there just needed to be a cooling period.

She knew it was only temporary, didn't she?

He remembered how barren her eyes looked after their fight. After he said what he did about her past ways and how she treated people. Her entire face looked like someone who was watching the ending of something they had not anticipated. Admittedly, it may have been unnecessary on his part. She's been hurt, he knew. But she hurt him, too.

Lavender's detachment from Caleb was another matter. It was like she didn't care. Katherine had called and inquired about the boy's well-being more in the last few weeks than the aunt who'd helped raise him.

Caleb had been asking for his "Tee Amášte," and they had no answers for her absence, other than she was "busy looking for a house."

"She don't wanna live with us no more?" Caleb asked, confused and upset. "I want to play the song, too," Caleb would murmur.

The song? What song? They wondered.

"The song we play. The fast song."

Čhetáŋ realized he underestimated her influence. She always set aside time for CJ, exuded patience with him, and imparted lessons and information from their father that he didn't even know.

Čhetáŋ sat back in his chair, rubbing his hands together and staring at the wall. He repeatedly bounced his leg up and down like subconsciously keeping the frantic rhythm of a song only he heard. This was the agitation Gloria walked in on, while holding her head and clutching her stomach.

"I don't feel right. Something's wrong," she said.

She was only thirty-two weeks along. *The baby can't be coming now, this is too soon,* he thought. Her worried look made his stomach sink and he rushed to her side.

Čhetáŋ helped her to the car before calling for CJ. Under usual conditions, Lavender would be home from work at this time. He thought of that as he gathered Gloria's purse and shawl and strapped her into the passenger's side while securing his crying son into the car seat, trying to calm him all alone. And, *blood?*

He was now seeing blood.

Shit's falling apart, he whispered to himself, and hopped behind the wheel of "Blue Magic," hurling himself towards another unknown.

Chapter 32

Animatronics

"Insane" - Summer Walker

IT WASN'T LAVENDER'S INTENTION TO GET DRUNK THE PREVIOUS night when she opted out of Chris' event and ended up hungover and missing work. In fact, ever since she'd been living under his roof these two months, her partying had subsided, even while the dishonesty about a range of other situations grew.

Her evening began by lying to Chris about helping her nephew to avoid attending his show. She still hadn't spoken with Čhetáŋ much. Just a few text messages where she understood CJ to be fine, which gave her a guilt-free conscience for tying his condition into her lies. Instead of showing up to support Chris, she went to Renée's house to wait while Kiara twisted Renée's hair to start her dreadlock journey. Lavender tagged along there and planned to only stay a few hours, then be back in time for Chris' return and for work the next day. Just long enough to give the illusion that she'd been away with CJ. Instead, she ended up arguing with Renée, walking two miles to a nearby watering hole to escape the feud and taking a cab back to Chris' place.

It was a silly dispute over what to view on Renée's SmartTV. It ended with Renée wondering aloud why a person "without a pot to piss in, nor a window to throw it out of" was at her house arguing about anything.

When Renée stated that Lavender was "shitting on the one home, someone was dumb enough to offer her," meaning Chris, and suggested she wasn't raised right; it nearly came to blows. Instead of having to explain away bruises or other evidence of a fistfight later to Chris, Lavender regained her composure and simply left.

She called Angie and got no response. She tried Caesar, who'd mostly ignored her since she started spurning their sexual exchanges after moving in with Chris. Since it was a Sunday when buses didn't run, Lavender was left to either hover about the exterior of Renée's home and neighborhood until Kiara had finished. Or, salvage a bit of dignity and find her own way to manage the situation and get back to Chris' by herself.

She walked to the closest refuge she was familiar with, the Mexican restaurant just off the main highway. She knew two of the bartenders there, and they slid her free drinks for hours while she tried to find a ride. When that failed, she eventually had to spend forty dollars to take her all the way from the south side to East Montgomery. Fortunately, she managed to beat Chris home, less she had to conjure another lie to explain her inebriated state from the "babysitting" she was supposed to be doing during those hours. Lavender went to bed and barely stirred when he arrived. She mumbled about coming down with something when he laid beside her for the night.

Supper the following evening began as uncomfortable shallow banter between the two about the chicken not turning out how Lavender wanted and about how Chris' activities before the Fall break were piling up. While not highly interesting for either, it at least moved them beyond the awkwardness of that morning. She was almost comatose in his bed and heaved throughout the night. Lavender was still lethargic and queasy when Chris woke up, and she called into work. Her explanation was "sinuses," which, in hindsight, she realized was inadequate to explain the upchucking. It was the first thing that came to mind in her squeamish state.

"Give what you can when you can. No big deal," Chris' initial attitude toward their cohabitating arrangement was gracious. It was a little over two months into that graciousness now. Lavender had begrudgingly relinquished her stance on not being involved with the band and ended up playing some gigs with them as an alternate. These consisted of a couple's anniversary party and a show at a community clubhouse for a woman's 65th birthday, where they played Franky Beverly and Marvin Gaye sets most of the night. She just stood at both and played rhythm like an animatronic. *I look like Billy Bob Brockali,* she thought.

The money from those events was minuscule, but between that, her job, and the free rent, she was able to start replenishing her savings. They were small steps toward a more permanent solution. However, it made her stomach ache with anxiety. She was grateful to Chris but felt trapped in his world—one she wasn't particularly inclined to. She had never lived with and been this susceptible to a man before. Where even something as valuable as Joshua's recordings rested with him. Everything was all *tangled.*

Lavender couldn't articulate her feelings, only that she did not care much for band life. And, she loathed to say so since it was all tied up with a man who felt sorry enough to take her in.

Playing with the band was everything she knew it would be—long boring practice hours rehearsing the same repetitive covers, most times without guarantees that she would even play at all. She was just a backup. Most musicians in her position wouldn't have to endure that drudgery on a consistent basis. But she lived with the band's leader, the one allowing her to live rent-free, the one keeping her father's things, the one who must have *love* for her even if he hadn't said those words. She only agreed out of gratitude. Even ending her long-standing job at the club to be available for rehearsals and travel, to support him, and on the off chance that she *may* get to play. Even if the bar work had dwindled to part-time hours since she began her custodial job, it was still something that was hers. Still, the way she had known to get by. This was a new world now.

"This is gonna be good. You'll see," Chris assured her in the beginning. "What else you got to do?"

Basin Street didn't have the opportunities he promised. She almost felt duped. There were other local bands, more established ones they had to compete against for gigs. And there wasn't the pool of shows available for all those legacy bands and a fledgling one like Basin Street in a small city. They were relegated to leftover jobs: the *old people's* parties and anniversaries. The *country* shows that were at some "rinky-dink" establishment in some hard-to-pronounce town, fifty miles this way or that. It was even less interesting than she originally imagined.

Now they both sat, brooding over barely palatable chicken in silence because she couldn't be honest sooner.

"You feeling better?" Chris asked.

"Oh yeah, just a little allergies." Lavender gave a dry sniff.

He sucked his teeth. "I missed you at the show."

"Yeah, I'm sorry."

"Hopefully, that means you'll make this event we got coming up. Putting together a little thing with Basin Street for promotion but also, you know, a fundraiser for my students. It's an opportunity for you to play. It's Sunday when Travis nor the backup can be there."

"Oh yeah? When is it?"

He frowned, "I literally just said it's Sunday." Chris turned up the palms of his hands. "Are you even listening?"

"Of course." She chewed her food slower than any normal mastication required and swallowed before more stalling. "Sunday, huh."

"You know what... don't worry about it," Chris said.

"What now?"

"Don't act like you're actually considering it if you don't wanna do it."

"I'm not acting like anything."

Chris shrugged his shoulders. "Have I done something or said something to you that I just don't know about?"

"Can I chew and think for a second? I gotta check with Čhetáŋ and make sure he's good with CJ and all. That's it. He got a lot on his plate."

Once again, she offered her go-to excuse whenever she wanted to escape any dealings with Basin Street. He never questioned her on it, even knowing she and Čhetáŋ were still at odds. Instead, she spent most of those dates hiding away at one of her friends' places like she had when Renée sent her away walking. Or, more recently, it was to cover for a more noble cause—completing her DUI school hours. She hadn't disclosed that to Chris either. He didn't need to know any more of her *fucked up shit,* she decided. Let her quietly get this back, at least, all on her own. Then she could move on without him knowing that "tidbit."

It was her second attempt at rejoining the ranks of drivers. The first time she tried she had to quit because she missed a class and was subsequently out of the $400 the course cost. This time she was determined to finish.

"How's he doing? Your nephew?" Chris asked.

"He's doing good. I'm just happy to spend time even though me and my brother still shaky."

"Hmph."

In the face of blatant lies, Chris still managed to be caring. Her lies were acrid in her mouth. The words made her sick each time he *made* her perform them.

They both went to bed early, each to a side. The figurative gulf between them was unconsciously manifesting into reality. When Lavender rose the following day, it wasn't to her usual alarm sounding off. It was to the buzz of text messages and a voicemail from Čhetáŋ.

"Hey, it's me. I think you're up this time of morning or will be. We're at Jackson Hospital with Gloria and the baby. I might need somebody to look after CJ for a minute while I deal with all this. Call me."

She didn't know what "this" was; if it was serious or just an overly precautious ER trip. However, it was an opening.

Chris dropped her off at the hospital.

"Thank you." She kissed him on the mouth and watched his dissatisfied eyes stare back into hers.

"Let me know any updates or what I need to do," he said.

"I will." Then he drove away.

Lavender walked into the Emergency Room waiting area to find CJ sitting in Čhetáŋ's lap, sound asleep; his hand clutching his Spider-Man action figure.

"Hey," Čhetáŋ said as she approached. "Thank you for coming."

"Of course."

"Shit got crazy so fast, I ain't have nobody else to call," he explained.

Lavender thought about Gloria's sister and mother. There were others to call, but he chose her.

"I understand. What happened? What are they saying?" She asked.

"I don't know a lot until I can get back there. Gloria was bleeding, but I don't think in pain. I don't know." Čhetáŋ paused and squeezed the back of his neck. "We were back there for a minute, but Caleb started freakin' out. Gloria was talking, though, and they got her situated in a room and all, so I came out here to settle him down. I'm going back now if you can go on and get him."

"Sure."

"I mean, I can give you the keys to the car, and you can stay with him at the house until later. That'll be good too."

"I ain't staying at the house Čhetáŋ," she said with a definitive look.

He sighed and pulled his hands down over his face. "Ok fine, whatever. Stay here then."

"I can take him to my place." She offered, but Čhetáŋ twisted his face at the suggestion.

"Your place? I don't even know where you staying. At some dude's I don't know? Nah."

"Ok, ok." She thought for a second. "I'll go to the house long enough to get some things for him, get us some breakfast, and go to Liz's. Cool?"

"Cool." He handed his small drooling bundle over to her. Caleb only roused long enough to wrap his legs and arms around her before going back to sleep, never once loosening his grip on Peter Parker.

"I'll call you soon as I know something," he said.

Before she departed the room, Čhetáŋ whispered another "thank you" and navigated his tired body back through the double doors and into the hospital's main floor. Caleb didn't wake up until they got to Mary's, and it was then that he saw her smiling brightly at him.

"Tee Amášte!"

He and Lavender spent the better part of the day at Elizabeth's, where Keshia was also visiting. Elizabeth was so excited to be with her granddaughter Laila for the first time since Keshia's graduation that she hardly even grumbled at Lavender and Caleb's surprise appearance at her door in the wee morning hours.

Laila and Caleb giggled and played for hours, with Caleb assisting his younger cousin in taking clumsy, wobbling steps. He helped feed her McDonald's biscuits and shared his toys. When he wasn't in leadership mode, he was never more than a foot away from Lavender, like he feared letting her leave his sight.

"You're gonna be a good big brother CJ," Lavender said but almost instantly wished she hadn't.

"You heard anything yet?" Keshia asked, "From Chase?"

"He said something Placenta... Placenta P-r-e-v-i-a," Lavender was unsure if she was pronouncing it correctly. "She was bleeding a lot. Doctors want to keep her."

"Oh, Previa. I knew someone with it, but it went away on its own."

"Can that happen?" Lavender asked.

"This late? I'm not sure."

"All that stress," Elizabeth blurted out while looking in Lavender's direction.

Keshia groaned, "It ain't stress related, momma."

"You don't know everything. You don't even live here to know what's going on. This girl here moving out, Kathy moving in. You gon' try to tell me...." Frown lines formed deep hollows across Elizabeth's forehead. She caught herself getting worked up and sat back, reaching out for Laila. "Look at this juicy thang here!" She picked her up and sucked on her cheeks with loud slurping noises and nuzzled her neck until the baby squealed with laughter.

Keshia whispered to her cousin, "This why I don't never come home," and laughed. But Lavender wasn't attentive to her.

"What you say Aunt Liz? Kathy moving in?"

Elizabeth smiled a wide self-satisfied grin. "Yep."

"Nah," Lavender rebutted.

"Yes, she is."

"Well, when then?" Lavender asked, doubtful about the announcement.

"Hell, I don't know when. Soon. I talked to her and everything when Chase was 'round here one day. She sounded good too, for whatever that's worth."

"You talked to her?" Lavender asked.

"What I just say?"

Lavender looked just as puzzled by the revelation as she was that her aunt and mother had shared words.

"I ain't have nothing else to do," Elizabeth continued and shrugged.

"And what she say?"

"Hell, that's our business. Just you know she coming and to stay. This the first time I'd bet on it."

Čhetáŋ retrieved Caleb later that evening to drop him off with Gloria's sister before taking Lavender to her new quarters. CJ cried and screamed when he was forced to leave his Tee Amášte, and a piece of her broke. She missed him. She missed their shed playing despite the nonsensical rift it had caused with Gloria over his health. Lavender promised she'd see him again the next day, not knowing if it was a pledge she could keep.

The topic of Katherine didn't arise while CJ was in the car, but the moment he was discharged to Gloria's family and the car door slammed shut, Lavender dove into it.

"Tell me about momma," she demanded.

"Damn. Can I get in? And where am I taking you?"

"Just hit East Boulevard," she responded, then turned her body as far as her seat would allow to face him. "When were you gonna tell me that this is for real this time? She's really coming, like Liz said?"

"Considering everything, I didn't think you wanted to know, or cared. You wave me off anytime I mention momma anyway, right," Čhetáŋ offered.

"I just think it's something I needed to know."

"Ok. You know. Now what?"

"Go down Troy Highway," she directed. "So, what's going on with that?"

"Man, I got so much on my plate right now, I honestly ain't thought long about it. Until a couple months ago when she was all serious and giving details, I thought it was gonna be the usual bull-shit. She says she has a job lined up at a bakery, cause that's what she's doing now in the work release. And that, she plans not to be with us no longer than a couple weeks or so."

"Pffft," Lavender exclaimed. "Ain't no way."

"Well, that's what she says."

"And you're prepared for when that few weeks turns into months, or that bakery job doesn't happen, or she starts back with pills or whatever. If Gloria can't handle weed, she damn sure ain't..."

"Stop," Čhetáŋ raised his voice. "First, she has to have a job for this transfer thing to even stay intact. So, if that shit fails, she's going back anyway. Second of all, momma long done with that other shit."

"If you say," she moaned.

"I do say. She hasn't messed with it the last years she was in. She hasn't since the state rehab program and she been at the transitional house this whole year. On top of all that, she's sick anyway. Hell, she scared to do anything to add to that."

"Sick? Sick how?" Lavender asked, surprised by the revelation.

"An issue with her heart," he said.

"The irony."

Čhetáŋ narrowed his lips, and she could hear him grind his molars. "Tell me where I'm dropping your ass off at."

"Don't be like that. I'm just saying, other than the sick part, this sounds like the same shit."

"Maybe, but you know how we talk. Yeah she got a condition now, but she also talking clear, being accountable, not blaming anyone else. I mean, she knows she only hurt herself with everything and..."

"What? She didn't just hurt herself! She hurt us all!" Lavender countered fiercely, then turned away from him.

"Well, I ain't just throw her away like you and Aunt Liz. I listened to her and know she sound sincere."

"Nah, you ain't throw her away. You just did that to me," she said. They grew quiet.

Lavender guided Čhetáŋ across the other side of town, up the Eastern Blvd., down Vaughn Road, towards Ray Thorington Road. The homes and acreage became larger as they traveled. The clusters of pine trees grew thicker and taller, and the streets were either newly paved or repaired. There wasn't a pothole or piece of trash or an out-of-place blade of grass along the pristine highway or landscaping. Čhetáŋ was quiet, but his face revealed the intrigue that spun in his thoughts over the manicured scenery and how she'd managed to find herself living here.

"This where you been staying, huh," he muttered when they pulled into Chris' neighborhood. Čhetáŋ was genuinely curious when they reached the driveway, and he saw the navy Acadia SUV with an Educator license plate and New Orleans Saints decal. "Who is this dude? Where you meet him?"

"Work."

"Hmph."

She looked at him, hoping he'd return the gaze, but he didn't. "It's the same guy I was with that night y'all kicked me out, remember? I haven't been back and forth with anyone else. Just him."

"We'll see... that ain't what I hear."

"And what you hear?" She inquired.

Just then, she saw the blinds of the front room lift and knew Chris was peeking to see who his visitor was.

She exited Blue Magic, trying to avoid an interaction between the two. She was happy that Chris bore witness to the drop-off. It helped continue the facade of her being with Caleb all of those evenings she'd lied. *But these two can't meet right now.*

"Call me and let me know about the baby. Call me for CJ. I'll find a way to get there if you can't come," she said. Lavender went to the back door, and Chris was waiting at its threshold. He gave a two-finger wave to Čhetáŋ, who barely acknowledged it.

Čhetáŋ didn't call her about CJ or Gloria's situation for a few days. He only sent a series of texts offering minimal information:

- *Gloria being kept and monitored until the baby strong enough to be induced.*

- CJ is with his aunt and grandma.

- Spending the night at the hospital, CJ with his aunt.

That was it. She wondered if he was being curt on purpose or if that was all that was going on.

She was submerged in frayed relationships. Caesar was still not answering her sexless calls. Angie wasn't estranged but exhibited one of her disappearing acts—usually due to a feud with one of her baby's fathers. There was also whatever was happening between her and Chris. Kiara was around but had a man and child and her own affairs.

Lavender thought about how she was living the most physically comfortable she ever had, in Chris' posh home, but it had turned into a sumptuous island.

Lavender rushed to answer the phone when she heard it buzz, hoping it was Čhetáŋ. Instead, the caller ID displayed a 973 area code. Numerals she had not seen flash across her screen in over five years. Numbers that, even before then, she tried to block or ignore. She almost rejected it but thought, *fuck it*. Everyone else had apparently spoken to her. She may as well get it over with.

"Hello?"

"Hey... yes...." The voice wavered.

"Yes?"

"Lavender? It's me, momma."

"Yeah, I know. Čhetáŋ gave you this number I guess."

"Yes, he did. Well... how you been?" Katherine's voice was jittery and low.

"Fine."

"I know you've been hearing about me coming home. I... just wanted to talk to you."

"Go ahead." Lavender knew the soft carpet Čhetáŋ would roll out for her return. She was not sure what or if any reconciliation had occurred between Elizabeth. However, she wanted to make sure

Katherine understood, with her, it would not be so easy, no matter how much time had passed.

"I'm happy to be seeing you soon. Glad you picked up. It's been too long since I heard your voice."

"Yeah, well, I guess I couldn't avoid it any longer. Now that you're supposedly moving down. Might as well get this over with so we'll know where we stand."

"And where is that?" Katherine asked.

Lavender laughed, "I think you know. Why we playing?"

"Ok. Let's go."

Lavender paused, somewhat surprised by Katherine's directness in wanting to confront the issue. "What you want from us? From me?"

"I don't understand. I'm just trying to get home, is all."

"You wasn't trying to *get home*, no other time," Lavender said.

"I was, baby. I just went about trying to do that in the wrong way then."

"Oh yeah? I think you want us to take care of you now. In your old age? Cause you sick, I heard. You coming down here with nothing," Lavender continued.

"No. That's not..."

"You want me to forgive you?" Lavender interrupted. "Again?"

"I want you to know all the regret I have on how I went about things, for a long time pitying myself. I knew I was wrong and thought y'all was better off. But I didn't know how to fix it." Katherine paused and gulped for air. "I eventually got a clear head, but I was hurting, I was wrong. I wish I woulda done better by y'all. You forgiving me, that's your choice."

"Cool. I don't choose it then. You have no idea what it was like."

"I think I do, I..." Katherine began.

"Like hell you do! You don't! So much shit fell on me, that your son don't even know, while y'all best friends sharing everything, talking about me, and still not knowing shit."

Katherine took a moment, digesting Lavender's words before

adding, "I know you fell into bad habits like I did."

"Don't you ever compare us, cause I was here!" Lavender yelled. "We ain't the same!"

"I know I fell on the climb, and you never saw a climb as anything worth trying."

Lavender found her mother's words to be cryptic and laughed. "What the hell is this psychoanalyzing metaphorical shit? What climb?"

"I failed you in a lot of ways, I know. But the one I hate the most is how you see yourself in this world. To give in before trying. That nothing is worth pushing for. That it'll all burst before it amounts to anything. And you get in your own way and cause the thing you fear. I know. I felt like that too after everything."

"Stop saying that! Stop saying we're alike, like at all," Lavender snapped at her. "You did what you wanted to do, cause that's what you wanted to do! I did what I had to do! That's different!"

"And what you doing now?" Katherine asked.

"What you mean?"

"You still doing what you have to do? Or you getting in your way so you can go back to the aching you know. 'Cause you understand that pain. And it feels good to soothe that pain. I know."

"Fuck you. You don't know me."

There was a pause.

"Hmph. You're right. I know me," Katherine said. "It took a while to."

"Well, glad y'all acquainted now," Lavender said, choking back tears of anger.

"Nothing you say to me, gon' make me not love you, Lavender. Them days of beatin' myself up over wondering if I could ever get that back and meet your approval are done. I've prayed to God about it. I know He forgives me. I got His grace. I'ma love you regardless. So will He. One day you gon' learn to let go of those things, whatever they are, so you can feel and know that too."

Lavender ended the call.

Chapter 33

Momma Knows

"I Love You More Than You'll Ever Know" - Donny Hathaway

LAVENDER FELT UNBALANCED AFTER THE CONVERSATION WITH Katherine. She did not think it possible she would leave a discourse with the woman for the first time in so many years, angrier with her than before. *How dare she reach in whatever book of therapy lessons she picked up in prison and analyze and prophesize,* she thought. None of that felt like Katherine sought forgiveness.

Lavender toiled over the call for days, wondering what the next months would be like with this large ever-present figure finally returning to their lives. It almost rattled her during her examination that morning at DUI School. She had spent too much energy and Alka-Seltzer on those thoughts she considered while lying across his bed.

It was mid-afternoon, and she heard Chris get home several minutes earlier. They still weren't on the warmest of terms, but she wanted a palate cleanser from everything between Čhetáŋ and Katherine.

He was reclined in his favorite chair in the living room when she walked in, his face buried within the pages of "Between the World and Me." She entered without greeting and knelt before him and began rubbing his knee, then up to his thighs and reaching underneath his shirt. When that garnered no response, she then attempted to separate him from Ta-Nehisi by grabbing at the book.

"Stop, ok," he said in a hostile voice she didn't expect.

"What's up with you," she questioned. He'd been rather reticent with her ever since the morning she'd awakened hungover after the fight at Renée's. Yet, this was different. "Chris?"

He finally closed his book and folded his arms; every movement further unnerved her. "Where were you this morning?" He asked.

"This morning?"

"Yes, this morning."

She'd been so blindsided by his coarse tone and considerations over her mother that she had to think for a moment to recall for herself. Then she remembered she'd taken the bus to endure the final grueling hours of her DUI class for her license reinstatement.

"I was helping with CJ, I told you."

"Yeah, you did. But after two of my members couldn't make practice, I canceled and rode through your old spot, assuming to see you, maybe get y'all lunch or something since I was close by."

Shit.

"I pull up, your brother on the porch looking at me crazy, one of your homegirls too, and some big dude, Caesar, is that his name?"

Shit.

"Like an idiot, I go I'm looking for Lavender, and they tell me you aren't there. I look at your brother like, didn't you pick her up? Your brother stutters his way through some bullshit before the big nigga, smiling, starts playing with me. Telling me about y'all being close old friends, how he wasn't a musician but knew how talented you were. Talking other shit too. Clearly, I know where this is going. I tell them I had my days mixed up, and I leave."

She didn't understand how all of this could've happened and she not receive one call or text of warning from Angie or Čhetáŋ. Then it dawned on her that she'd placed her phone in *Do Not Disturb* mode that morning for class. Any warnings they may have sent still languished in that limbo.

"So, where were you? Cause it damn sure wasn't with your nephew."

She was tired of lying at this point. "DUI school," she whispered.

"What?"

"DUI school." Then she showed him her documentation, the progress she'd made each weekend through the twenty-hour course.

"Why didn't you tell me all that before? When the hell did you get a DUI?" He asked.

"Cause," she shrugged. "That shit is embarrassing. It happened a few years ago."

He rolled his eyes.

"I don't know what to say. It ain't something I wanted to share. I wanted to take care of it on my own."

"You could've told me that."

Lavender looked at him with abashed eyes. "Why? So you can feel sorry for me some more? You know how often I wonder why you fuck with me? I don't offer you anything. So now on top of everything else, I should tell you the main reason I'm on buses and thumbing rides this entire time, isn't just because I can't afford a car, but also because I got arrested for driving high as shit on cocaine? Oh yeah. Cause that's what it was. Coke. You cool with that? That make you feel better?"

Chris was taken aback, but then regained his position. "Doesn't matter about how I'd feel. It was the truth," he said. "Instead of me finding out like this. I told you when we started I ain't judge you."

"Well, ok, I didn't tell you then. It wasn't major. I was almost done with the class, so it wouldn't have mattered."

"But it did matter. I could've helped you."

"There it is," she sighed. "I didn't want your help. I wanted to fix something myself."

"There what is? I've never made you feel any type of way about none of your shit."

"*My shit*," she scoffed. "You don't mean to, but... like in New Orleans, you had your friend thinking I was some professional musician and teacher at your school. That ain't sound like 'not judging my shit.'"

He paused, perplexed, and tried to recall the incident. Then his puzzled gaze turned into an annoyed snarl. "Don't try turning this on me. What about that dude Caesar?"

"What about him? It wasn't anything."

"Really? Cause he had some interesting ass facts," Chris countered.

"What you mean?"

"He made sure I overheard before I left. Saying y'all had spent some time a couple weekends ago. Specifically, turned to your girl about the 'fun' y'all had after the Bama-Florida game. The game that was the same weekend you couldn't be bothered to come with me to the festival performance in Opelika. 'Worn out' from dealing with your nephew you said. But, what? That ain't what wore you out huh?"

Caesar was being the petty asshole she always found entertaining when it landed on other people. "It wasn't like that at all. I..."

"So, you've been lying to me this entire time? Is your nephew even still sick? Am I a fool you've been playin' all along?" His veins were engorged, spittle flew as he spoke, and it crossed her mind that she had ruined this man's decent nature. The thing she was afraid would break was undone by her hands. Just like Katherine said.

"No. Chris. It's not.... Look, I was with them that time and some others. But all together. I wasn't with Caesar like he trying to make it seem. I was with Angie, him, their crew. They had a watch party."

"Why the hell would you lie to me about being with them?"

She hesitated several seconds, each feeling like a punishing hour.

"Answer me!" Chris demanded.

"I just didn't want you to think I wasn't grateful for everything you've been doing. But, it just ain't for me. The band, really. I don't want to do it. I didn't know how to tell you, so I just been, making excuses. CJ was sick, but not like that. Not as bad right now with the meds he's on. I was kinda using that to get out of those shows, so I wouldn't make you feel bad."

He laughed.

"But I wasn't fucking Caesar," she continued explaining. "Not then. I haven't since we really been together. Since I moved in. That's the truth."

"So why is he talking shit to me if y'all ain't? I've literally just caught you in these big ass lies in less than fifteen minutes." He slapped one fist inside the palm of his other hand. "Why the hell would I believe what you're saying about him now is true?"

"Cause it is!" Her eyes turned into pools. "He's just being that way because I don't mess with him anymore. I'm with you!"

"Man stop," he said. His usual soft demeanor when it came to her was gone. No tenderness at all. "You're not shedding them tears for me. You shedding them cause you got caught. About to lose your free room and board. Your free chauffeur and shit. Your free gullible nigga service."

He stood to his feet to leave, stepping over her as he did. She still knelt on the floor. She reached to grab him and delay his exit, and he pulled away with a sharp jerk that, while barely touching her physically, had bludgeoned her ego.

"You know how wild it is that you would lie to me about your four-year-old nephew being sick, and you helping, just so you could avoid me and my band and shows? Shows I was trying to help you get put on with," he chided. "And not only are you not with a sick child, like you said... you're with other niggas!"

She remained on her knees sobbing, swallowing the lump in her throat that kept returning. She tried clearing her eyes of desperation, but they, too kept emptying their reservoirs.

"Chris, please... I, I love you. I swear I do! I swear I ain't never told no nigga this shit!"

It's true, she never said that to anyone, but now she felt she had to. She needed to tell him like she was plunging into a canyon, and those words were grappling tools. It felt like a descent. She had to because the words were true and she just came to understand why she'd struggled with submitting to them, disarming herself for him. The words that were a reflex and didn't need authentication because the feeling behind them had mass and existed.

He looked at her and breathed in deep steadied breaths, closing his eyes before glancing away. She thought she must look pathetic, weeping, on the floor begging like lyrics from the Blues she loved playing.

"This is all too much," he said, standing beneath the threshold which led down the hallway. "I can deal with a lot, but lying like this... Like who are you? In my house? After everything? Nah. I don't trust it. You need to start looking for somewhere else to be." He said with a somber tone. "You ain't gotta be gone tomorrow, but... you gotta go."

Chapter 34

Renovations

"Do Better" - Ab-Soul and Zacari

"You sure you don't want none of this?" Čhetáŋ pointed at his cup of chicken Ramen Noodles, devouring the simple dinner like he hadn't eaten in days.

"Nah. I'm good on that," Lavender said. She'd actually gone without sustenance since a quick pastry that morning, but she wasn't hungry at all.

Much that had transpired felt like lead in the pit of her stomach, disrupting her appetite, disrupting her sleep. The eviction, the unexpected feelings for Chris, trying to process them, then suddenly losing the source of those emotions, the situation with Katherine, then another eviction. Of all those issues, the one that landed hardest was the fifteen-second "lesson" from her estranged parent. That sat with Lavender the heaviest. Chewing over all its various meanings, having to swallow that coarse dish, and reckon with how exact certain portions of it were and what that meant that it had been correct. Fifteen dense and loaded seconds. So, she had no hunger watching her brother slurp down his food.

"So, it's next Saturday. I know you don't care, I'm just saying,"

Čhetáŋ said to Lavender between bites while they sat together in his living room.

"No. I don't care. I got bigger concerns," she murmured.

"I bet you do," he said with a smirk that he subdued after seeing her face. "I mean, if you don't have no place by then, you can stay here... on the floor... hiding from momma and Gloria," he smirked again.

She sat wordless, looking at CJ, who slept after they had enjoyed a few hours of guitar. The toddler's day was long as he'd spent the early part of it with Čhetáŋ visiting Gloria at the hospital.

It had been weeks since Chris had kicked Lavender out, but... not kicked her out. Now she was most comfortable spending her days and nights while she still could, back at Mary's before Katherine, before Gloria and a newborn would arrive.

"Don't you have something else happening next week you need to be more concerned about," she asked.

"Nah. They start the steroids then. It's five days later for the real event. Praying everything still works as they say."

Between searching for a new living space, she'd helped Čhetáŋ ready the house for the two new arrivals. The nursery—her old room— was now pink, cream, and coral, with art hanging of little Black girls wearing generous afro puffs framing the sides of their cheeks. There were butterflies painted intermittently over the walls that Gloria started in the months she'd been gone. There was a mahogany crib still in its box and the bassinet they still needed to move into the master bedroom. Lavender's dresser, armoire, bed, and nightstand were crammed together like puzzle pieces along a side wall; an exhibition of confusion over what would become of the set. They didn't get a chance to decide the sleeping arrangements, whether Katherine would get CJ's small bed or if she'd rest in the nursery for her stay. The "Jenga blocks" of furniture skewed the otherwise swanky aesthetics Gloria had created.

They'd been busy in the months she'd been gone.

"Damn, Gloria ain't waste no time when I was out. Almost like, y'all definitely wasn't letting my ass back for nothing," Lavender said to Čhetáŋ the first time she had seen her room after being away. It gave her a weird feeling. Yes, this was always the eventual plan, but the swiftness with which Gloria seemed to have *erased her* from the house was jarring.

"Don't be like that. I'm the one that told her to go on do whatever painting while it was empty and could just cover your shit up. So even if you came back, it could already be done. Gloria ain't even want to. She just knew you would be back, smoking out her 'new paint smell,'" he laughed.

Gloria had added white crown molding and new baseboards to the house a few years before. She also added track lighting in the kitchen and recessed lighting in the living room. All touches that stood out against the rest of the old home's decor, which Gloria hadn't gotten around to sprucing up yet.

She got "some" class, Lavender admitted as she looked over the additions. Whatever faded memories Katherine had of her old home, might've been painted over, rearranged unrecognizable phantoms now when she returned. Lavender originally saw the upgrades as unnecessary flourishes on an old place that didn't know where its next burst pipe or faulty wire lurked. Gloria must've only been trying to make the best of the cards she was handed.

None of this could've turned out the way she planned. Gloria's beau, as sweet, affable, and promising as he was, could never catch whatever wizardry was necessary to elevate him to that next professional baseball level and livelihood. After all those years, no Major League, no Yankees, not even a stint as a triple-A shortstop in some more exciting location. She still ended up in Montgomery, sharing an old house with two children, her man's sister and now his mother, recently out of prison. Gloria was bound to the family's circumstance now almost in a way that even she wasn't. Lavender almost felt sorry for her, but then thought that was extreme.

"You should marry that girl," Lavender said as she picked up the instructions for assembling the changing table for the nursery.

Čhetáŋ's eyes were wide and he tapped his ears like they needed clearing. "Say what?"

"You heard me. Real talk. It doesn't matter how I like her or not. I won't be living here anyway. It's been ten years. What you waiting for?"

"I'm gonna marry her. I was just trying to see how all this was going to pan out. Get done with school. You know."

"Well, you done with school now. If daddy was here, he'd want you to," Lavender said.

"Yeah, but just waiting for the right time."

She unfolded the instructions and moved towards him so they could begin the assemblage, playfully hitting him across the face with the pages, "Ain't no right time," she said.

They worked at the house together until he had to drop Caleb off with Gloria's family and return to the hospital. Lavender stayed, scrolling through the internet on Čhetáŋ's laptop, looking for affordable apartments. Listings in neighborhoods like Carmichael, Capitol Heights, and Old Cloverdale populated the search engine's page.

Old Cloverdale. She thought about the friend that Chris tried to put her in contact with. *He lived in "Old..." something,* she thought but couldn't quite remember what she'd written on the paper scrap that had his other information. She remembered it felt too far to go and too weird for her to attempt teaching white teenage boys. *But now, what the hell,* she shrugged. It couldn't be much different than what she already did for free with CJ in the end, no matter how outside of her comfort zone it had seemed.

Why is Old Cloverdale showing anyway? Lavender thought after several more seconds of glancing at the screen. It was in an area of the city of "old money" with lush lawns and aged, renovated but well-kept cottages and mansions. How it landed in her price range results, huddled among options like public housing, single rooms for rent and complexes she knew to be sketchy, made her guffaw in a way she hadn't laughed in weeks. *Must be shit,* she thought. She saved the result anyway and added it to the list of places to investigate.

Chapter 35

Good Bones

"Cranes in the Sky" - Solange

THE AC HAD GONE OUT IN THE GREYHOUND SOMEWHERE around Virginia, making an already long ride even more unbearable. Although it was mid-September, it was a muggy day for traveling with a bus full of bodies and no air circulating. Katherine imagined she looked like the polished, soapstone figurines in her parole officer's office—her bare, deep brown shoulders and arms dewy with perspiration. Her stomach growled, and she only had one-half of a peanut butter sandwich left and a bag of pretzels that she had grabbed from a vending machine prior to departure. Katherine was trying to hold on to the last ration until she was closer to home. *"Home"* being the thing she prayed she would find once she arrived.

When she spoke to Čhetáŋ on the phone, the conversation was not the warm anticipation she'd dreamed of for their reunion. His voice was tense and raspy.

"Ok, about three P.M. on Saturday? I'll be there, or my homeboy Ian if I can't," he said.

"Ian?" She supposed it would've been too much wishful thinking to expect Lavender in his stead.

"Yeah Momma, Ian. I gotta run."

He was matter-of-fact and short. She knew her timing was imperfect, but when would it have ever been *perfect*? Waiting on an elusive place known as *good timing* was her undoing.

When her bus got to its Atlanta stop, her stomach no longer felt hunger but twisted and inflamed. The void that had craved morsels of whatever food was left now only screamed anger in the form of gurgles and acute pain. The tension in her neck and back added to the discomfort of it all. She nibbled on the pretzels and tried stretching her arms up with the breathing exercises her counselor had shown them in their pre-release classes to quiet the storm of anxiety.

She hadn't seen Čhetáŋ in over four years. The last time was when he made the trip up to her facility for Christmas and sat with her through the allotted holiday visitation hours. They laughed and ate bland turkey and pumpkin pie. He was all smiles and tales of school and traveling, playing in the minor league.

Never far from her thoughts were those of the daughter who she hadn't seen in almost two decades and barely exchanged words with since Mary died.

"How's Lavender?" She'd always ask him.

"Oh, she's making it," was his typical response. It was dry and empty, *like how she thinks of me*, Katherine concluded.

So do not fear, for I am with you; do not be dismayed, for I am your God. I will strengthen you and help you; I will uphold you with my righteous right hand.

She repeated Isiah 41:10 over and over as they grew closer to Alabama. She wasn't the most dedicated adherer to the good book, but the last few years had made her want to recommit.

When the Greyhound hit the outskirts of Montgomery, the clock on the refurbished, older model flip phone she was given as a parolee read 4:08 PM. It was much later than she'd told Čhetáŋ her arrival time would be due to traffic. So, she concentrated and brought the device closer to her face, readjusting her bifocals. "Jus got outside city should be thre soon luv u," *Send*.

She sighed and rubbed her stiff, arthritic thumbs after typing. Even that simple task was laborious. Age and years of abuse were toiling enough, but grappling with learning new technology and terms she didn't understand felt daunting. She didn't know this new world and dreaded the time it would take to figure it out. But she knew she had to if she wanted to succeed at all. The tingling of doubt tried stretching its cold tentacles around her shoulders again. The pain in her upper belly radiated out and into her chest, burning. *So do not fear, for I am with you; do not be dismayed, for I am your God... Breathe*, she whispered.

Katherine looked out from her window seat, and she didn't recognize this place. It had changed even since that one Thanksgiving visit. There were new interstate interchanges with lofty flyovers and overpasses. Long stretches of I-85, she remembered as not being more than pine trees and barren fields as a child, were now bustling new centers of development. The sleepy city with its reputation as being resistant to change, had managed to transform itself into something more updated. It was no Newark or megalopolis with scores of pedestrians on crowded walkways and bike lanes, but it had new energy. It pleased her to see the downtown landscape had preserved much of its original and historical architecture. Many old, dilapidated buildings were renovated and reimagined. The old facades were still there and recognizable but made clean and like new; people still had faith in them. Someone recognized they had *good bones*. She smiled at the idea.

When they finally pulled into the station, it took several minutes to get her stiffened legs moving, and one young man helped her with her only bag as she slowly disembarked. She hadn't received a text back from Čhetáŋ and then realized her phone was dead. She frantically looked around and was reminded of her anxiety by the gnawing in her gut. The cold, tingling feeling of dread tried crawling its way back around her neck. This time, it was stunted when she saw him.

His face had aged slightly, and he had more facial hair. His dreadlocks now hung just past his shoulders. And there was his smile, just as bright as she remembered. That smile obscured the sun's afternoon radiance, and all the tension in her body began to evaporate.

Čhetáŋ hugged her tightly without speaking a word of greeting and collapsed into her small frame. He brought his hand up to her crown and got a hand full of short gray curls. "You cut your hair. I like it," he said.

"You grew yours. I like it too!"

They embraced until most of those who'd arrived with her were long gone.

"I've waited on this day so, so long! God is good. I missed you so much," she said through streaming tears.

Čhetáŋ's face glowed with emotions, and he struggled through his words. He finally uttered a "Come on" as he grabbed her bag, and they walked towards "Blue Magic."

A look of amusement and confusion briefly flashed on Katherine's face at the vehicle, wrapped in all its advertisement, but she didn't speak a word. She just continued to beam, trying to revel in every bit of the afternoon. She inhaled deeply. It was a part of her meditation practice, yes, but she also wanted to remember the smell of the moment. The aroma of baked bread and basil wafted in from the brick oven pizzeria on the corner. She remembered that place had once been an old bank. Yet here it stood, all new, made fresh and appealing again, even if in another form.

"You ready to go?" Čhetáŋ asked.

"Yes. I'm starving!"

When they arrived home, Katherine could smell the lemon and scents of Pine-Sol, and it returned her to her childhood and afternoons of cleaning chores with Elizabeth. Even with the alterations Gloria made to the interior design and the updated furniture, *this was home*.

"This where we're putting you for now, I guess," Čhetáŋ said as they walked to CJ's quarters. "It's sorta tight with this twin bed, but at least it's more space to get around. Unless you wanna sleep in the baby's room. It's a regular bed but, it's still some sorting out we need to do. I didn't know what would be easier..."

"Anything easier," she laughed. "I can sleep in the baby's room, so I don't run my grandson out."

The bed was made. Soft pillows and a comforter covered it. The bassinet was moved to the master bedroom, adding at least some additional space while they still worked out what would happen with Lavender's furniture.

"Well, this is quite nice," she said. "This was my old room actually-ly." She touched the finished butterfly figures on the wall.

"Yeah, we know. Lavender helped me finish getting it together."

"She did?"

"Yep." Čhetáŋ said.

"Well, I'm sure she excited about the baby," Katherine went on.

"Yeah, but she helped like make the bed and stuff for you too."

She blinked, a bit surprised. "She alright? You know if she coming by later?"

"That I don't know. I doubt it. She didn't say she was. She busy trying to find a new place."

"Oh. Where she staying now then?" Katherine asked.

"With some dude. But they fell out." He sat her things on the dresser and closed the curtains to the room.

"You ready to ride with me to meet your grandson?" Čhetáŋ asked. The announcement broke her from a state of reflection.

"Now you know that!"

Tap, tap, tap... Light knocking sounded on the door of the guest room. Lavender straightened up and sat alert on the bed. "Yeah?"

"I'm coming in," Chris said. He slowly opened the door and

searched for her in the dimness. Lavender reached over and turned the lamp on.

"This was in the mail," he said and handed her an envelope that read, Driver License Division.

"Thank you."

He paused for a moment and looked around the room. Her things were in a transitional stage of organization for the move, though she was still in the process of figuring out where to precisely. They'd not had any length of conversation since he delivered his ultimatum. Both avoided each other, which wasn't difficult in the spacious dwelling. Lavender felt it was almost meant to be this way because their end also coincided with the start of the school year, and her work schedule changed. She now went into her custodial job a couple of hours later, so they missed each other readying in the mornings for work and afterward at departure. How awkward it would be for him to arrive with her every morning. She knew Chris. She knew that rather than watch her lumber into the darkness towards a cold bus stop at dawn every day as her old schedule would've required; he just would've gone to work sooner and driven her himself. How *fortunate* they did not have to endure that.

Their summer together had felt like a span of years and a flicker of a moment. She missed him next to her every night in a way she never craved another body's proximity. It was safety and warmth she didn't know she needed until it was absent. The wound felt even deeper because she'd caused it. And maybe he wasn't the first or the last of her destruction of things. She didn't know if it was her nature to avoid that yet, but she recognized herself in this ruination.

When Chris hesitated rather than leave the room with any urgency, Lavender exploited the brief misgiving and grabbed his hand, holding it without words until it no longer felt reasonable to remain silent.

"Chris, I... I'm sorry. Again. See..." she flashed the envelope as though he wasn't the one who'd just handed it to her. "I wasn't bull-shitting with that. I wasn't bullshitting about Caesar..."

He turned his head and pulled his hand away.

"I wasn't lying about loving you. Even when I didn't know what to do with all that, when it scared me. That gotta be what it is, cause I've never felt this.... like I don't have my lungs no more. And that might scare you, but, I don't even care." She avoided his eyes. "You made me figure out what I wanted, shit I haven't thought on in years. Reminding me about myself. I ain't have to always be waiting on the bad. I just wanted to make sure you knew that too."

"Well," he cleared his throat. "It's just a lot going on right now anyway. We shouldn't have rushed into none of this. That's on me, right. That was my fault. So, it's best we just, wipe all this clean and have some separation."

It was the last thing she wanted to hear but knew of no other way anyone else would've reacted.

He told her he would be leaving for a gig over the weekend so that if she was doing any moving, he wouldn't be around to assist. He shut the door and left her to her silence again.

He was still so cold, she thought. Cold in a manner she did not think was even possible from him. She wanted to fix it but didn't know how. There was nothing she could give him. There was nothing he ever wanted from her.

Lavender returned her smartphone to her face and continued scouring rental listings again when an unidentified number rang her phone.

"Hello? Yeah, this Lavender."

Chapter 36

You Got a Lifetime

"Coming Home" - Leon Bridges

KATHERINE KEPT HER EYES ON HIM, THEN HER, AND THEN BACK to Caleb again. He ran rambunctiously around her legs, giggling and screaming "Grandma!" as though she'd been in his life from the beginning. His voice was the sweetest sound she'd heard since, maybe, her own children ran about. The new baby, Skyler, was sound asleep and the direct copy of her mother—a woman she didn't quite know what to make of just yet. All she cared about was she was here. It felt almost dreamlike. There was only one missing element.

"You talk to Lavender yet? She say anything?"

Čhetáŋ and Gloria glanced at each other.

"Ma, you know what I told you. If she wanted to come, she would've called."

"Ok, ok."

Gloria had delivered the baby by C-section a couple of weekends before. And while Lavender did visit during her hospital stay, it was when Katherine was not there. Since Gloria and the infant were home, Lavender had not yet shown her face.

Then, as though on cue, keys rattled near the entryway, and the deadbolt turned. The door swung open, and the afternoon autumn sun obfuscated the details of the person's face and figure, casting the body as a silhouette.

Lavender, Katherine thought.

If Katherine still questioned who had entered, the answer arrived when Caleb ran towards the figure, shrieking as always, "Tee Amášte!"

Lavender lifted and kissed him on the cheek, whispering something in his ear. Then she stepped inside the foyer and shut the door behind her. She was tall and fit. Her hair was braided into two long plaits that framed her face, hanging below her cleavage. Her eyebrows were thick but arched, and she wore lip gloss that accentuated her full, slightly discolored lips around a smile that was Joshua's, Katherine thought. This was her Lavender. None of the pictures she had seen of her daughter from Čhetáŋ over the years could match the vision of the flesh.

Lavender spotted Gloria first, holding the baby, as she rested in the chair facing the front door. She gave Gloria a feeble smile and a nod of acknowledgment before turning her eyes to the woman on the sofa by the window. Katherine rose to her feet with tears in her eyes and approached with slight apprehension.

"Lavender," she said.

Lavender didn't have time to respond before Katherine embraced her, and Caleb, who still clung to his aunt, pressed against her shoulder.

Lavender hesitated and offered an aloof hug around Katherine's waist. It lacked commitment. It lacked awareness of what embrace even was. Performative is how it felt, but Katherine happily accepted it.

Čhetáŋ entered, "Hey! How you get here? I thought you were gonna call for me to get you if you were coming."

They planned this dinner at the last minute, after Gloria finally felt up to it. It wasn't fancy. It was simple offerings of store-bought baked chicken, which Katherine tried to fix up with additional seasonings and a dressing of barbecue sauce. She also sat and snapped the green beans, preparing them as Mary used to, and made sure there was macaroni and cheese, what she remembered as one of Lavender's favorites. Lastly, there were the hoecakes. It filled the house with fragrances that were reminders of moments that spanned distances and squelched the appetites of generations of Freemans.

Lavender unlocked herself from Katherine and Caleb and stepped into the room, towards Čhetáŋ, and patted him on the shoulder.

"I drove."

"You drove?" Čhetáŋ and Gloria said in sync.

Lavender flashed her temporary license and Čhetáŋ smiled. "Look at you."

"I'm in a rental truck, taking a few things back and forth to my new spot."

"Oh. Who you moving in with now?"

"My damn self," Lavender said with wide eyes and a nod. "What Keith Sweat say? Nobody!"

They both laughed, rousing Skyler to momentary wails. Gloria quickly readjusted the pacifier and rocked her back to sleep.

Katherine stood back as an onlooker, not understanding the subtext between the siblings. She had her moments to reunify with Čhetáŋ and to work towards acclimating to her new reality, but she still felt the stranger. She mostly kept quiet and unseen within her son and Gloria's family dynamics. However, when asked or when she felt it appropriate, she took the initiative to help as much as possible. She prepared meals, did laundry, washed bottles, kept her space and every common area cleaned. She also learned the regimen for Caleb's medication.

When Gloria's own mother and sister visited, having their own methods and opinions for assisting the new, second-time mother and newborn, she stayed out of their way. Katherine would joke, "I know y'all want the money, but y'all gon' miss me when I start working and leave." Katherine was earnest about everything she shared with Čhetáŋ in the lead-up to her arrival. Even the employment at a local bakery was near finalization after a hiccup on the employer's end. Everything was coming together, *slowly but surely, almost.* Katherine watched her daughter move about the room, awkwardly avoiding her.

"Can I see Skyler?" Lavender asked Gloria.

She handed the napping, babe to her aunt; a copper-toned girl with a head covered in dark loops of hair, thick and opaque as molasses. She was delivered early but was strong and healthy.

"She's a doll," Lavender smiled. "Your damn twin."

Gloria beamed, then tugged at the base of the baby's onesie, "Let me check her diaper," she said as Caleb began his onslaught of requests for his aunt.

"We playing today? Outside? You can use my guitar," he said. He had noticed she was without her case.

"Come here, boy," Gloria directed. "Help me with your sister."

They exited, as did Čhetáŋ, back into the confines of the kitchen. All reasonable delays and interruptions were removed from the space between the mother and daughter.

"Sit down," Katherine said. "How are you? How are things?"

"They're fine," Lavender said without elaboration.

"So, um... well you got a place of your own now? Chase said you'd been living with your boyfriend. But I guess you wanna go out on ya own?"

"Something like that."

"Sometimes you gotta do that," Katherine suggested.

Lavender yawned.

"I'm 'bout to get lined up with a bakery and, well, I'm happy to stay here long as your brother will have me and I get to be 'round my grandbabies, but if not, I'll be looking for a place too, soon. After I get settled. They gon' need the space."

"Yep."

"I actually like the bakery thing. Did it in Newark in the work release. Remember when I had that catering business? Me and my friend. Didn't last long. But I get to bake the cakes and get to be a little creative with the decorations. I'm enjoying that part. But, what about you? You liking your job? Still playing the guitar, I hear..." Katherine was nervous, rambling in the same way, Lavender would when she lacked the words to bridge an uncomfortable distance of two beings attempting connection. "I know you getting your own place, but tell me about your friend. Your boyfriend you was staying with. How was all that? He have kids? Thought about your own one day?"

"Momma," Lavender finally cut in. "Nobody summarizing twenty years for you in three minutes. At least, I'm not."

Fair, Katherine thought.

"And nah, I never thought about kids. Cause why would I have babies I wasn't ready to take care of?

Wasn't nothing to say about that. "I... I understand," Katherine swallowed hard. "Well... you look good. Look well."

"Yep."

Everyone was appreciative of the minors present at the kitchen table during dinner. Their obliviousness toward decorum—loud burps, suckling, smacking sounds, and lack of concern over the adult drama —kept the room from unbearable silence between fragmented conversations.

"Where you moving to?" Gloria asked, sitting across from Lavender.

"Old Cloverdale. I found this lady needing to sublet for a year."

"Oh, that's cute. I like it over there," Gloria smiled.

"Old Cloverdale? You gonna be able to afford that on your own?" Čhetáŋ asked.

"I mean, yeah. I guess. I'll find out soon," she shrugged. "I'm good, though. I picked up another part-time job."

"For real? Doing what? Another bar?" Čhetáŋ inquired.

"Nah. It's in music. Teaching some," Lavender said before gulping her sweet tea.

Čhetáŋ and Gloria glanced at each other.

"How the hell you get a job teaching music?" He asked. "You ain't nobody's certified."

Gloria nudged him hard with her elbow. It made him rock in his chair yet never disturbed the baby at her nipple.

"It's more tutoring. You don't need a degree for that," Lavender said, turning her fork in the macaroni.

"I'm just surprised that's all. I'm happy for you," he said. "You almost done moving? You didn't need help?"

"I really didn't have much. I mean, my furniture is still here. I was gonna keep some of it and sell the other pieces when y'all are done with it... if, y'all get done with it," she said in a low voice before looking at Čhetáŋ and giving a quick peripheral glance at Katherine.

Katherine understood this subtext and tried responding, but Lavender continued.

"Chris is letting me keep all Daddy stuff there for a little while at least. Until I can figure something else out on that. I don't have room at my place, and I'm not bringing all of that back here. It's gon' finally make me come up with a plan."

"Hmph. Well, you could've buried it again," he smiled. "That's what's up though. Happy for you. Proud of you, sis."

"Thanks. My place ain't fancy. It's one of the older, smaller duplexes. I still got it at a steal, though. The lady was desperate. Had a family emergency and gotta be out of state for a minute."

"That's a blessing," Katherine interjected, then realized her statement landed in an awkward moment in the discussion. "A blessing for you, I mean." She felt the need to lend her voice to the procession of conversation passing her by.

Lavender ignored her and marched forward with her point. "The lady's mom got sick, and she just, like, dropped everything. Moved back to Missouri, just like that. Taking care of her own. Some people will do that."

Čhetáŋ sighed, and Caleb dropped his spoon into his seat.

"Oops!" He exclaimed, nearly falling from his chair to retrieve it.

"Be careful, CJ," Gloria said, but the child's disruption was not enough to pivot the trajectory of the simmering discourse.

"It's good she can do that," Katherine said. "Some people are more able to make a way."

"Some people make making a way a priority," Lavender fired back, never lifting her eyes away from her plate.

"Sometimes, it is hard to know the best way to go 'bout prioritizing things, 'specially when you got other commitments and problems you going through. Like, what to fix first. That's the burden—for some people," Katherine added, recalling her early days in New York working while Ernest was ill. Then she thought about the hours she stood on her feet at the diner trying to keep the apartment after Joshua was gone and couldn't decipher which was being held over her head now.

"Everybody got problems they go through, but don't always make excuses for just doing what they want, or doing nothing," Lavender stirred her macaroni.

"Sometimes it's not always what it seems to be," Katherine insisted.

"And sometimes it is!" Lavender jabbed her fork of baked cheese and pasta into her mouth.

The verbal parade had devolved into a duel of passive-aggressiveness and Katherine decided to allow her daughter the last word so they could all finish their meals in peace.

Lavender consumed her entire helping. Katherine picked at portions of hers, only finishing half.

They cleared the table and Katherine began washing the dishes as Lavender stepped away with Caleb while Gloria and Čhetáŋ put Skylar in her bassinet and walked outside.

"That went well," Gloria joked with him. They stood on the back patio, absorbing the breeze of the first tepid day of early Fall. They watched Caleb go down the slide of the outdoor play set that he'd almost outgrown. He was running, laughing, and falling as though he hadn't been in an emergency room with his first symptoms of juvenile arthritis only a few months ago.

Lavender had briefly exited but returned through the side gate with the guitar case she had in the truck the entire time.

"Look what Auntie has," she said, and Caleb's eyes shined.

He ran from his slide, past his parents, and into the house as Gloria warned him not to wake his sister.

"Where he going like that?" Katherine asked, joining them after cleaning the kitchen.

"You'll see in a minute," Čhetáŋ responded with a deep yawn.

Caleb returned with his ukulele.

Gloria laughed, "He really thinks he's doing something, too."

Lavender pulled out their chairs from the shed.

"You gon' do the song?" Caleb asked.

"Let's do a different one first. Then we'll do yours, ok?"

He shook his head, excited.

"You can learn this. It's easy. Your granddaddy taught it to me. You ready?"

E3, A0-A2... down, up, down... G, E-minor, C...

The notes rang out clearly, over the busy street and resounded out and over Mary's garden, only yards away. The patch had lost some of its definition, but it was still detectable. Stems of lavender flowers continued to sprout in and out between weeds even as autumn approached. The footprint of its borders was still apparent.

After more than an hour of "Redemption Song," "Dueling Banjos," and more "Dueling Banjos," Gloria and Čhetáŋ could only get Caleb inside once Lavender promised she would return in the next few days when she was done moving. It satisfied him for the moment and he hugged her and went inside with his parents, leaving the mother and daughter pair alone again. Katherine rested in one of the chairs, and Lavender straightened up the informal concert area.

"You're real good with him. Real patient," Katherine commented.

"That's my baby. I owe him for the last couple months I was away."

"You're still really good with the music. You was always gifted there. It came easy to you."

Lavender nodded, almost done with her chore and she packed the nylon-stringed guitar back into its case.

Katherine took a heavy breath. "I'm sorr..." She stopped, then started over again after a pause.

"When I was nineteen and moved up north, Daddy gave me all the money he had. And even borrowed some we didn't have against the house I learned. He told me to do good and make him proud up there."

Lavender groaned, already exhausted with the tale. Katherine noticed but proceeded anyway.

"That was a rare thing for a Black man to do, 'specially back then with everything goin' on. Send one of his only two daughters that far away to do, who knows what in the end. But he believed in me, and that was good enough. I was his baby girl; honor roll, in the school papers, in the local papers, acting, modeling, all that. He trusted that whatever he put in me, he was gon' get back with every success I had."

Lavender never quit moving, still shuffling and rearranging things in the shed. Katherine watched her. But she never paused her story. She didn't wait for her daughter's *performance* to finish.

"I was doing good at first," Katherine smiled, thinking about those younger days and all the ambition and talent, strong lungs and heart and spine, and the time she believed she had. Then her face turned from its pleasant state. "He got down, real bad. I asked, but he didn't want me to come back for that. Come all the way back for what? That sounded crazy to him, not with what it took to get me up there. He had Momma and Lizzy, he said. He didn't send me all the way up there to get started, then come right back for a sick man. Guess he felt he'd sacrificed too much for that. I worked, and I had some good things going before he died. But I don't know that I ever felt like any of it was worth it. Not worth what I missed here. Not at that point. So, I pushed even harder. And there were ups and downs and then. Then, I had the best thing to ever happen. I met your daddy and had you."

Lavender paused, just inside the shed, turned and said, "That's when it all went downhill right?"

"Lavender, hush dammit!" Katherine slapped her hands together. "Won't you listen for one time?"

For the first time all evening, she allowed her frustration with Lavender to boil over. It was the first time since she arrived that she'd been frustrated with anyone at all.

Lavender stopped and took a seat on the lower step of the shed. She folded her hands in her lap and beckoned for Katherine to continue. Katherine cleared her throat and regained her thoughts.

"It broke me some when he died. And your aunt was mad I wasn't here. And she would tell me what he was going through. All of it. I never knew he was gonna go like that. He'd been sick for a while. I didn't want to see him like that. He'd been sick before with his lungs and part of me just wanted to believe it was gon' be that again. But I still would've tried if I'd known how quickly it would be, after the stroke and all. Or how bad, I would've quit everything." Katherine's face turned anguished. "Then... I just, I kept getting stuck on everything having to mean something after that. It needed to be worth it. Like I was trying to make up for it. I couldn't ever get back right with that in my mind. It played like a record skipping. Same thing after Joshua." She took a contemplative pause and picked at the insides of the palms of her hands.

"Having y'all was the best thing I ever did at the end of the day. The only thing, really. But I was in my own head about not living up to and not being or not doing enough. I was young, and what seems like the world to you when you young ain't really all that important when you look back. I coped in real bad ways. And that's my fault. I should've never started it. Cause then that led me to worse places and people and down holes I never dreamt I'd be. And everything that's happened, I blame myself for. And everything you and Chase had to deal with. That's my fault. Everything—the things I know about and whatever things you went through I might never know about. All is my fault. That's why I'm so proud of you. And I know I'm supposed to be being a better Christian, but I'm so fucking proud of you." She began to weep and then wiped her face.

Lavender looked up from where she had been staring at the ground the entire time, confusion covered her eyes.

"I know that boy in there, and my grandchildren wouldn't be here without you. I know that. Čhetáŋ is one of the best men and fathers I've ever known. And you did that. I know Momma was here for him and everything, but it was you. You, here the longest, you filling in cause there was nobody else. You being the mother. You being the sister. You giving of yo'self in ways even when you couldn't see it. And I know a lot of that don't go recognized by most, cause that's how it is. Nobody sees who's pushing and pulling or taking all the blows. And most of them blows came from me and my shit. Me, putting even more on you. And despite all that, you still here. Better than I ever did with anything in my whole life. Better than I ever was or dreamed I could be. Cause I couldn't even do what you did and still be, beautiful, and strong, and humble like you. In one piece like you. And be in this world alive and still growing, still with everything to offer it and get from it. A lifetime of more you gon' have. That's all you."

Chapter 37

Joshua's Daughter

"All Night" - Beyoncé

LAVENDER'S HEAD THROBBED. AFTER TWENTY-PLUS YEARS OF disappointments, broken promises, and arguments, she expected apologetic words and excuses. There was some of that, but she didn't quite understand what the words swirling in her mind from Katherine meant. Whatever it was, it caught her unprepared. Her face burned, and the tears fell as a deluge. The reaction flustered her further because she hadn't wanted to give any emotion. She tried avoiding Katherine's gaze. She still wanted to despise this woman. Lavender had planned for whatever words of remorse Katherine had to land with flat effect. But this was some trick, some new *wrinkle* she'd picked up from all the therapy and rehab sessions.

Katherine approached and stopped just before Lavender's feet. Then she lowered herself to be at eye level with her daughter. It was a slow, deliberate drop to her knees, especially for a woman nearly sixty years.

"What you doing?" Lavender asked, but Katherine ignored her.

She wanted to look at her child's face. She needed to kneel and look into her eyes. It was almost a curtsey, a clumsy curtsey to her progeny who'd conquered terrains and distances she'd failed to traverse.

Katherine wrapped her in an embrace so firm that it almost felt like restraint to Lavender.

"I was the cause of it all. Give that to me," Katherine said. "Give it to me, ok." It sounded like an incantation to Lavender as her mother pulled her in tighter and tighter, nearly stealing the few breaths she had left from sobbing.

Give what to you? Lavender thought.

"Give me that pain and that hate. That fear you wear. Give me that darkness you been carrying. That was the shadow I cast. It ain't yours. Let that shit go. You ain't this shrinking thing. You're Lavender Amášte—the best of me. Joshua's daughter. Black, Oglala, gorgeous, gifted. The best of us both."

Lavender's chest could no longer stand the pressure and spilled out from her eyes, mouth, and nose along with a guttural sound that escaped from some deep cage. She crumpled inside Katherine's full cradle as they swayed, and her mother rocked her like the twelve-year-old girl she had sent away all those years ago. The girl who'd forgotten all of this. The girl who'd abandoned herself. The one who had forgotten that luminous possibility was even conceivable for herself. Who had only wanted to survive and live without remembering it was her right and inheritance to dream and fight for and have too.

The fact that this vision and retrospection had come from Katherine... Lavender didn't know what to do with those feelings.

They remained that way without words for what felt like hours. When they untangled, Katherine wiped Lavender's tears and braced herself on the ground to rise to a standing position. She assisted her mother until Katherine's footing was sure.

"I gotta go, Momma," Lavender said. "I gotta go and... I gotta have this truck back before a certain time." It was a lie, but she needed an escape. Somewhere else to be with whatever she was feeling. Somewhere other than in this space.

Katherine kissed Lavender's forehead, then her cheeks, then her hands, and tried holding her in place.

"Momma, I gotta go," Lavender said, slowly pulling away. "Tell Čhetáŋ I had to leave."

Lavender left and stopped two blocks down the street at the intersection where Freeman's Grocery used to operate. She was a wreck once more, unable to proceed after the signal light was green. Sheets of tears obstructed her vision. Drivers behind her honked and cursed, but she could not move. She had to sit through another cycle of the traffic signals before she was composed enough to apply her foot to the accelerator.

Lavender spent the next few days decompressing from the weekend and that moment with Katherine in the yard. It had helped that she was still busy getting her new place together and the arranging and decorating of everything kept her busy and offered an imminent goal to focus on. The duplex was old, possibly built in the 1940s, if not before. Nevertheless, whoever renovated it had labored to modernize it as much as possible. It wasn't a luxury model apartment, but the hardwood had been restored, and, from their appearance, all the countertops and fixtures were added within the last five years or so. It was called a "two-bedroom apartment," but the reality was the primary bedroom was small and the adjacent "bedroom" much smaller. Lavender imagined that if someone attempted to place an actual bed in the smaller room, you'd be unable to open the swinging door for entry. She guessed it could serve as her music room. Nevertheless, it was the most she'd ever had. At thirty-six, it was the first place that was all her own, procured entirely in her name, minus any family loopholes or exceptions.

She was about to relax after days of unboxing and bookshelf assemblage of suspicious durability when someone knocked on her door. Čhetáŋ was working, and the only other person who knew her new location was Chris. He only knew it because, as inconsiderate as she'd been to him, he was still the kind of man that helped her with her first load of moving on the initial day of relocating.

She couldn't fathom why he would be back, but when she looked through her peephole, she saw skewed dreadlocks and a Nike suit through the fisheye lens.

Lavender opened the door for Chris, "Hey, what you doing here?" She tried to tamper her enthusiasm, unsure if she succeeded.

"I was in the neighborhood. Ain't that what people say?" He smiled. She had missed that face, those dimples. "I see you getting it together in here."

"I'm working on it. I might bring my dresser over from the house. But I'm good with the air mattress for a while."

"Interesting," he said. She hated when that was his response to anything and was glad to hear it again.

"That doesn't meet with your approval?" Lavender asked.

"Not up to my approval. This is your spot. I just think it's interesting."

She shook her head and grinned. "You're wondering why the hell I would bring a dresser over and not a bed."

He shrugged.

"My mom's finally out. Well, parole under something called courtesy supervision. She's at the house, using the bed now. I need my dresser. I can't let her have everything, but she can keep the bed. She's old."

"Interesting," He rubbed his beard.

"What do you want?" Lavender asked with a smile.

"Not much. I just have something for you." He reached into his pocket and placed its contents in her hand. She looked down at it and glanced back at him, confused.

"You got me an old ass, scratched-up smartphone?"

"You don't want it?"

"Um. I don't understand what you want me to do with it."

He took it back. "Lemme see..." Chris touched the screen on the phone a few times. "This one right here. I like this one."

An audience applauds before music comes in, eventually drowning them out. The volume of the melody decreases slightly, and introduces an engaging voice on the microphone. "Hey... is everybody alright? You alright, Miss? This Rhapsody, and I am Joshua Adair, or as some call me, Jo'. We will be serenading you all tonight with a little Miles... or Ella or, hell, Quincy if I feel like it."

Joshua's voice was clear and ringing and boomed through a tiny, contemporary device, not the bulky artifact she was used to hearing him sound from.

She covered her mouth, stunned. "How'd you? When?"

"My band ain't big time, as you well know," he paused with a bit of sarcasm in his tone. "However, one thing about being in this business, even as a small player, is you make connections. I have a couple of those. I spoke with an acquaintance a while back with a studio. Found out he had a nice setup where he could do mass transfers of analog to digital. The kind of thing you needed."

The first night after he allowed her to fill part of his home with all of Joshua's Fujis, Memorexes, and Maxell brands of cassettes, she complained about how expensive and overwhelming it would be to transfer the entire collection. She would have to do them in small batches at a time. Even then, it was hundreds of dollars for each increment.

"That shit cost thousands! What you do?" She asked.

"Hell, I ain't do *that*," Chris laughed. "My friend owes me a couple of fifty favors, and as often is the case, you're really paying for what you don't know and can't do yourself. I had a source in both instances. So, it wasn't cheap, but it wasn't thousands of dollars either."

Her eyes stung again. "And you got all of them?"

"Not all, not yet. But most. Still waiting on like two more bins, but you're on your own with those 8-tracks 'cause even he couldn't do that."

She laughed, "That's fine, that's fine!"

"And, yeah, this my shitty old phone. I wasn't buying your ass a new mp3 player, but the music is all in the cloud. You're good. I can send you the link in a second. It's in my email. One sec..." Chris scrolled through his phone.

Lavender shook her head in disbelief and turned away from him before covering her face, trembling. He was preoccupied with searching his mailbox before he noticed. Once he did, he stopped and held her.

"Are you crying?" He asked.

"Why'd you do this? Why? After... Why?"

"Cause, for one," Chris began, "when I saw all the shit you went through to keep them, I knew how important your old man's music was to you. I respected that. I felt that." He rubbed her back, comforting her. "And then, two, honestly, this shit is a process. I'd already started sending my homeboy your bins before you fucked up, and they're just now done."

They laughed almost in sync. Lavender's face turned a rosy shade.

Chris continued, "You didn't even know I was sneaking them joints out when you were at the house. I started with the ones at the bottom, figuring if you went in there, you'd go for the easiest ones on top, but hell, I didn't know. I was going to surprise you." He pulled back to look at her. She tried to hide her eyes behind her hands, feeling as though she looked a puffy mess, but he pulled them away. "Lastly, I need to get my space back. So, see, I did this for me," he laughed.

Lavender stepped back and studied him for a moment, shaking her head. "Christopher Daquin," she said, smiling. It was as if his name was a testimony or wish.

"Oh, yeah. I got a message from Patrick the other day. He said you sounded like you knew your shit when it came to the music tutoring, and y'all were gonna work something out as far as schedule and travel. Like he might scoop you from the bus intermodal downtown on those days, 'cause that's not too far?"

She nodded.

"Good. Glad that might work out. That's good for you," he said.

Good for me. Those words leaving his lips didn't ruffle her this time. Then he looked at her with a mischievous stare.

"He said you kept going on and on about me, though. How I was a great person, a generous guy, how I reminded you of what you used to love about playing and how music made you feel and all this ol' gushy shit. Dude was like, 'well Goddamn Chris, what you down there doing to that girl?' So I was like, you know me."

They both snickered again.

"You fucked me up is what you did," she said, embarrassed.

Chris' visit was brief because he had a show to do. He had dropped in and unburdened her of a massive, decades-long predicament she'd carried and then was gone in an instant. Like, she'd imagined it.

Lavender listened to Joshua the rest of the night, lying awake on her air mattress in the empty bedroom. She played track after track, sometimes on repeat, excited not to have to mess with rewinding and fast-forwarding or the paranoia that used to cause about what that repetition would eventually do to the ribbon of the cassette. She didn't worry about running the battery down after unyielding, consecutive listens. Or, breaking whatever antiquated music player she listened on—concerned that as technology changed, she wouldn't be able to repair or replace it. If this already used and dinged contraption were to give out tomorrow, she still knew where Joshua's voice was safe and preserved. She smiled and cried again, thinking of the irony that the collections' past redemption had been her burying it beneath the soil. And how that grace now belonged to "the cloud." It was *corny* but true. She was that girl again, back in her room, at Mary's, at the foot of her bed, cradled in her father's words and dreams but with air, lacking the barricades of the bins—free.

Chapter 38

Not Forever

"Here Comes the Sun" - Nina Simone

"I heard 'bout y'all little dinner the other day," Elizabeth said as Lavender cornrowed her hair.

They sat in the kitchen as usual, surrounded by remnants of the lunch Lavender brought and Elizabeth's medicine bottles, already emptied of a portion of their contents for that day's regimen.

"Uh huh. What you know about it?" Lavender asked.

"Your momma told me."

"Oh, so y'all talkin' like that now? Y'all best friends now?" Lavender was curious. This was the second time Elizabeth casually mentioned conversing with Katherine as if their discussions were light banter. Lavender wanted to know what was said between those old adversaries. If Katherine had similarly rattled her aunt, nursing some buried injury that had been neglected under layers of impotent fixes.

"Nah, not like that," Elizabeth added.

"Sure, Auntie. You full of shit, you know that?" Lavender said. "I'll find out what y'all are talking about, though. Čhetáŋ tells everything."

"What? Ain't nothing." Elizabeth said. "I started to come over there and get me a bite that day. But you know I can't drive."

Yes, you can. Lavender shook her head but moved past that persistent narrative. "I wish you would've. You could've saved me some energy from having to read your sister. We could've done that together."

Elizabeth shifted in her seat and glared at her niece. "Now, you full of shit."

"How?" Lavender asked.

"You might've started like you was fixin' to read her, but your ass was all hugged up later as I hear."

"Hmph."

"Besides, y'all ain't want me over there," Elizabeth continued. "The neighbors gon' have to pay for my shows now. I gave 'em enough free ones when you was little."

They got a hearty laugh from that, thinking of all the chaos Elizabeth used to cause between fights with Kenneth and her general penchant for disorder.

The doorbell rang, and when Lavender answered, she opened it to see Čhetáŋ standing beside Katherine. It was a surprising interruption to occur during this standard hair appointment.

"What y'all doing over here?"

"We got invited, that alright with you?" Čhetáŋ asked before thumping her shoulder.

She looked at Katherine as they entered and whispered, "Hey," then retired to her position hovering over Elizabeth's chair.

"Tell me about your new place," Elizabeth went on, tilting her head as Lavender worked on the back row. "You know, if you just had to, I woulda let you have one of these rooms. If you just had to."

Jesus Christ, Lavender thought. "What? You say that now, after I already have somewhere?"

"You need tough love," Elizabeth shrugged.

"Is that what you been giving us our whole life? For damn sure wouldn't have minded some soft love," Lavender said, looking at

Čhetáŋ with a crooked smile and disbelief. Then she moved past this latest example of *Lizisms*, to discuss her place. "My place is cool. It isn't spectacular and all, but hell, it's mine. All mine."

"I heard it's barely bigger than this table, though," Elizabeth added, slapping the furniture in the process.

"Liz..." Katherine shook her head. "Let my child alone."

"It's alright. Whoever told her that was lying anyway," Lavender fired back. "This table is way bigger than my place."

They all burst into laughter. It felt correct but dreamlike and fragile. Lavender only allowed herself to mull over how surreal it was for a moment.

"I don't know why you always say what 'you heard' anyway Aunt Liz, wasn't nobody but Chase's talking ass. That boy could never keep nothing."

"I don't know what you're talking about," Čhetáŋ responded. "All I said was when you walk through the front door, you're in the backyard."

More howling ensued, filling the room and echoing past Elizabeth's open windows as far as the air would carry it.

"Y'all terrible, don't do my baby like that," Katherine added. "She doing good. Real good."

That *baby*, hearing it in person and not through cold fibre optics, was still abnormal. The word seemed to still everyone in the room, including the voice that had spoken it.

"We all gotta start somewhere," Katherine said before a short coughing spell took effect.

Lavender stopped braiding, went to the refrigerator, and grabbed a bottled water. She poured it into a glass and handed it to her mother.

"Thank you."

Elizabeth turned around and faced her stylist, "That better not had been my last cold water in there, Lavender, I'm for real. I ain't have but a few already cold. She could've had some regular iced tap water. That girl been in jail, and I know they wasn't handing out no Fijis in there."

"Oh my God," Čhetáŋ said.

"Y'all don't worry about it. I ain't thinking 'bout Lizzy," Katherine said with a grin. "She ain't changed when it comes to some things. And I don't mind that. I missed some of that."

"You know I ain't changing, now."

"You ain't lying, Momma. Cause if I'd gotten you ice, she would've said something about that too."

"And you know it," Katherine agreed, and she and Lavender shared corresponding nods.

"Y'all just too sensitive," Elizabeth said before adding. "Well... You do get carried away with my ice, though, girl, I ain't lying. Knowing my ice maker don't be workin' half the time."

"That's your sister," Lavender said, facing her mother again.

"I know it."

"Nah, sis, I ain't changed on everything," Elizabeth eventually said. "But you can't do the same shit forever, either."

They continued in this manner for hours, into the afternoon and then past sunset before Čhetáŋ dropped Lavender off at her place. It was empty inside her new abode but not lonely. Her cupboards were still mostly bare, all except the lone bottle of tequila gifted as a housewarming present from Angie. She bypassed it and instead grabbed one of the cans of soda Gloria and Čhetáŋ had sent over. It was a Sunday evening, and she had work the following day. It would also be her first evening in the role of *music tutor for privileged boys*. She smirked at the title she'd given it but felt surprisingly less nervous about it than she once had.

She entered her scrunched music room where her classical guitar rested. It was the same one Kenneth had gotten for her. The one that, for years, she believed was from Mary and had played all their duets with it. She kept the guitar even with the mixed feelings which surrounded it. Given those attached memories with her grandmother, it was hard to depart with the instrument.

Lavender nestled on the floor with the guitar against her body and began playing some of those same gospel songs, reminiscing. Then she pulled out her new-old mp3 player of Joshua's recordings and scrolled through, listening to his voice, and playing until her eyes were too heavy to continue.

Acknowledgments

Thank you to...

My father (SGJ): a man of massive personality who bragged loudly about my tiniest accomplishments. I lost you in 2020. Your sudden absence reminded me of our ever-present mortality and is probably the sole reason I finally completed this story.

My mother (MG): You have believed in every dream I've ever conjured. Everything good and genuine found in me comes from your unyielding love, support, and resolve. You have inspired me more than you will ever know or understand.

My husband (CB): my loudest cheerleader! I appreciate your unwavering support even when you're uncertain about what this tiny person with a big imagination is doing exactly. Your whispers of encouragement always pull me out of self-doubt.

Special thanks to...

Jessica Carter

Marie Coichy Dauphin

Kimberly L. Poole

Nicole L. Price

Justin Green and Diamond Duke Wayland (*for helping to keep me straight on these guitar licks!*)

Christie Glascoe (*editing*)

Ashley Shepard (*marketing*)

About the Author

Monica is a visual artist and emerging author. Based in Atlanta, Georgia, and a native of Alabama, Monica enjoys steeping much of her fiction writing and artwork in Black southern heritage and its ties to modern culture. As a student of history, she aspires to convey the connecting fibers of the past and the present and how they coexist within the contemporary human condition. Whether in a spirit of rebellion against systems or reflected in the psychological struggles we carry and struggle with daily. "Songs of Lost Things..." is her first novel and will also feature a series of original art pieces to accompany the story and its themes.

Please follow Monica on Instagram and TikTok: @moni_shywriter, Facebook: @moni.shywriter, linktr.ee/moniartist and at monicamccollough.com.